Planetarity from Below

# Planetarity from Below

## DECOLONIAL ECOPOETICS OF MIGRATION AND DIASPORA

*Emily Yu Zong*

UNIVERSITY OF MICHIGAN PRESS
*Ann Arbor*

Published in the United States of America by the
University of Michigan Press
First published January 2026

A CIP catalog record for this book is available from the British Library.

*Library of Congress Cataloging-in-Publication data has been applied for.*

ISBN 978-0-472-07781-6 (hardcover : alk. paper)
ISBN 978-0-472-05781-8 (paper : alk. paper)
ISBN 978-0-472-90542-3 (open access ebook)

DOI: https://doi.org/10.3998/mpub.14600018

The University of Michigan Press's open access publishing program is made possible thanks to additional funding from the University of Michigan Office of the Provost and the generous support of contributing libraries.

Front cover illustration: "Feng Shui, 2004" by Guan Wei

The authorized representative in the EU for product safety and compliance is Easy Access System Europe, Mustamäe tee 50, 10621 Tallinn, Estonia, gpsr.requests@easproject.com.

*For my parents*

# Contents




Digital materials related to this title can be found on the Fulcrum platform via the following citable URL: https://doi.org/10.3998/mpub.14600018

## Acknowledgments

This book has been a journey across landscapes, cultures, and conversations. As a migrant in Australia and Hong Kong, I am deeply grateful to my companions in the animal world. Cats, goats, and cows have taught me about wonder and mutuality beyond words. My gratitude also goes to the landscapes: mountains, beaches, creeks, wetlands, and bushlands. They provide refuge, strength, and boundless imagination to diasporic lifeworlds and call me into a lifelong journey of learning

I am indebted to Merlinda Bobis for her climate fiction and the conversations we shared, which seeded my research on planetarity and from which it later grew. I would also like to thank Rita Wong, Kazim Ali, and Chen Quifan for their words of encouragement, and the other authors and filmmakers in this study for their ecologically expansive perspective on Asian diasporic belonging and responsibility that have been a source of inspiration.

I have shared chapters and received thoughtful feedback from many colleagues. I dearly thank Emily Potter and Brigid Mangner for inviting me to present an ECR-Keynote talk at the 2023 Association for the Study of Australian Literature and Association for the Study of Literature, Environment and Culture–Australia and New Zealand conference, which gave me an opportunity to receive valuable comments on refugee ecologies. I thank the German Association for Australian Studies, particularly Patricia Plummer, Katrin Althans, and Bill Ashcroft, for inviting me to present and engage in conversations. I presented the decolonial water ecology chapter at the Association for the Study of Literature and Environment conference in 2023 and benefited from intellectual inspiration from Asian American colleagues, particularly Jeffrey Santa Ana, who offered generous advice and support.

I owe my passion for diaspora studies to my doctoral mentors David Carter, Sneja Gunew, Carole Ferrier, and Wenche Ommundsen, who guided me to the importance of cultural plurality and speaking up from the margins. Many other people have offered valuable insights that developed my thinking about environmental humanities and academia, including Scott Slovic, Astrida Neimanis, Cajetan Iheka, Marisol De la Cadena, Xiaojing Zhou, Serpil Oppermann, Andrew Baldwin, Stephen Muecke, Tony Hughes-d'Aeth, Hsuan Hsu, Christof Mauch, Kiu-wai Chu, Serena Chou, Li-hsin Hsu, Winnie Yee, Daisy Tam, Jamie Wang, and Belinda Smaill.

I am grateful to the Department of Humanities and Creative Writing at Hong Kong Baptist University and my dear colleagues there for providing a vibrant intellectual home. I want to thank Kwai-Cheung Lo and the Anthropocene Studies members for the annual symposiums and invigorating conversations. My commitment to the environmental humanities flourished during those formative years of lecturing courses and experimenting with practice-led art exhibitions. These adventures strengthened my faith in the arts and the creative commons from the ground up. This research was supported by funding from the Hong Kong University Grants Committee Early Career Scheme Grant (no. 22614922).

Sincere thanks also go to the University of Michigan Press and to my editor, Marcella Landri, for her dedicated editorial support and to Sara Cohen for her insightful guidance. I appreciate Delilah McCrea, Danielle Coty-Fattal, and Marcia LaBrenz for their assistance during the publication process. I am grateful to the two anonymous readers of this book for their generous time and invaluable feedback.

An earlier version of parts of Chapter 4 was published as "Post-apocalyptic Specters and Critical Planetarity in Merlinda Bobis' *Locust Girl.*" *Ariel: A Review of International English Literature* 51 (4) (2020): 99–123.

This book would not have been possible without the unwavering love and understanding from my family and friends. My parents and siblings have supported my academic journey across continents, and my mum's Tai Chi practice has been a holistic reminder of the vital flow of *qi*. Last, my heartfelt thanks go to my husband and intellectual companion, Alex Gearin, who has read many chapters of this book, consistently brings humor into my life, and cooks countless meals that nourish my work and soul.

# Introduction

## *Toward a Decolonial Ecopoetics of Migration*

> I am stateless but I belong to this Earth that is my mother. I am a stateless person, but I am a free man because the Earth is for me. I belong to nature, belong to mountains, oceans, seasons, jungles, deserts and I belong to those societies where I have breathed with them, smiled with them, cried with them or lived with them. I am a free man.
>
> —**Behrouz Boochani, "Dialogue"**

What would migrant stories and lifeworlds look like if they were to diverge from a modern humanist narrative of freedom? The Kurdish Iranian writer and asylum seeker Behrouz Boochani offers an ecopoetic provocation. In an interview, Boochani expresses that out of statelessness he has formed a sense of planetary freedom by pledging solidarity with the earth. Escaping from Iran in 2013, Boochani soon encountered Australia's stringent borders and was exiled to Manus Island detention camp, an experience that shattered his belief in liberal humanist ideals of freedom. By saying, "I am a stateless person, but I am a free man because the Earth is for me" ("Dialogue"), he invites us to an ecological notion of life that embeds refugees within the natural world, where mountains, oceans, seasons, jungles, and deserts are terrains for refugee belonging, despite state borders (2020). Boochani's memoir, *No Friend but the Mountains* (2018), imbricates biopolitical and ecological imaginations to animate a thickening of refugee mobility. In one scenario, he describes witnessing flowers growing near a sewage drain in the camp, interpreting their persistence as life's immanent resistance and zest. Against the violence of the camp, a landscape haunted by sovereign ghosts, capitalist greed, and ecological impoverishment, Boochani sees an interspecies ethic that can strengthen refugee political agency against oppression. Freedom, as he depicts it, involves a political and imaginative negotiation of collaborative survival through ecological interdependence.

This book examines narratives of collaborative survival with the natural world and explores their decolonial potential to delink migrant and refugee struggles from a modern telos of freedom, alongside its colonial, racial, neoliberal, and technocratic designs that have caused planetary ruins on land and sea. A decolonial call, however, raises questions about migrant and refugee resistances that have traditionally emerged from struggles for justice, rights, and freedom against a measure of Western modernity and liberal humanism. I argue that even as existing migration and diaspora studies have critiqued inequality to promote inclusivity within and beyond the nation, justice-oriented methods do not sufficiently address the colonial roots of modern humanism. What tends to be overlooked is how migrants and refugees become embedded in modern (settler) colonial structures—ongoing material and subjection regimes of property, individualism, and progress that reproduce racism, sexism, speciesism, and Indigenous dispossession. A profound tension and political predicament implicate migrant and refugee communities globally, including Asian immigrants and refugees entangled in the structural inequalities of nation and capital by claiming belonging to settler-colonial states such as Australia, Canada, and the United States. *Planetarity from Below* is a book that takes up this challenge to ask what decolonization might mean for migration studies, and how migrant ecological knowledges, imaginations, and praxes can contribute to unlearning colonial ways of inhabiting the earth toward alternative collective futures against and beyond the Anthropocene, this epoch of human-driven ecological crises.

A decolonial approach to restorying migrant ecologies would involve, first and foremost, understanding how the modern colonial divide between nature and culture has constructed migration and ecology in conflicting terms. In my use of "ecology," I am inspired by the late anthropologist Deborah Bird Rose, who insists ecology means thinking "with, and from within the world," in contrast to thinking "from the outside, over and above and against the world" (2022, 15). Thinking with the world dismantles colonial fantasies that alienate persons from the environment. It embraces a relational understanding of life as webbed flows of interdependence and coemergence. Thinking with the world also means the stories with which we perceive the world have the power to remake worlds. Yet the modern narrative of freedom posits that to migrate is to attain emancipation, where such emancipation is measured by one's proximity to an Enlightenment ideal of a rational, autonomous, and property-owning liberal individual.

Modern freedom has shaped global migration patterns and entrenched the epistemic coloniality of migration. Since the fifteenth century, migration has been deeply entangled with colonialism, starting with the historical rise of European empires and settler colonialism, the "discovery" of new worlds, enslavement, indentured labor, and Indigenous dispossession. This colonial legacy continues in the ongoing dehumanization and governance of migrants through colonial power structures of racialization, capitalism, and bordering practices (Collins 2022, 1242). Colonialism is embedded in the fabric of contemporary migration, although migration studies and policies are typically preoccupied with "the unprecedented present" of new crises, migration trends, and control mechanisms (Mayblin and Turner 2021, 2). Only recently has migration studies begun to address decoloniality as crucial to rethinking what is (un)freedom during migration movements, and how liberal humanist discourses have interpreted migration in anthropocentric, economistic, and individualistic terms that overlook the ecological connectivity at play.

The concealment of coloniality in the current politics of migration is embedded in the racialized economy of liberal possessive humanism. In modern liberal narratives, migrants, refugees, and other racialized groups are expected to gain human freedom by translating alienated labor into the capitalist property regime, whereby differences are supposedly resolved by a politics of recognition. I join scholars like Elizabeth Povinelli, Lisa Lowe, Kathryn Yusoff, Aileen Moreton-Robinson, Jodi Melamed, and others in arguing that modern freedom and liberal personhood rely on a structural collaboration between the colonial divisions of human and life, capitalist economies of alienation and extraction, and liberal (multi)cultural politics of domestication and management (Melamed 2011; Moreton-Robinson 2015; Povinelli 2016; Yusoff 2018). As Yusoff explains, modern liberalism has been forged by the extractive grammars of white geology and racial subjection, creating a hierarchy between the human and the inhuman—racialized people, plants, animals, matter—and exposing colored bodies to toxic harms (2018, xii). Thus, the Anthropocene, this epoch of humanity's geological agency, must be reinterpreted as a colonial racial formation. Colonial racial hierarchies fuel the capitalist inequality, reproduction, and accumulation that in turn develop freedom for the Euro-American individual. Lisa Lowe describes an "economy of affirmation and forgetting" to name the colonial processes through which "the human" is freed by liberal forms, while the variously colonized and dispossessed peoples whose labor and resources potentiated that liberty are either assimilated or forgotten (2015, 3). A modern telos of (un)freedom, alongside liberal promises of equality, reason, and progress, severs migration from global asymmetries of life. It privatizes these inequalities by racializing migration as a matter of state control and border security.

Racialized representations of migration loom large in contemporary border politics. Today, human disruptions of ecosystems have led to extreme temperatures, sea level rise, melting glaciers, floods, storms, and toxic pollution, displacing millions of vulnerable people and wildlife. The extensive relocation of people, capital, or non-native species may also disturb landscapes and worsen existing environmental challenges. Considering both the new possibilities and new risks, Serpil Opperman asserts that migrant ecologies carry a kind of "ghostly doubleness," gathering mixed stories that undermine anti-immigration apathy in the Global North but also signal the risks of wildlife displacement and traveling viruses defying human borders (2023, 80). But this doubleness often slips into a binary of either/or in media and government discourses of the Global North, which enlarges migration's environmental threat to redraw humanist hierarchies at a time of rising climate precarity. For instance, the green population movements by various far-right parties in Europe, Australia, and North America blame immigrants for resource depletion, environmental degradation, and harming the way of life of first-world citizens. Such ecobordering draws on colonial, neo-Malthusian, and racialized environmentalism to justify border violence and protect the "nativist stewardship" of national nature (Turner and Bailey 2021, 110). By depicting borders as an ecological fix, these green gatekeeping agendas naturalize Global North privilege, while separating such privilege from its systematic exploitation of the Global South. Beneath the racialized spectacles of contemporary border crises, the migrant figure and the environmental fear it provokes, rather than entirely new, is an outgrowth of longer processes of colonial and racial disposability generated by modern extractive capitalism (Ahuja 2021, 11).

Underlying green border politics is a stereotype of migrants as environmental polluters. To their modernizing ambitions are attributed an unjust amount of blame for nature's decline. Simultaneously, another stereotype casts migrants as ecological victims. Their plight signifies an upcoming racial future threatening the Western humanist subject at the end of the world. These two contradictory images of the migrant—polluter and victim—are paradoxical figurations that shape the contemporary environmental narration of migration as cause and effect of crisis. They index two sides of a racializing coin that effectively strips migrants of ecological awareness by projecting them as modernity's structural "other": Either migrants assimilate into Western humanism and its global racial order, or they are tragically displaced by it. Adding to this duality is also a third story of "migration as adaptation," taken up by major actors like the Intergovernmental Panel on Climate Change, which reframes climate migration as an individual opportunity for economic advancement, shifting the focus from systemic change to personal entrepreneurship (Faber and Schlegel 2017). These images depict migrants and the world's poor as *resource misusers* (incapable of sustainable development), *helpless victims* (disposable in the global economy), or *exemplary adapters* (agents of neoliberal capitalism). Thus, the figure of the migrant has come to represent the limit, anxiety, and ecological other of the modern humanist subject at a time of planetary breakdown.

"The twenty-first century will be the century of the migrant," writes Thomas Nail to highlight not just the record number of migrants but also how overlapping techniques of social expulsion have become ever more active (2015, 7). Nail challenges us to develop new accounts of the migrant not as a "type of person" or failed citizen but rather as a mobile position people move into and out of due to social conditions of mobility (2015, 235). The migrant allows us to historicize social techniques of expulsion and to understand society as a dynamic process of redefining the structures, agencies, and borders of mobility. *Planetarity from Below* argues that the migrant operates as a mobile figure connecting, and reshaping, the discourses of humanism and capitalism in the Anthropocene. Modern migration has embodied the inhuman and racial techniques of colonial labor, land, and resource extraction. The colonial invasion of the new world, slavery, indentured servitude, Indigenous land seizure, neoliberal displacement, and climate racism are examples of how migration names the inhuman property praxis of colonial earth-writing (Yusoff 2018, 2). Yet migration has also served as a generative nexus for desire and longing, exchange and collaboration, and passage into the unknown. If migration were to remain a creative force for social change, migration studies scholars must approach mobile subjectivities not simply from a politics of control by state and capital but from the *excess* of mobility—the manifold subjective desires, agency, insurgence, and living labor of migrants—that structurally exceeds the "laws" of supply and demand and thus can be rearticulated to counter colonial injustices (Mezzadra 2011, 126). It is to the excess of mobility that my decolonial study of migrant ecocriticism turns. To decolonize would create tensions and opportunities for both unearthing how migration has been embedded in the extractive economies of modern subjective life and assembling a non-anthropocentric cosmopolitics by the so-called ecological "outcasts."

If migration is a defining feature of our unpredictable era, we need ecologically nuanced migration stories beyond modern master narratives. Politicians and policymakers seeking to control migration from above tend to rely on stories of abstract data, labor productivity, and border security, neglecting the thickness of migrants encountering altered landscapes from below. Simplistic views of migrants as polluters, victims, or adapters reinforce the white liberal subject as the default agent of environmental stewardship and world history, disregarding the green practices by migrant and diasporic people. In mainstream globalization discourse, migration embodies techno-economic and transnational cultural flows that are often rendered placeless by the very mobility and fluidity across national borders. This tendency to consider migrants as placeless is conjoined by the recent scholarship from various contexts reflecting on how migrant and refugee claims for place in white liberal democracies risk reinforcing settler colonial norms and Indigenous erasure. This work calls for redirecting migrant belonging beyond established frameworks like "integration," "claiming the nation," and "multicultural diversity" (Wong 2008; Fujikane and Okamura 2008; Suzuki and Bahng 2020; Favell 2022). But there is less work on how ecological and place-based imaginations could expand migrant ethical and political stances beyond a modern dichotomy of victimhood and threat to show their relevance to planetary concerns at large. *Planetarity from Below* seeks to explore the planetary ethics and collective visions within migrant ecologies through decolonization. What are the stakes and prospects of reconceiving migrant and refugee freedom beyond liberal possessive humanism? What forms of migrant subjectivity, mobility, and community are worlded by a more-than-human approach? How might ecology foreground conversations between diaspora and Indigeneity? What literary aesthetics and cultural forms articulate these movements?

Boochani's earthly statement resonates with the many other short stories, memoirs, poetry, speculative fiction, and documentary films analyzed in *Planetarity from Below*. Within these cultural expressions of migration, I identify a planetary ethos that springs from, and in turn supports, migrant and refugee communities in resisting a colonial hierarchy of life and things. These narratives revise an emancipatory tradition of diasporic and transnational literature by reflecting on how migrant freedom has been measured against modern progressive narratives—property, nation, Man, technology—that commodify, displace, and stratify migrant bodies, labor, and homelands as the surplus of capitalist extraction and exposure. This book traverses a constellation of "surplus landscapes" that provoke the radical ambivalence of modern excess, from Australia's pastoral interior and oceanic refugee camps to resource frontiers on unceded Indigenous Canadian territory, to futuristic climate-ravaged worlds, and to migrant labor sweatshops in China. These landscapes tell stories of how a planetary commons of land, water, energy, and minerals has been exhausted and militarized by colonial and neoliberal resource regimes to accumulate wealth and enforce borders against the dispossessed mass for the benefit of the possessive individual. The universal privilege of the propertied human subject is reproduced by the racial, class, and ecological disposability of migrants, Indigenous peoples, refugees, migrant workers, and nonhuman ecosystems that have sustained the global economy.

Against normative modern subjecthood, the literature and film engaged herein imagine alternative subjectivities that reorient migrant agency toward wondrous, decolonial, affective, nomadic, trans-species, and deviant forms of connectivity, fostering life and survival through situated kinship in more-than-human worlds. If more-than-human relations have shaped modern biopolitical governance in forms of oceanic borders and racist rhetoric, they have also shaped the material substance of migrant collaborative survival across species and borders. Modern progress blocks attention to "patchy landscapes, multiple temporalities, and shifting assemblages of humans an nonhumans"—to notice them in the shadows we must reorient our attention (Tsing 2015, 22). Mapping the generative, although uneasy, kinship between migrants and nonhuman agencies (animals, plants, water, fire, minerals, waste, and technology), I argue that contemporary migrant ecopoetics shifts environmental ethics from individual moral concerns to a political ecology of sustaining life in precarity. In other words, instead of treating environmentalism as a matter of liberal humanist stewardship, the book traces narratives in which ecological interdependence is a precondition for migrant and refugee agency rather than its rational effect. A perspective shift unfolds in this study that resets the goal of migrant and refugee struggles from a politics of modern recognition to a perpetual "queering" of modern freedom: constantly negotiating ethical alterity and transversal alliance that undo the liberal humanist master subject and its binary logic of inclusion or abjection.

This ecological reorientation of political subjectivity from the margins, along with the relational ethics and alternative futures it iteratively affords, contours a bottom-up worldmaking project that I propose as *planetarity from below*. Simultaneously ecological and social, planetarity from below offers a collective imaginary to counter the modern human conceit of separating nature and culture. Instead of romantic unity at the end of the world, planetarity from below involves a pluralist worlding of multispecies coexistence by ecologizing and democratizing an ethics of alterity at the limits of knowledge. The "planetary" dimension invites ecosocial and geosocial conceptions of earth beings that affirm the human as part of a living and interconnected web of life. The "below" aspect attends to everyday, situated, and micro-scale experiments of ecological "doing" and "commoning" that widen cracks in modern colonial systems. Rather than imposing global models to remake a damaged world from the outside, a planetary relational collective is constructed from within, by responding to ongoing state and capitalist violence, and by reclaiming the inhuman intimacy and decolonial conviviality from the excess of modernity to create alternative possibilities of life. Uncanny and unknowable yet immanent and irrepressible, it is prompted by the ghosts of the planetary commons collecting debts from global agents. It is the nonhuman-within and the becoming-world.

In this book, I offer planetarity from below as a framework to uphold the often overlooked relational ethics and worldmaking projects in contemporary migrant ecopoetics. The concept of poetics—derived from the Greek *poiesis*, meaning "making"—as Kate Rigby reminds us, is not limited to poetry or human practice, but can refer to the craftsmanship of all earthly life, thus inviting us to consider what we make with words and creative practices might help sustain the other-than-human poietic processes on earth (2006). An ecopoetic analysis, then, understands knowing as a praxis of doing and considers environments not as passive property but as ecosocial sites of narrativity and more-than-human becoming. I embrace a broad definition of migrant poetics that encompasses the epistemic errantry and nomadic becomings afforded by the diasporic condition, migration literature and aesthetics, as well as the open-ended encounters between self and surroundings that resist the totality of possession. Édouard Glissant's conceptualization of poetics of relation as a transformative mode of history that "remains forever conjectural and presupposes no ideological stability," "opens onto the fluctuating complexity of the world" and "the evolution of the planet Earth," and "safeguards the particular" and "the energy of Diversity" is a source of inspiration for the expansive sense of migrant ecopoetics here (1997). A migrant ecopoetics that partners decolonial politics with the creativity, wonder, and opacity of more-than-human worlds is the focus of this book.

While existing scholarship in migrant and ethnic ecocriticism has focused on environmental justice (Hayashi 2011; Ray 2013; Fitzsimmons et al. 2015; Zhou 2021; Santa Ana et al. 2022), *Planetarity from Below* builds upon this body of work by coupling justice concerns with planetary ethics. I conceive of ethics not as fixed moral norms but as the ongoing practices of sustaining and caring with more-than-human worlds (Puig de la Bellacasa 2017, 6). On this view, migrant ecopoetics of planetarity from below presents decolonial methods of ethical doing and political remapping through which to refuse colonial codes of disposability and recast matters out of place as the fertile soil for an ecologically expansive notion of life. Migrant ecocriticism can offer a critical framework for reimagining the planet through embedded and embodied ecologies of hybridity, movement, and emergence that disrupt modern fantasies of purity, bordering, and transcendence. Migrant and diasporic senses of place can redefine territories and identities with storied, porous, and mobile meanings. Planetarity from below materializes the ongoing process whereby ecological collectives are constructed by the borderland subjects exposed to colonial racism and extractive capitalism. It also addresses migration artists' search for cultural forms and aesthetics of alterity and nonhuman agency that rearticulate the *excess* of mobility for transformative poiesis in the Anthropocene.

My analysis unfolds an insurgent poetics of excess that gives shape to a decolonial planetarity interwoven by movement. Movement refers to both the expulsions that render migration central to the capitalist reproduction of modern (un)freedom and the margins of liminality within which migratory and surplus subjects reimagine political communities and reclaim movement as the intrinsic condition of life. The book's chapters examine how migrant ecopoetics unmoors the inhuman property relations of colonial extraction and redirects the residual forces of mobility toward ethical ecologies. They range from Indian Australian placemaking stories that invoke a decolonial ethics of wonder to destabilize settler colonial possession; to Asian Canadian water memoir and poetry that unlearn capitalist resource imaginaries to foster diasporic-Indigenous solidarity; to refugee ecocinema and memoir that assemble affective responses to interspecies extinction and solidarity at oceanic borders; to climate fiction in which the ghostly return of nomadic subjects implodes fossil fuel capitalism; and to Chinese migrant worker literature that depicts "geo-cyborg" characters emerging from the toxic debris of neoliberalism, industrialization, and technocracy to animate geosocial and mineralogical agency. Together, this corpus of migrant ecopoetics from below decolonizes a universalist concept of the Anthropocene to historicize unruly, incalculable, and more-than-human ecologies of migrant and refugee lives that exceed techno-capitalist control from above. A poetics of planetarity from below goes beyond a reductive critique of capitalist modernity and Western coloniality. Rather, it pluralizes knowledge by recuperating the networked agencies embedded within the current world order and situating migrant subjects at the unstable geos/bios/machine interfaces to offer alternative cosmovisions of coexistence.

While the concept of planetarity might imply a sense of wholeness, I approach it as a pluriversal world imaginary to counteract the old universalism that neutralizes local histories, subjects, and places into a telos of modern totality. Romantic images of the planet, like those found on Google Earth or within globalization's narratives of time-space compression, tend to celebrate an abstract sense of unity as a product of the homogenizing effects of capital and technology. These global abstractions still hinge on a colonial divide between nature and culture. Instead, planetarity composes a relational ontology of emergent naturecultures from thick material interdependencies. It multiplies singularity and nonexploitative modes of interspecies mutuality against globalization's machine of sameness, domination, and extraction. Whereas the globe is a humancentric construct, the planet is ecocentric and what decenters the human (Chakrabarty 2021, 19). In conversation with Gayatri Spivak, who coined the term "planetarity," my initial concern is to conceptualize the planet as ethical alterity, one that shifts from the globe as a rationalized techno-capitalist system to the planet as an incalculable ecology of lived encounters (2003, 72). A figure of the (im)possible, planetarity entails Derridean "teleopoiesis," or imaginative making from a distance, to call forth inhabitable futures to come.

While emphasizing that literary and artistic imaginations hold open the epistemological unknowability of the planet to suspend global capitalist consumption, the narratives in *Planetarity from Below* deviate from Spivak's conception of planetarity as the textually undecidable to articulate a materialist poetics of planetarity. These narratives invite us to consider ecopoetics as a material-discursive practice for remaking migrant and refugee subjectivity, mobility, and freedom from state and capitalist abstraction to thick sites of more-than-human emergence. They open up affective and multispecies worldings of migrant flourishing embedded in everyday lived ecologies of survival, wonder, and labor. These stories are planetary because they translate the inhuman and nonhuman matters—land, water, energy, animals, plants, minerals, and technics—currently policed by colonial capitalist property regimes, back into the vibrant substances that always already constitute the human. Living into a planetary relationality, differences and otherness become moments for ethical transformation rather than reasons for fear, enclosure, and commodification. Moving beyond romantic unity, planetarity from below uncovers how an alternative cosmopolitics of radical coexistence are immanent to the material interconnectedness of plural life-forms that emerge from and survive through state and capitalist injustices. The planet is always in excess of the globe.

Tracing material shimmers of planetarity on the uneven geographies of state and capital, *Planetarity from Below* triangulates a decolonial dialogue at the intersection of diaspora, migration, and critical race studies, ecocriticism and environmental humanities, and the planetary turn in the humanities. Offering "planetarity from below" as a decolonial ethos of worlding, this work diverges from familiar tales of globalization and liberal humanist recognition to explore migration cultural expressions that register the colonial differentiation of human geological agency. It helps extend critical frameworks of environmental ethics and political ecology by attending to how migrant and refugee cultural works creatively reimagine society as where posthuman ethics and multispecies coexistence can flourish. A comparative inquiry into contemporary migrant ecopoetics across settler colonialism, racial capitalism, Indigeneity, refugee biopolitics, climate migration, techno-capitalism, and neoliberal globalization—with geographical focuses on Australia, North America, and China—*Planetarity from Below* presents a translocal and transnational study of emerging planetary aesthetics. It sheds light on a developing body of migration literature and arts that has taken an ethical stance for a shared planet.

## A Decolonial Approach to Migrant Ecocriticism

Over the past two decades, a notable shift in ecocriticism has focused on moving beyond canonical nature writing to address the intersection of environmental justice and social justice within postcolonial, Indigenous, and migration literature and arts (Huggan and Tiffin 2006; Adamson and Slovic 2009; Hayashi 2011; DeLoughrey and Handley 2011; Nixon 2011; Iheka 2017; Suzuki 2021; Santa Anna et al. 2022). This critical shift has facilitated a reflective awareness of nature and the environment beyond white settler imaginaries of pristine wilderness to recognize them as historical formations shaped by colonial and racial powers. Postcolonial, Indigenous, and Asian diasporic ecocritics examine how nature has been mobilized as a material and ideological instrument of social control, how space and place offer recuperative tools for histories of empire and capital, and how environmental violence is tied to the structural violence of global neoliberalism. Emerging at the outset of the twenty-first century, with recognition of the human's geological agency, this intellectual trend grounds narratives of disjunction and rupture to "provincialize" a universalist geologic of the Anthropocene (Deloughrey 2019, 2). In *Slow Violence and the Environmentalism of the Poor*, Rob Nixon describes how literary writing can make visible, fracture, and give human dimensions to the insidious and instrumental ways that neoliberal development imposes displacement upon the Global South, not solely by physical removal but through the slow violence of resource extraction and outsourced toxicity rendering people's homes uninhabitable (2011, 19). The environmentalism of the poor disrupts a seamless logic of "free market" neoliberalism, exposing the colonial logics of developmentalist enterprises that spatially and temporally mark the marginalized poor and their landscapes as expendable for capitalist elite profit.

Decolonial ecocriticism reconceives migration beyond Eurocentric epistemologies of governance, bordering, and (un)freedom to reveal how the modern colonial matrix of power degrades the ecosocial livability of raced, gendered, and subaltern peoples. As Malcom Ferdinand poetically writes, decolonial ecology is "a *rising up from the modern world's hold*," in search of a new world where emancipation from colonial rule cannot be reduced to human relations, but must imply a disembarking off the colonial ship of inhabitation (2022, 175). Coloniality names the extraction of human and nonhuman ecosystems by the capitalist property relations as limitless resources. When coloniality is located at the heart of ecological crises, environmental issues like climate change, pollution, and species extinction are never simply "natural" disasters, but the material symptoms of empire, settler colonialism, racial capitalism, militarism, fossil fuel capitalism, and technocracy. Decoloniality, as Catherine Walsh and Walter Mignolo remind us, brings to light occluded histories, subjectivities, struggles, worldviews, and bodies to unlearn, undo, and disobey the abstract universals of the modern colonial order for a pluriversal *otherwise* (2018, 17). The experiences and imaginations of the displaced offer a political genealogy that counters the apolitical, acultural, and dehistoricized sense of place in modern environmentalism (Ferdinand 2022, 179). *Planetarity from Below* stories this insurgence of a political ecology of the wretched of the earth for otherwise ways of inhabiting the earth. Specifically, I construct a transnational sense of place by interconnecting decolonial projects across a spectrum of migration contexts including diaspora, Indigeneity, refugeehood, and migrant labor on a global scale. This integrated approach moves beyond national boundaries and a lopsided view of South-to-North migratory flows, linking the causes of displacement and internal migration in the Global South with the symptoms and effects of migration in the Global North.

A decolonial migrant ecocriticism must also grapple with how contemporary migration border regimes reproduce a colonial hierarchy of life and animacy. Concerns about environmental justice, mobility, and histories from below characterize the fledgling field of migrant ecocriticism. In 2017, the journal *ISLE* published a special cluster on "migrant ecologies in an (un) bordered world," with essays tracing diverse border crossings—refugee and asylum seeking, climate and environmental migration, migrant labor, and animal migration—to examine the concomitant ecological and social disposability in processes of migration. By establishing a relationship between the mobile body and the environment, migrant ecocriticism troubles the disciplinary power of borders and exposes how colonial racial structures mobilize environmental discourses to institute stasis, displacement, and exploitation (Iovino 2013; Oppermann 2017; Zhou 2022; Baldwin 2022). Borders are biopolitical technologies that categorize migrants according to rubrics of race, class, gender, skills, and health; they also present ethical opportunities for reimagining nonexclusionary and hybrid modes of belonging. At a time of mass extinction, borders also raise questions of multispecies justice to underscore the plight of displaced nonhumans. For example, the US-Mexico border wall, built during the Trump administration to deter human migrants, impedes the freedom and seasonal migration routes of various animals, including mountain lions, javelinas, black bears, foxes, coyotes, and visiting jaguars and ocelots (Nugent 2022). In this context, considering the excluded migrants and animals in shared vulnerability and solidarity can offer powerful decolonial and antiracist critique.

Conversant with critical border studies that understands borders as constantly becoming and exchanging between inside and outside (Parker and Vaughan-Williams 2012, 728–29), migrant ecocriticism further reconceives borders as material and discursive spaces enabling an environmental politics of becoming-with. As Oppermann notes, borders are "ethical sites that confound save-the-day political solutions" because unexpected human and animal crossings give rise to dynamic ecosocial geographies that defy discursive closure (2017, 248). Attending to Australia's oceanic borders and refugee ecology allows me to illustrate this point (see Chapter 4). Oceanic borders and refugee camps are ecosocial interfaces where land and sea, humans and nonhumans, stories, affects, bodies, and places converge to world a relational ontology of refugee (im)mobility, whose ambiguity contests territorial finality. A decolonial migrant ecocriticism, as this book conceives it, departs from discrete selfhood to reconsider migrants and refugees as being corporeally and affectively embedded in vital relationships to more-than-human environments. These body-place exchanges are political. They materialize but are also capable of disrupting biopolitical structures. Thus, decolonial migrant ecocriticism diverges from reproducing Western humanist narratives that externalize the mobile body itself as security threat, border spectacle, and abstract data. Instead, it recenters impurity, movement, and contingency as the defining rhythms of a migrant environmental ethos.

While ecocritical and migration studies have illuminated the interconnected vulnerabilities between migrants and nonhumans by foregrounding how racism and speciesism share similar roots in colonial structures of "othering, domination, and governmentality" and capitalist exploitation, these projects sometimes stop short at a narrative of victimhood, leaving unexamined the generative political kinship between migrants and the nonhuman (Hage 2017, 14). That such kinship is a tricky issue is frequently stated in claims of a linear progression of humanity (dehumanized—human—posthuman) that emphasize the humanity of migrants before their ecological and more-than-human traits. A progression claim is addressed by Sandro Mezzadra and Brett Neilson in their analysis of the "We are humans" rallying cry from Lampedusa, a Mediterranean island switch spot for North African asylum seekers en route to Europe. They suggest that this "to be human" slogan by the most vulnerable of mobile subjects exposes the poignancy of "*all too human* politics," whether these politics "celebrate technological prosthesis, explore the environmental consequences of human exceptionalism, or assert the independence of object from human thought and perception" (2018, 230). The assumed tension between the "yet to be human" and the "all too human" expresses how struggles over mobility in our global present are deeply intertwined with colonial borders and hierarchies that define what it means to be human.

There are several counterarguments to the narrative of progression, the idea that the dehumanized must be recognized as human before ecological considerations. First, as humans who breathe, drink, and exchange with the world, migrants are ontologically entangled with other humans and nonhuman actants of air, water, nutrients, and toxicants. Second, more-than-human entanglements are political tools for both revelation and resistance within the carceral confines of modern bio- and necropolitics. Admittedly, entanglement is not always strategic and enabling. It can manifest as toxic intimacy corroding migrant bodies and dreams, such as the use of toilet hygiene and long queues to impose domesticated animal status on refugees in Australia's offshore detention camps (see Chapter 3), or the toxic waste of globalization that materializes in the diseased bodies of Chinese migrant workers (see Chapter 5). But it is precisely the game of state and capitalist biopolitics to deny the embedded and embodied nature of disenfranchised migrants that justifies the making surplus of these living subjects via uneven exposure, hazardous waste, and exploitative labor. Here, a more-than-human politics becomes a way of critically revealing "the biopolitical technologies of racio-speciesist boundary marking" and the embodied acts of inhuman subjection inscribed by the military-industrial prison complex at borders, which casts nonstate outsiders as the bestial nonhuman other of the tautological human citizen subject (Pugliese 2020, 54). Rather than moralizing a push to transcend the human or risking an all-too-human tendency of depoliticization, this book is written in search of renewing migrant justice through a more-than-human lens: These inhuman intimacies and alliances are political sites for identifying existing humanist precarity and political accountability, and for composing coalitional and multispecies futures where migrants become with a lively world full of agency.

Considering migrant kinship with nonhuman nature is compelling in a decolonial context because it opens possibilities for an alternative environmental ethics that does not depart from individual morality or liberal humanist ecological stewardship. These notions of stewardship and virtue reinforce Christian humanist notions of the individual as a disembodied being detached from an external environment (Alaimo 2016, 82). While environmental justice research has focused on identifying bodies of color as sites of environmental injustice and correcting those injustices, these studies often assume, and thus fail to adequately dislodge, a habitual bonding between a whole, healthy body and a pure, healthy environment (Ray 2013, 8). Colonial injustice can be enacted at the very moment of environmentalism through what Sarah Jaquette Ray calls the distinction between ecological "subjects"—those (Euro-Americans) deemed stewards and rightful inhabitants who belong in nature—and ecological "others"—those considered impure, dirty, and disabled and thus threats to nature and nation (10). In other words, modern environmentalist reliance on individual morality has reinforced existing social hierarchies along racial, gender, and class lines. This is exemplified by the "trash talk" at the US-Mexico border, where media and government blame undocumented immigrants as "those who trash America," referring to discarded survival objects such as food, clothing, and water bottles (Sundberg 2023, 875). Such trash talk takes immigrants out of context and blames them for individual decisions that contaminate the purity and health of American wilderness. Anti-immigration sentiments and militarized borders are then justified by the practice of waste labeling, as migrants are demoralized as filthy, environmentally irresponsible, and akin to trash. They are cast as the opposite of ethical middle-class American citizens, while the wider geopolitical contexts compelling them to cross certain landscapes remain obscured.

Decoloniality invites us to rethink Euro-American environmentalist traditions that equate ethics with high morality asserted by the rational individual in response to an external other. An individualistic tradition of ethics privileges conscious intent and the cultivated, capitalist, and biopolitical individual, whose reasoning, human exceptionalism, and self-regulated ethical behavior are predicated on the inferiority of "spectacular, binary, and constitutive 'Others'—the disposable bodies of the sexualized, racialized, and nonhuman" (Braidotti 2006b, 130). A politics of assimilation and sameness will not disrupt these universalist views of humanity and morality. I align with Priscilla Ybarra's critique that popular US environmentalism and civil rights activism, in their claims for rights and justice for the marginalized, tend to appeal to a utopian ideal of universal humanism, which prevents a more radical interrogation of the destructive coloniality of modern humanism that perpetuates both racism and environmental degradation (2016, 27–28). This critique is applicable beyond the United States to contexts like Australia, Canada, and China, where environmental justice narratives can similarly reinforce the normative modern human subject and attendant notions of hope and victimhood. Bringing migrant and ethnic studies into a revisionist project of environmental ethics poses the question of reclaiming local lived alternatives and embodied ecological agency by marginalized peoples that expand traditional ethical frameworks.

Staying with the unresolved tension between the dehumanized and the more-than-human, *Planetarity from Below* tackles the challenging yet necessary ethical task of migrant situated kinmaking across species and material boundaries. To do so, what we need is not merely reiterating the necessity for making kin, but rather ask first what is forcing many migrants and racialized people to choose between human needs and the natural environment. What is responsible for limitations on one's kinmaking ability, as Katharine Dow and Janelle Lamoreaux have explained, lies with a heteronormative, white supremacist, capitalist political economy and its inherent structures of inequality, not with individual decision-making (2020, 487). With this insight, this book moves away from an individualist convention of ethical and moral agency toward reconfiguring environmental ethics as an ongoing process of troubling power infrastructures and value systems that hinder a more collective, planetary horizon of diversified kinship.

Displacing an individualist tradition of environmental ethics, decolonial migrant ecopoetics proposes to weave entangled narratives of migrant alliances with more-than-human kin that are reciprocally life-enhancing. Feminist, new materialist, and posthumanist scholars have broadened our conceptual tools to reconceive ethical agency, not as a discrete attribute or biopolitical morality, but as ongoing "responsibility and accountability for the lively relationalities of becoming of which we [humans] are a part" (Barad 2007, 393). Puig de la Bellacasa urges us to reconsider ethics as everyday ecological doings in the continuation and fostering of life at the corporeal level of naturecultural interdependency, where reconnecting ethical commitment to an ontology of distributed agency without reverting to classic humanist categories requires a speculative effort (2017, 16–20). Multispecies scholarship teaches us that "making kin" is a life-saving strategy in the Anthropocene (Haraway 2015; Rose 2011). In this light, a truly planetary ethics of migrant ecologies would involve viewing displaced humans as part of a broader community of displaced beings, across the living and nonliving (Chu 2021, 580). The migration writers and filmmakers in this book ecologize the unexpected alliance and practical kinship between displaced humans and nonhumans (fox, peacock, river, crab, flower, insect, mineral, and ghost). These kinships encourage an ecological ethics of mutuality and nonhuman agency without slipping back to colonial capitalist relations of property and mastery. The asylum seeker Boochani witnesses in a flower the zeal for life and freedom (Chapter 4), and the migrant worker poet Zheng Xiaoqiong forges mineralogical affinity with iron against the industrial mechanization of geologic matter (Chapter 6). Although such kinship building may carry political stakes and embodied dangers, it holds much political promise for a migrant sympoietic ethics, an ethics that cares with the intrinsic agency of the cosmological world for multispecies flourishing, against the anthropocentric individualism behind ecological plunder.

In bringing together environmental justice, critical border studies, and more-than-human scholarship, *Planetarity from Below* denaturalizes the claimed authority of modern humanist biopowers in knowing and managing migrants. Writing about migrant ecologies in the age of planetary undoing involves demystifying the environmentally ruinous colonial legacies of capitalism and its possessive reproduction of racial and class hierarchies across local and global contexts. Here decolonizing entails ecologizing. In response to Bruno Latour's provocative question, "To modernize or to ecologize?" I suggest that ecologizing serves multiple purposes in contemporary migration studies: challenging universalist tendencies of Western environmentalism with situated colonial, racial, gender, and labor histories; offering an ecomaterialist corrective to the abstraction of fluidity and flow in previous diaspora, transnational, and globalization studies; and discerning critical moments of impasse due to colonial and capitalist codes of possession and enclosure. Ecologizing migration also involves cross-mapping literatures and geographies of borderlands and migrants en route alongside those of diaspora and settler experiences. Such cross-mapping, as explored in this book, allows us to identify how the modern Man persists as a systematic dividing measure between the included and the excluded, while also propelling a shift of migrant cosmopolitics from a humanist ethics of cosmopolitanism to a planetary ethics of ecological coexistence.

Migrant ecopoetics attests to the entangled tensions and anxieties that come with living with precarity and difference in a world of man-made borders. If ethics entails the response-ability to relate to and care with alterity, and if, as Rose reminds us, "Ethics precedes ontology . . . to be enmeshed is to bear responsibility" (2022, 5), then migrant ecopoetics enlarges our ethical senses of being responsive to the vulnerability *of*, and *to*, human and nonhuman others. Vulnerability and precarity do not necessarily reinforce victimhood; as Tsing invites us to ponder, "Precarity *is* the condition of our time. . . . What if precarity, indeterminacy, and what we imagine as trivial are the center of the systematicity we seek?" (2015, 20). It is with this focus on sustaining life in flux that this book takes up the larger question of what constitutes worldmaking practices from below. Worldmaking projects arise from the thickness of life in lived flows and untidy contingencies. They show us the nontotality of the present and pluriversal histories in the making. Migrants become with places and nonhumans through ecological wonder, ancestral memory, affective attachment, interspecies sociality, and diasporic-Indigenous relations. But these ecologically attentive aspects of migration have been obscured and foreclosed by modern colonial apparatuses of property, person, and progress that mythologize the liberal possessive individual. Rather than telling stories of exceptional migrant success, or perpetuating migrant placelessness, it is urgent to start a new narrative trajectory: a story of earthly migrants.

## Planetarity from Below: Migrant Cosmopolitics beyond Human Exceptionalism

The globe and the planet are concepts of imagining the earth. Global modes of picturing the earth often reflect modern humanist desires to master alterity. The history of how globalization becomes a dominant world vision is the history of modernity dreamed by empire, capital, and technology. Global visions of the one world have manifested through European colonial expansion of territories and oceanic routes, the invention of world standard time, Cold War–era satellite imagery, and narratives of globalization—including time-space compression, the free market economy, and digitalization. In these abstract visions of intelligible oneness, the globe is figured not only as a physical enclosure but also a historically embedded ideological projection to orient the self with respect to the world, the unknown, and the other. Mary Louise Pratt in *Imperial Eyes* describes such projection by analyzing how Enlightenment-era travel writing and natural history produced a Eurocentric global or planetary consciousness during European imperial ventures (1992, 5). Today's neoliberal globalization promotes a world unified by human capital and technology, reducing time and space to regulatory grids of progress. As much as these globalist images and imaginaries evoke a romantic sense of interconnectedness, they simultaneously perpetuate an epistemic position of externality, of humans detached from Mother Earth, from where to grasp an illusory humanity as a whole (Spivak 2003; DeLoughrey 2014).

The planet intervenes in humanist globalism with ecological alterity and the limits of knowledge. Whole-earth thinking has been a prevalent theme in modern environmentalism facilitated by science and technology. During the 1960s and 1970s, iconic satellite photos like *Earthrise* and *The Blue Marble* galvanized the environmental movement by appealing to shared human history, vulnerability, and responsibility. In the 1970s, climate scientist James Lovelock and biologist Lynn Margulis developed the Gaia hypothesis, which posits the earth as a self-regulating system of living and nonliving elements whose interactive balance sustains planetary habitability. From the 1980s onward, earth system sciences have expanded to map, model, and scale the impacts of human activities on the earth's climate, atmosphere, and ocean ecosystems (Steffen et al. 2020, 54). Planetary frameworks have provided holistic, integrated, and big-data views of the earth, elucidating the reciprocal relationship between human and nature, predicting ecological thresholds and potential catastrophic ends, and pressuring global solidarity toward collective action to counter the Anthropocene.

Current planetary crises, such as climate change, species extinction, and rising toxicity, manifest as interlinked phenomena of inhuman agency and cycle breakdowns that defy mastery by scientific modeling or technological quick fixes. Facing the radical otherness of the planet, many earth system scientists assert a globalist sense of historicity by framing its habitability as a question of human governance and (in)action, but this may also obscure the planet's profound otherness that moves through but ultimately exceeds human exceptionalism (Chakrabarty 2021, 89–91). The convergence of planetary and global timescales produces what postcolonial historian Dipesh Chakrabarty describes as "being political at the limits of the political," where the Anthropocene entails a constant conceptual traffic between geologic events of deep time and political actions in human historical time, and an extension of politics and justice to the nonhuman (2021, 8–13). In the face of climate change, political thought must grapple with the tension between planetary and global perspectives, recognizing how the planetary exists both *within* and *beyond* human existence. Spivak proposes to reimagine ourselves as planetary subjects rather than global agents because the planet resides "in the species of alterity . . . we inhabit it, on loan," yet the globe is "in the gridwork of electronic capital . . . [which] allows us to think that we can aim to control it" (2003, 72). In the decolonial Anthropocene, engaging the planetary, then, is not so much about abstract interconnectedness at the world's end, as about materializing alternative epistemologies, aesthetics, and cosmovisions from the ground up. This requires a situated politics to rupture the global designs of modern colonial narratives by cultivating a planetary subjectivity that ecologizes an ethics of alterity in local places and an earthly poetics that keeps imagining unimaginable futures at the limits of representation.

As a defining feature of globalization and the abject other of the liberal human, migrants are uniquely suited to call us to planetary and emergent forms of unlearning, insurgence, and coexistence. Having researched Asian diasporic literature for over a decade, I have observed the divergence between the multiplicity of Asian diasporic identities and the Western literary market's reluctance to register such multiplicity. The contradictions of liberal hospitality and colonial structures of race and nation both enable and commodify an ethnic politics of representation under self/other binaries and domesticating labels of cultural exotica, authentic victimhood, and multicultural enrichment (Gunew 1994; Palumbo-Liu 1995; Huggan 2001; Chow 2002; Zong 2016, 2020, 2023). Although migrant and ethnic writing tends to be recognized as testimonial and particular rather than universal and transcendent, the political specificities in this literature are frequently read by the mainstream to confirm non-Western victimhood against a humanist notion of the subject and individual rights in universal white norms (Bow 2012, 558–59). Studying migrant planetary imaginations and ethics offers a valuable corrective. It not only shows that minor subjects and literature are capable of theory and worldmaking but also illuminates the creative potential of a subaltern cosmopolitics of planetarity, making visible how migrants from a variety of social contexts resist the neoliberal master subject of biopolitical life and embody the motive force of alternative futures that are already underway.

Planetarity offers a renewed vision for migrant cosmopolitics that challenges anthropocentric and capitalist framings of mobility in the broader fields of globalization, transnationalism, and cosmopolitanism. In response to significant waves of migration in the late twentieth century, diaspora studies and cultural theories of globalization gained prominence. Foundational scholars like Homi K. Bhabha, James Clifford, and Stuart Hall have explored how migrancy and diaspora afford cultural alternatives of hybridity, difference, and fluidity to territorialized notions of race, nation, and culture (Clifford 1988; Hall 1990; Bhabha 1994). Diasporic experiences enable these scholars to envision a cosmopolitan ethics of otherness, cultural exchange, and political belonging that fosters coexistence among differences. Concomitantly, many critics have doubted the figurative freedom of hybridity and cosmopolitanism, especially the proclaimed separation from colonial structures of race and labor and the tendency to frame culture as an antidote to structural inequalities. Many have exposed how Western liberalism depoliticizes cultural differences, rendering differences as consumable goods under seemingly benevolent rhetoric of multiculturalism (Hage 1998; Chow 2002). Other scholars like Pheng Cheah critique the anthropocentric tendency of hybridity theories for positing migration as a mode of transcendence into human linguistic and cultural freedom from the givenness of nature and material constraints in the Global South (2006, 86). By privileging cultural transcendence, theories of hybridity and cosmopolitanism risk reinforcing modern "rifts between nature and culture, the Real and its representation/signification, matter and language/form, necessity and freedom" (Cheah 2006, 8). In addition, many scholars have troubled cosmopolitanism's reliance on liberal humanist notions of intentionality, rational agency, and moral stewardship that presuppose a colonial separation between human and the environment (Latour 2004; Ahuja 2012; Elias and Moraru 2015b). These debates present a nuanced perspective on the often celebratory discourses of cultural hybridity and cosmopolitanism in migration and diaspora theory, which may fail to trouble, or even privilege, human exceptionalism and neoliberal mobility.

Questioning the desirability of neoliberal subjective life, a planetary poetics cultivates ecocentric modes of migrant and refugee subjectivity and mobility, where collective survival is sustained by going beyond human exceptionalism. Planetarity, in the words of Amy J. Elias and Christian Moraru, ethicizes the world through a bioconnective structure of awareness that subverts globalization's homogenizing tendency and makes up for cosmopolitanism's lack of care for nonhuman life (2015a, xi–xii). Deliberately provocative, Elias and Moraru concede that planetarity has yet to inspire a world culture of relational localisms that would make up its postnational, geocultural, and nonhierarchical formation (2015a, xii). Indeed, previous thinkers such as Spivak, Chakrabarty, Ursula Heise, and others have called for a planetary imaginary that remains inclusive yet rejects completeness, a mode of worlding that I explore more concretely through migrant situated imaginations of more-than-human alliances. Interlacing my analysis of migrant ecocriticism between globalist abstraction and planetary alterity, I turn to decolonial ecopoetics for crafting planetarity in process. The merit of speculating on planetarity lies not in building conclusive solutions but in training our capability to constantly imagine otherwise. Despite dominant sociality shaped by property, nation, and neoliberal values, the migration literature and film discussed here recuperate borderland experiences of the colonized and racialized to compose the planet as method and imperative, rather than entity or destination. Reading the planet as method attunes our attention to a micropolitics of everyday, vernacular, and nested ecological experiments by the otherwise "excess" subjects exposed to colonial racism and capitalist extraction in open-ended becoming. Migrant ethical agendas of planetarity from below imagine into being a pluralist ecoculture of more-than-human solidarity while sharpening critique of the world's differential powers.

Aware of the limits of representation, *Planetarity from Below* contributes to the recent material-discursive turn in literary and cultural studies by thickening transversal accounts of migration to overcome the coloniality of knowledge. I write during a period of vigorous debates in literary and cultural studies about the narrative and cultural forms that can better accommodate human agency at the timescales and materialities of the Anthropocene. These include reconsidering the limitations of the realist novel and its themes of individual moral growth (Ghosh 2016), recalibrating genre and speculative fiction to unsettle anthropocentrism and neoliberal capitalism (Clark 2015; Ghosh 2016; Bahng 2018), addressing the representational challenges of slow violence and environmental justice (Nixon 2011), and investigating the overlooked textuality of transcorporeal natures (Alaimo 2010; 2016), storied matter (Iovino and Oppermann 2014), oceanic passages (DeLoughrey 2017; Suzuki 2021), elements (Cohen and Duckert 2015), and fossil fuels (Balkan and Nandi 2021). I consider these discussions as efforts to move storytelling and literary criticism away from traditions rooted in human exceptionalism, individualism, and representation, toward an ecomaterial paradigm that accounts for the coemergence of culture and nature, language and matter, and form and reality.

In this vein, my study places at the heart of planetarity an imaginative poetics that calls into being relational collectives of which humans are already a part. Planetarity resonates with what Timothy Morton terms "ecology without nature," or the "mesh," which expresses the ecological state of human society as enmeshed within a relational web of life, in which life-forms compose uncanny collectives of coexistence that are at once familiar (intertwined) and strange (singular) (2009, xx). The mesh implies a dynamic ecological collectivity both "to come" and disturbingly "there," because we are it (Morton 2010, 278). Similar to Morton's notion of the mesh as what is beyond concept and externality, the planet as relational collectives is uncanny, nontotalizing, and in excess of meaning. But differing from Morton's aversion to an environmentalist language of "embeddedness" and "immersion" as what reinforces separateness (2010, 281), I insist that planetarity needs active construction by environmentalist language, culture, and arts that iteratively invoke embeddedness to resist colonial capitalist alienation, imagine alternative worlds while describing the existing world, and bring forth disenfranchised bodies, times, and ecologies against their domestication and annihilation. If there are inevitable tensions between worlds and words, ecological embeddedness and aesthetic distance, and planetary ethics and global politics, then the migration arts assembled in this book demonstrate how new immanent experiences of coexistence can be negotiated through storytelling as a generative act of creating the multiplicity of bodies, selves, and worlds that potentiate conditions and care for social change. Between the familiar and the strange, self and other, and the yet-to-come and the uncanny present, planetarity can be cultivated through a diasporic sensibility of internal migrancy or a place-based poetics without telos.

Imagining planetarity compels epistemes, ethics, and praxes of alterity and unknowability in human relations with more-than-human nature. These epistemes of the unknown take myriad shapes in the book's chapters—wonder (Chapter 1), water (Chapter 2), affective ambiguity (Chapter 3), haunting (Chapters 3 and 4), metamorphosis (Chapter 4), and toxic deviance (Chapter 5). By ecologizing an ethics of alterity and nonhuman agency, the migration literature and arts explored here can be understood as expanding epistemological tools for a pluriversal cosmopolitics of coexistence: acquiring embedded knowledge yet aware of the limits of knowledge, appreciating differences without capitalist possession, and becoming with the world at the unpredictable interface of matter and meaning. The planetarity thus performed and produced departs from the one-world modernity of techno-capitalist globalization toward knowing, caring, and collaborating for lifeworlds in the plural. On one level, these narratives can be interpreted as giving historicity to the excess of mobility in the shadows of modern subjective life; on another level, they orient our attention to the wonders and terrors of life's entanglements during modernity's environmental making of the "planetary uncanny."

The migratory sites and authors I engage in the book convey a comparative and translocal approach. The book transgresses a nationalist tradition in the study of literature, following critics like Elias and Moraru who proclaim "reading planetarily, then, is necessarily reading comparatively" (2015, xxiv), and Wai Chee Dimock who holds literature answerable not to the nation-state but deep time and the planet as a whole (2008, 4). The book's scope expands from its initial focus on migration cultural expressions in and about Australia—where migrant and refugee ecocriticism is yet to gain traction—to contemporary Asian North American and Chinese literature to engage a heterogeneous cast of marginalized migrant ecologies across empires. This translocal perspective reveals the fractures in a progressive rhythm of neoliberal globalism by showing how migrant and refugee subjects are capable of post-anthropocentric ways of being. It is my hope that the translocal structure of the book reflects the decentralized fabric of planetarity from below, where constellations of site-specific local resistance against colonial and capitalist disposability incrementally world an ecocentric commons and the cultural-aesthetic geographies of the planet.

The migration literature and cinema I analyze refuse essentialist notions of belonging defined by race and nation, while they also share a desire to embed migrants in local places against placelessness, whether it is a farm, river, detention camp, desert, factory unit, or waste dump. Rather than stable territories, these places are portrayed as porous contact zones infiltrated with global and inhuman crossings. Writers like Merlinda Bobis allegorize climate futures and refugee migration beyond national borders. Others, like Mena Abdullah, Kazim Ali, Rita Wong, and Behrouz Boochani, disturb the territorial claims and telos of settler colonialism through nonlinear processes of diasporic placemaking. For Ali and Wong, embodied and embedded knowledge is crucial for unlearning immigrant complicity in settler colonialism and engaging diasporic-Indigenous collaborative ecologies. For Zheng Xiaoqiong and Chen Qiufan, Chinese migrant workers embody the transscalar, molecular, and geosocial intimacies between the globe and the planet, including unwanted and toxic ecologies. Chen's sci-fi novel *Waste Tide* (2013) depicts a biomedical e-waste object whose migratory trajectory connects American militarism in the Asia-Pacific during World War II, globalization, waste imperialism, techno-capitalism, urbanization, and migrant labor exploitation in China. Rising from historical debris to haunt the future, the novel's waste matters and migrant bodies expose biochemical afterlives that are irresolvable by progressive narratives of modernity, technoscience, and the free market. Chen's novel, then, alerts us to the nonlinear temporalities and geosocial formations over the *longue durée* that pose challenges for artistic expressions, epistemologies, and ethico-political practices in an epoch of planetary unraveling.

In this book, I put forward two decolonial praxes—*ecologizing an ethics of alterity* and *thickening mobility*—to characterize how migrant ecopoetics reconstitutes life and freedom in the cracks between the globe and the planet. The book is divided into two parts that connect the decolonial ecologies of diasporic settlers and transient migrants. This conceptual design underscores the continuity of, and insurgence against, colonial humanist borderings. Part I reads diasporic narratives of land and water that decolonize settler colonialism. What does it mean for migrants to inhabit land and drink water haunted by colonial ghosts? An ethics of alterity foregrounds onto-epistemological practices of wonder, humility, and unknowability when prioritizing nature's immanent agency. This part analyzes how wonder and water, as ambiguous ecologies that destabilize knowledge and possession, might animate migrant "unsettler" poetics of ethical placemaking, interspecies mutuality, and Asian-Indigenous solidarity. Asian diasporic authors Mena Abdullah, Kazim Ali, and Rita Wong identify possession as an *impasse* for a diasporic politics of difference in settler colonial states like Australia and Canada, where Asian differences are commodified for racial capitalism and white anxiety projection. Decolonizing wonder and water provides an ecological counterpoint, enabling diasporic settlers to recognize and refuse the inhuman property relations imposed upon them by a colonial politics of recognition. This unsettling process also illuminates how diasporic modes of emplaced impurity contribute to ecological awareness and ethics that respect nonhuman agency. A decolonial analytic stays with the historical incommensurability among diasporic, settler, and Indigenous positionalities, while actively probing into the new stakes and solidarities that might emerge as diasporic placemaking shifts from "settler" to "unsettler" geographies.

This focus on unsettled ethos is joined by a second cohort of narratives that call for a poetics of thick mobility to story the entangled, contingent, and more-than-human lifeways of refugees and migrant laborers within and against biopolitical capture. What are the implications of decolonial and more-than-human methods for the displaced who are yet to attain humanity? The idea of "thickness" establishes the excess of mobility. Thickness addresses the ambivalent dynamics of mobility and immobility, where an emphasis on fluidity and flow in migration and transnational studies encounters state and capitalist bordering that dehumanizes refugees and migrant laborers as surplus, waste, and dead matter. While thick mobility acknowledges the slow violence and slow death by neoliberal capitalism, it also recuperates migrant worldmaking projects from lived and felt contingencies and everyday practices of sustaining life in messy materialities that express and elude posthumanist biopolitics. What alternative mobilities of life and animacy abound in inhuman landscapes of oceanic borders, refugee camps, climate-parched deserts, migrant worker sweatshops, and e-waste dumps? Thick mobility embraces an ethics of subsistence, exposure, and transversality to articulate a residual poetics that animates migrant and refugee movements and ecological collectives beyond humanist apparatuses of politics.

### Diasporic "Unsettler" Poetics

In Chapter 1, "Unsettling Possession: Diasporic Ecologies and Ethics of Wonder," I examine a diasporic ethics of ecological wonder, asking if and how diasporic memory and cultural hybridity contribute to an emplaced mode of wonder that does not view its objects possessively. I analyze Indian Australian writer Mena Abdullah's short story collection *The Time of the Peacock* ([1965] 2019), which recuperates diasporic mobilities to challenge white settler pastoral imaginaries on dispossessed Indigenous land. Set against the racial assimilation policies of the 1950s, the stories portray a Hindu-Muslim immigrant family whose placemaking practices remap an "Australian" landscape, the bush, as a space where natural history intersects with human histories of empire, nation, race, and labor migration in early twentieth-century Australia, with a focus on the history of Muslim hawkers. By tracing how the racial and cultural experiences of the immigrant child narrator interact with her embodied sense of wonder at the natural world, I explore how ecological wonder is vulnerable to the domesticating tendencies of racism and ownership. I argue that what distinguishes Abdullah's stories from existing environmental literature is her distance from an individualist tradition to decolonize wonder for antiracist and post-anthropocentric critique. To wonder, yet not to possess, is depicted not only as a practice of mapping nature's abundance against racial isolation, but also as an ethical challenge and opportunity for migrant settlers to realize the inhuman property relations imposed upon them by colonial racial subjection. Wonder's role in revealing the ecological uncanny and its interrogation of the tension between alterity and possession render it a vital praxis for decolonial migrant ecologies by invigorating debates about race, property, and settler humanist recognition. I explore the decolonial potential of the *diasporic settler*, positing diaspora as a helpful framework for problematizing settler claims to indigenization. Abdullah's stories express that diasporic ethics and ecologies of wonder can inspire new forms of unsettler responsibilities by delinking migrant placemaking from self-possessed modern mastery and shifting toward an ethics of alterity and unknowability with respect to nonhuman agency. It is also wonder's resistance against ideological calculability that moves diasporic liberatory politics beyond a colonial dichotomy of domination and survival to open space for playfulness, creativity, and interspecies mutuality within the planetary web of life.

Further unsettling possession, Chapter 2, "Decolonizing Waters: Indigeneity, Diaspora, and the Aqueous Commons," examines diasporic water narratives that unlearn capitalist property relations. I argue that migrant ethical ecologies within settler colonial contexts must address racialized people's participation in settler forms of citizenship, rights, and property ownership that perpetuate the systematic theft of Indigenous land. The works of Indian American writer Kazim Ali and Chinese Canadian poet Rita Wong draw us to water eddies of liberal dissent in recent diasporic writing that confronts migrant inheritance of colonialism and cultivates Asian-Indigenous solidarities. Water gestates relational ethics that flow across past and present, planetary commonality and situated politics, and life and toxicity, connoting a planetarity attentive to the limits of knowledge. Ali's memoir *Northern Light* (2021) and Wong's poetry collection *Undercurrent* (2015) illustrate how water's ambiguity to connect and differentiate enables decolonial community building, facilitating collaborations across knowledge systems while "staying with the trouble" (Haraway 2016). Ali's memoir counters settler colonial hydropower and amnesia by intertwining an immigrant's quest for place with reflections on his family's role in building a hydroelectric dam that displaces water ecosystems and the Cross Lake Crees in Canada. Wong's ecopoetics recasts bodies, cities, and landscapes into a liquid matrix of capitalist injustice, petrocultural modernity, and radioactive waste, seeking to dissolve settler colonial enclosure and call for system change. I suggest that the water stories by Ali and Wong perform a decolonial poetics of the *aqueous commons*, unsettling the modern idea of water commons as property rights management and moving toward an aqueous politics of watershed consciousness and more-than-human care. Approaching aqueous subjectivity from the coemergence of watery matters and watery poetics, this chapter reimagines water bodies as ecocultural archives of discrepant temporalities, knowledges, and solidarities that unmoor settler capitalist territoriality. The aqueous commons proposes an ongoing practice of ethical worlding, illuminating the centrality of embodied and emplaced knowledge for cross-racial environmentalism and decolonial modes of learning *with*.

## Thick Mobility: Excess Ecologies and Residual Forms

The next three chapters ecologize the excess of mobility in contexts of species extinction, climate change, and toxic waste. Chapter 3, "Refugee Thick Mobility: More-Than-Human Emergence at Oceanic Borders" considers refugees and asylum seekers within a planetary collective of displaced beings (minerals, wildlife, and ghosts) in an age of extinction. Public policy and media often reduce asylum seekers to abstract figures of security threat, faceless masses, or humanitarian rescue. While dominant bio- and necropolitical frameworks critique humanist hierarchies to counter sovereign erasure, they also risk reinforcing anthropocentric structures of life and foreclosing posthumanist and ecological understandings of refugee mobility. I propose *thick mobility* as a method to examine more-than-human biopolitics and emergence at migration borders and illustrate through analyses of recent refugee cinema and memoir what cultural poetics this new framework may take shape. Gabrielle Brady's documentary film *Island of the Hungry Ghosts* (2018) invokes the atmosphere of haunting to attach emotional thickness to the slow death incurred by Australia's governance of biodiversity and human diversity on Christmas Island. Behrouz Boochani's memoir *No Friend but the Mountains* (2018) conveys an affective ecology of (im)mobility where the author's anxiety, fear, hope, and wonder intertwine with the migration border regime. I argue that the atmospherics of haunting and affective (im)mobility in these works articulate residual ecologies of refugee worldmaking that animate an eco-ethics of excess, contingency, and ambiguity against a modern necropolitics of extinction. Refugee thick mobility reveals more-than-human relations not just as explanatory tools for posthuman biopolitics, but also as practical means for a multispecies politics of shared vulnerability, grievability, and solidarity. This perspective unfolds an ecologically expansive notion of life that decolonizes refugee mobility from an exceptional humanism toward cultivating affective and planetary collectives that resist colonial capitalist policing of life.

Continuing the discussion of refugee ecology, Chapter 4, "Climate Migration, Carbon Specters, and Planetarity from Below," proposes a nomadic praxis of planetarity from below. As climate change exacerbates border geopolitics, Filipina Australian writer Merlinda Bobis's novel *Locust Girl* (2015) reframes climate migration not as an external spectacle but as an implosive and entropic symptom of colonial subjection and capitalist extraction that reproduce inequalities at a time of Western humanist existential crisis. The novel allegorizes a climate future as the past-to-come, where the specters of colonialism, racism, and fossil capitalism return to haunt humanity in residual forms of desertification, climate migration, and militarized borders. Implosion offers a geosocial language to interpret the climate migrant as a vital figure in shaping decolonial understandings of climate change and to reclaim the ontological uncertainties of climate futures from paralyzing destruction toward reconfiguring systemic change. Placing Jacques Derrida's deconstructive spectrality in dialogue with Gilles Deleuze's nomadic ethics, I argue that, to dislodge the racial order of extractive capitalism, planetary subjectivity must ecologize an ethics of alterity beyond the discursive domain into immanent experiences of more-than-human existence. *Locust Girl* dramatizes the border crossing of a female climate refugee whose insect metamorphosis prioritizes embodied senses and intersubjective relations to stars, wind, rocks, water, fire, and other cosmic forces. The novel is a pertinent example of planetarity from below by linking a dispossessed woman's nomadic becoming to a planetary cosmopolitics of earthly multitude that is genuinely open to the inhuman and nonhuman dimensions of human subjectivity. I consider how the speculative aesthetics of *Locust Girl* develops planetarity as a decolonial episteme of differentiation that confronts the specters of extractive capitalism, and as a multispecies commons that thickens mobility and subjectivity through entangled assemblages of cosmic materialism. Climate fiction like Bobis's invites readers to imagine how transformative politics under climate change might arise from the excess of mobility and the exuberance of kinetic energy that implode state and capitalist calculations toward a new earth-to-come.

In Chapter 5, "Global Excess, Planetary Deviance: Migrant Workers, Waste, and the Geo-Cyborg," I show that migrant worker ecologies reveal the accelerated crossover between the globe and the planet in an era of self-devouring growth. As technological production and consumption continue to shape modern life, the global technosphere wreaks geological impact by consuming energy at an unprecedented scale, surpassing its ability to recycle waste and carbon. Grounding such planetary unmaking in the biochemical intimacies of neoliberal globalization, I analyze how Chinese migrant workers invite ethical and political attention to the deviant materialities of toxic waste and environmental illness that are exported to working-class bodies in the name of transnational capital. Drawing on the posthuman ethics of Karen Barad and Donna Haraway and the geosocial theory of Kathryn Yusoff, I propose that migrant worker ecologies prompt a new planetary figure—the *geo-cyborg*—an imaginary of techno-modernity that transmutes across the globe and the planet, the technosphere and the geobiosphere, and product and waste. Zheng Xiaoqiong's literary works and Chen Qiufan's sci-fi novel *Waste Tide* depict Chinese migrant worker geo-cyborg characters in global factories and e-waste recycling sites. Zheng's poetry and prose explore how the corporeality of female migrant workers intra-acts with mineralogical actants, industrial matters, and seasonal changes, pushing against state, market, and patriarchal powers that seek to discipline them into passive cyborgs. In Chen's novel, an e-waste object catalyzes the heavy metal toxicants in a female waste worker's body, transforming her into a geo-cyborg who leads a class struggle against local, national, and neocolonial forms of disposability. By enmeshing migrant workers within deep time, these narratives bring to light the recalcitrant matters and geomorphic collectivities that mobilize subaltern futurity and environmental justice from the residues of what have been stratified, literally and figuratively, as the wasted matters of neoliberal techno-capitalism. Traversing macropolitics and molecules, technology and nature, and accumulation and erosion, the geo-cyborg allows for transversal senses of temporality and corporeality that destabilize the *bios/geos/machine* interface. These transversal ecologies sharpen our perception of the uneven mobilities between global excess and planetary deviance from which to disrupt techno-capitalism and assemble ethical posthuman futures.

The book's epilogue reiterates the urgency of decolonizing migration and diaspora, resounding how such a project can bring about imaginative poetics and coalitional collectives that iteratively help us overwrite the Anthropocene. If the Anthropocene is marked by the inhuman geologics of colonial racism and capitalist extraction—in tandem with the myths and traps of modern (un)freedom and liberal humanist recognition—it is equally marked by an insurgence of knowledges, imaginations, and praxes that multiply new possibilities for coexistence beyond human exceptionalism. The book's chapters have tried to demonstrate how new forms of planetary subjectivity of migrants and refugees might emerge from historically specific and intersectional contexts, where borderland consciousness enables perceptions, memories, and cosmovisions that open, widen, pluralize, and plant seeds within the cracks of extractive, extinctionist, and one-world modernity. At the heart of this study is a decolonial worlding ethos based on a diasporic praxis of emplaced difference, movement, and excess in thick relational partnerships with nature's agency. As I have hoped to show, decolonization articulates ways of ecologizing migration beyond the possessive, individualistic, and assimilationist biopolitics of state and capital to confront the structurally colonial hierarchies of existence that continue to displace humans and nonhumans worldwide. Dwelling with the tensions, entanglements, and solidarities that arise from the decolonial shift, a diasporic poetics of planetarity from below expands the ethics of alterity, justice, and freedom for migrant and refugee cosmopolitics in more-than-human worlds, where freedom is reconceptualized as multispecies flourishing.

# Part I

# Diasporic Unsettler Poetics

We do not own the land, the water, the sky, the plant world, the animal world. They own themselves. The water owns itself.

—**Lee Maracle, "Water"**

Racialization is the process by which whiteness possessively operates to define and construct itself as the pinnacle of its own racial hierarchy.

—**Aileen Moreton-Robinson, *The White Possessive***

# 1

# Unsettling Possession

## *Diasporic Ecologies and Ethics of Wonder*

> *Wonder*, from the Old English *wundor*, might be cognate with the German *Wunde* or *wound*. It would thus suggest a breach in the membrane of awareness, a sudden opening in a man's system of established and expected meanings, a blow as if one were struck or stunned. To be wonderstruck is to be wounded by the sword of the strange event, to be stabbed awake by the striking.
>
> —Howard L. Parsons, "A Philosophy of Wonder"

Mena Abdullah's short story collection *The Time of the Peacock* opens with the enchanted and pastoral view of Nimmi, an Indian Australian child narrator: "When I was little everything was wonderful; the world was our farm and we were all loved" ([1965] 2019, 9). Set against the postwar assimilation policies of the 1950s, the stories center around an Indian family living on a rural farm by the Gwydir River in New South Wales, in an iconic "Australian" landscape known as the bush. This isolated family builds a pastoral haven with cultural memories, exotic plants and animals, and Hindu-Muslim beliefs. Written with potent lyricism, most stories convey an ecological sensibility through the dreamy viewpoint and imaginative inquisitiveness of a child in an animated world. Captivated by rural nature, its seasonal changes and inscrutable details, Nimmi is "the questioner" (13) and "the dreamy one" (18). She and her siblings are wonderers and wanderers who play in gardens, creeks, and paddocks and who befriend nonhuman animals.

Wonder unsettles place into an ecological experience. Philosopher Ronald W. Hepburn suggests that wonder can stimulate appreciative relationships with the phenomenal world that do not see its objects possessively such that "they remain 'other' and unmastered" (1984, 134). Unlike curiosity that vanishes after discovery, wonder can decenter the human by rendering one vulnerable to the unexpected whose meaning is ambiguous and can vary from joy to threat. As the epigraph to this chapter expounds, some etymologists propose that "wonder" may be cognate with the German *Wunde*, or "wound" (Parsons 1969, 85). Being wonderstruck, as philosopher Howard Parsons posits, is to experience a sudden opening in one's established system of meanings, to be "stabbed awake" by an ontological rift (1969, 85). For cultural theorist Jane Bennett, affective moments of wonder, or the mood of enchantment, might be crucial in prompting "ethical generosity," fostering an alternative ethical narrative of not just moral codes but also an affective, embodied openness toward others in everyday life (2001, 3). Often overlooked in a concept like "generosity" is not the moral virtue of giving but the collective feeling of abundance, which Bennett refers to as wonder's effects of "fullness, plenitude, liveliness" (2001, 5). To insist on an ethics of ecological wonder is to highlight an ontology of nature's abundance, a counternarrative to the modern capitalist ideology of scarcity that treats nature as a finite yet limitlessly exploitable resource. Wonder is ecological in how it diminishes the self by alerting it to the alterity of earthly things as they *are* and to the interrelatedness that conditions wonder in the first place. Because of this receptivity to otherness and the unknown, people in wonder are more responsive to the qualitative richness of things beyond fixed ideas of place—to notice the extraordinary in the ordinary, the uncanny in the familiar.

The ethical potential of wonder renders it an epistemic and affective disposition that is conducive to ecological responsiveness. But wonder itself is not inherently ethical. Wonder presents an ethical choice to care for the diverse ways others flourish, but such experiences are much constrained by ideology and ordinary habits (Willmott 2018, 54–56). Wonder is, therefore, morally and ethically ambiguous, contingent on specific cultural landscapes generous to its effects. Wonder can be restrained by modern colonial ideologies of nature/culture divisions and the domesticating tendencies of rationalism, objectification, and commodification. Scholars like Bennett (2010) have subverted the stereotype of disenchanted modernity, examining how to artfully cultivate a sense of wonder through an enhanced receptivity to vital materialism, or the inextricable interactions among humans, nonhumans, and things as vibrant, agential bodies. In addition to Bennett, Glenn Willmott argues that we must inspire wonder not only in the material world but through "acts of imagination," such as stories, songs, and arts (2018, 9). By extension, I seek to explore how ecological wonder provides a helpful framework for examining the shifting entanglement between stories and landscapes, humans and nonhumans, and receptivity and responsibility. Ecology challenges representations of wonder that cast the environment as exterior—in narratives of human stewardship, the romantic sublime, and settler colonial frontiers—and calls for a rethinking of wonder ethics through protocols of coexistence, mutuality, and open-ended ethical doings when acknowledging nature's own agency (Krøijer and Rubow 2022, 381).

Wonder's intersection with ecology and ethics has been deployed to deconstruct modern subjectivity and human mastery, but its relevance to racial and diasporic politics has hardly been examined. Colonialism has it that the capacity for wonder is something lost in the raced body, positioning it as lacking, deficient, inert, like nature, and in need of mastering nature for progress. In settler colonial discourses, "nature" and "wilderness" have been racialized as ideological and material terrains of power to privilege the white settler sense of place and imagined body politics. A certain fragility of wonder is all too apparent in migrant placemaking. In *The Time of the Peacock*, rural nature presents both safety and isolation for immigrants, and childhood innocence expresses wonder's vulnerability to instrumental reason and racialization. Labeled "nigger" by white children in town (Abdullah [1965] 2019, 21), Nimmi comes to understand a racial politics of place: "I, young as I was, could see the whole of my life as strange—a dark girl in a white man's country, a Punjabi Muslim in a Christian Land. . . . So strange that I, who usually chattered and was known as monkey, had fallen into silence" (25). Her perspectival shift disrupts a universal or individualistic notion of wonder to reflect on how wonder, or the lack thereof, can offer environmental justice critique. The immigrant child's restrained wonder interrogates the pastoral "bush" landscape as a powerful myth of belonging for settler colonial nation-building, a frontier myth that fabricates "real" Australian characters of egalitarianism, mateship, and pioneering spirit to establish white possession of Indigenous land (Ward 1992, 179).

It would be premature, however, to declare wonder's defeat by racism. Ecologies of migrant placemaking illuminate critical moments of overlap and disjuncture between diasporic and settler senses of place. Such ambiguity takes on literary expression in the diverse and incommensurate placemaking practices depicted in *The Time of the Peacock*. The stories' immigrant mother character carves out a new place attachment by building an enchanted garden, her "little walled-in country" (Abdullah [1965] 2019, 10), with Kashmiri rosebush, Indian jasmine, Himalayan violets, a pomegranate tree, and a white peacock from India. Yet the family's connections to land go beyond ethnocultural preservation and the Australian state to mark diaspora as what can ecologically intersect histories of empire, settler colonialism, and migration. The land is a storied landscape where immigrant characters remake ancestral ties, where Australian bushranger legend meets anti-imperial folklore from Pakistan, and where marginalized Indian Australian heritage resists racial assimilation. These plural sets of imaginations unsettle geographically bounded place with the spatial-temporal mobilities of diaspora, in which past and present, loss and reinvention, and mobility and enclosure converge to negotiate a multilayered sense of place. A consistent theme of cross-cultural fertilization as a lived adaptation and immigrant survival strategy in the stories expresses that cosmopolitanism need not be elitist or placeless. Specifically, diasporic remembrance and religious-aesthetic experiences of wonder can appreciate nonhuman agency and creativity. Nimmi and her siblings map stories of Hindu and Muslim deities onto mountains and animals, often with awe that imbues nonhuman entities with divinity, celebrates nature's immanence, and highlights interspecies mutuality. While an eagle is "a savage-looking brute" to a white farmhand (54) and a fearsome "wild creature" to their mother (55), to Nimmi and her siblings it is the "High Maharajah of the Sky" (56), a mighty king of the sky.

By attending to the diasporic placemaking practices in *The Time of the Peacock*, I place Mena Abdullah's stories in dialogue with recent scholarship on Asian settler colonialism and decolonization. A central argument of this work is to reflect how Asian migrants and refugees have been racialized in settler colonial states under the banners of liberal integration and multiculturalism, which have reinforced ongoing colonial structures of property ownership and Indigenous dispossession by white settlers; and how decolonization may bring new challenges and orientations for Asian diaspora studies (Fujikane and Okamura 2008; Saranillio 2013; Suzuki and Bahng 2020). While the theme of Asian-Indigenous decolonial alliances is explored in Chapter 2, in this opening chapter I dwell on the overlooked discrepancy between "diaspora" and "settler" positions rather than assuming a seamless transition from migrants to settlers. That is, I probe the decolonial implications of the *diasporic settler*, exploring settler modes of unsettling as ways of constructing diasporic methods of decolonization and problematizing setter claims to place that dispossess Indigenous peoples. Can diasporic placemaking create ethical and non-anthropocentric ecologies that resist settler possession? What does it mean to cultivate a sense of wonder toward land whose stories are multiple and contested? Can diasporic ecologies and ethics of wonder inspire new forms of "unsettler" relationality?

What makes the stories in *The Time of the Peacock* planetary, and not merely transnational or cosmopolitan, is their portrayal of how diasporic sensibilities of inhabiting place through cultural hybridity and ancestral memory may uniquely contribute to an affective-aesthetic landscape of emplaced impurity and defamiliarization, which enlivens ethical ecologies of wonder. Drawing on Catherine E. Walsh and Water D. Mignolo, who propose that decoloniality is not a static condition or destination but an ongoing response to "make visible, open up, and advance radically distinct perspectives and positionalities that displace Western rationality as the only framework and possibility of existence, analysis, and thought" (2018, 17), I investigate how a diasporic ecopoetics of wonder may function as an episteme and praxis with decolonial potential, one rooted in immigrant land-based survival, creativity, and cosmopolitanism from below that question settler territoriality. Set against the White Australia policy, before multiculturalism and on a racially exclusive pastoral geography, the stories in *The Time of the Peacock* recuperate culturally diverse stories in the land. Yet due to their reflexivity on colonial racial subjection and ownership, these stories are shaped by, but ultimately disrupt, a politics of inclusion. They reimagine Asian settler subjectivities that also resist assimilationist narratives of liberal multicultural diversity or national belonging. Instead, these stories may be understood under a conception of diasporic decoloniality, highlighting diaspora as a praxis of disturbing settler racialization, interweaving histories of empire and environment across translocal and intercolonial geographies, and opening up embodied wonder through unassimilable differences that destabilize possession.

The migrant ecologies in *The Time of the Peacock* demonstrate how place-based imaginations present a site of inquiry into the relationality between diaspora and settler, roots and routes, and locality and planetarity. Diaspora and place emerge as mutually imbricated rather than antithetical. Diasporic aesthetics of wonder, hybridity, and remembrance can diversify ways of perceiving human-nonhuman entanglement by nurturing "seeing eyes" in familiar land, which differ from settler colonial imperatives of discovery and possession. I argue that wonder's capacity to reveal the uncanny in the everyday and to underscore the tension between alterity and possession makes it a vital poetics for decolonial ecology, invigorating discussions about race, ownership, and human exceptionalism. It is when we locate possession at the heart of the diasporic impasse that we are able to attend to diaspora-settler intimacies and frictions, a critical step in disentangling migrant liberty and cultural politics of difference from colonial recognition and capitalist commodification. Abdullah's stories intervene in settler colonial pastoralism and proprietary frontierism through the diasporic mobilities of land. They portray diasporic ecologies, movements, and ethics of wonder to imagine nonexploitative modes of emplaced belonging and interspecies mutuality, through which diasporic people may scrutinize modern colonial ideas of race, animality, and liberal possessive individualism.

## Between Freedom and Possession: Space, Place, and the Diasporic Impasse

"Place is security, space is freedom: we are attached to the one and long for the other," writes cultural geographer Yi-Fu Tuan ([1977] 2001, 3). According to Tuan, space is more abstract than place and becomes place once meaning and "felt value" are ascribed to it (4). The two concepts also rely on each other for definition: "From the security and stability of place we are aware of the openness, freedom, and threat of space, and vice versa" (Tuan [1977] 2001, 6). This dialectic between abstract space and stable place is a recurring theme in settler colonial studies. As a powerful signifier of roots, place can appear reactionary. Homogeneous place identities have given rise to defensive forms of nationalism, competitive localism, sentimental heritage, and antagonism toward newcomers (Massey 1994, 147). Colonial and nationalist ideologies worldwide have instrumentalized and racialized space to "naturalize" the dominant group's sense of place against those who do not belong. "World history is a history of space becoming place," writes Lawrence Buell, who traces how settler colonial conquest in America deterritorialized Native American lands into abstract spaces and then reterritorialized these lands into social places for modern "democratic" nation-building (2005, 64). Similar production of abstract spaces characterizes the colonial imaginary of *terra nullius*, or "land of nobody," with which British colonialism displaced Aboriginal Australian culture to justify land discovery, theft, and property possession. The process of how certain landscapes, such as the bush and the beach, become mythologized and racialized in the Australian national imaginary is another example of how place encodes unequal powers and can help recuperate excluded histories in the land.

Diaspora is the realm of space and dispersal. With the rise of global migration movements, diaspora studies proliferated in the 1980s and 1990s as a field exploring cultural alternatives to homogeneous identities like the nation-state. Scholars including Paul Gilroy, James Clifford, Stuart Hall, Robin Cohen, and Bruce Robbins have examined how transnational exchanges and a politics of difference unsettle place-bound identities. Highlighting the ambiguity between "the location of residence" and "location of belonging" (Gilroy 1994, 207) and the interplay between "roots and routes" (Clifford 1994, 308) in the lived experiences of scattered peoples, diaspora scholars emphasize how diasporic consciousness of dispersal and hybridity breaks away from the absolute political sensibilities of modern citizenship and racial purity. Whereas scholars largely agree on the tugging of a conceptual homeland, they disagree on whether diaspora should ideally be defined by an eventual return, as proposed by William Safran. Gilroy argues that diaspora challenges linear narratives of assimilation or return and illuminates "mutable itinerant culture" (1994, 212). Clifford critiques a teleology of return through analyses of Jewish, African American, and Caribbean British cultures that demonstrate diaspora as involving the heterogeneous and back-and-forth reconstruction of historical memory, not necessarily oriented toward roots in a physical place (1994, 306). Stuart Hall asserts that the diaspora experience is defined not by essence or purity but by "a conception of 'identity' which lives with and through, not despite, difference; by *hybridity*" (1990, 235). These claims are characteristic of the transnational literature on diaspora and difference, which views hybridity as the cultural logic of globalization in a world whose identities are increasingly mobile and synergetic.

While this transnational turn to diaspora has opened up important discussions on cultural alternatives to the nation-state and racial assimilation, it is not without its problems. As Roger Brubaker observes, diaspora theories of hybridity tend to homogenize a teleological idea of the timeless nation-state against which diaspora is celebrated, while themselves often lapsing into "groupism" to define distinct identities that prefigure hybridity (2005, 10–12). The inherent tension between boundary maintenance and boundary crossing within diaspora still presumes a metaphysics of "identity," which can fail to account for the mixed belonging and uneven degrees of loyalty among different generations of immigrants. Moreover, diaspora theory has been accused of losing sight of power asymmetry in its pursuit of floating cultural differences that are easily appropriated and ghettoized by state and market multiculturalism. As David Leiwei Li argues, the evocation of difference "does not represent a true departure from identitarian thought but rather its privatization," where structural difference is depoliticized as an internal contradiction within the autonomous subject and the historically abject Asian diasporic subject is suddenly believed to be a sovereign individual in full possession of identity choices (1998, 193–94). The commodification and individuation of difference mystify capitalism through the logic of what Donna Haraway has termed Western possessive personhood, "to have ownership of the self, to have and hold a core identity as if it were a possession" (1991, 135). Within the liberal imaginary, property encompasses not only the rights to own land but also broad concerns about self-ownership, bodily integrity, and autonomous personhood (Nicolas 2020, 118). If diaspora studies were to maintain difference and otherness as its currency of counterhegemony, it must then critically confront not just the telos of assimilation or return but more fundamentally its own complicity with the subjection logics of capitalist possession and, by extension, colonial nature/culture dichotomies that commodify difference while obscuring material racism.

The relation to property and possession seems to be where diaspora theory reaches an impasse, where it gets settled. This impasse goes beyond individual identity to unearth the systemic entrenchment of migrant liberty within colonial racial capitalism and liberal-humanist apparatuses of person, property, and progress. Liberal possessive humanism—the notion that owning property makes one a subject—underpins global processes of settler colonialism, slavery, and colonial labor through which British and American national formations sought to universalize the Euro-American liberal individual at the end of the eighteenth and the beginning of the nineteenth centuries (Lowe 2015, 21). Postcolonial, Indigenous, and feminist scholars have critiqued how the universal liberal human subject legitimates divisions of the world and humanity into modern and backward categories and rationalizes the exploitation of "uncivilized" bodies, practices, and geographies through developmentalism. Race and racialization are pivotal in naturalizing human inequalities and reframing the dispossessive logics of global capitalist accumulation in liberal languages of development, freedom, and multicultural inclusion.

Simultaneously, capitalism reproduces racial subjectivity because capital's ever-expanding accumulation depends on inequality and possession as modes of production. Racial capitalism is always already colonial capitalism, as Susan Koshy et al. explain, because it arises from recursive processes of possession and dispossession, where settler colonial land thefts, the hierarchical production of global spaces and populations, and the expropriation of labor are global capital's conditions of possibility (2022, 7). Thus, the formal abolition of slavery in the nineteenth century did not mark the end of imperialist capitalism but the advent of new exploitative practices of indentured, plantation, and migrant labor that reconstitute capitalist world ecologies (Robinson 1983). Postwar liberal multiculturalism and the new racial politics of recognition in settler societies like Australia, Canada, and the United States construe and contain difference in ways that do not eliminate but conceal material inequalities, even as they have enabled new forms of neoliberal and extractivist violence (Melamed 2011, xvii; Povinelli 2019, 169).

When refracted through the dispossessive analytic of colonial racial capitalism, the right to property is one process by which immigrants assimilate into liberal promises, yet it is also a primary technology of liberal governance that promises emancipation in order to cement white settler possession. A structural collaboration across liberal consent, racial hierarchy, and capitalist labor lures immigrants into willingly accepting that upward class mobility and possessive individualism lead to freedom. But property functions less for equality than for perpetuating racial captivity and settler colonial capitalism. Asian American scholars Colleen Lye, Jeffrey Santa Ana, and Iyko Day have variously discussed the economism of Asian racialization, elucidating the ways in which settler colonial capitalism dehumanizes Asiatic bodies and labor into abstract capital while simultaneously displacing onto this body settler anxieties about capitalist monopoly, polarizing Asians as both an evil threat and an economic exemplar (Lye 2005; Santa Ana 2015; Day 2016). The model minority myth is a poignant example of how settler states like the United States essentialize hardworking "Asian values" and middle-class property to conceal structural racism, defining yet also denying the Asian subject's claim to intraracial diversity (Li 1998, 10). Through capitalist mechanisms of callings and rewards, Asian model minorities are hailed as honorary whites and ideal neoliberal subjects, detached from antiracist and anticolonial politics, and pitted against other people of color, yet they shall never achieve liberal personhood and must forever remain its structural other (Zong 2016, 246). The promise of racial liberation via property is, therefore, ridden with political dilemmas of self-negation and perpetual lack. Possessive individualism also hinders meaningful collective action and social responsibility that are urgently needed for tackling the planetary ecological crisis. Unraveling this structural contradiction inherent in liberal settler humanism reveals how divesting from modern colonial systems of land possession and economic extraction opens avenues for reimagining diaspora otherwise.

If diaspora studies were to undergo critical renewal, it might benefit from reconceiving diaspora as "a category of practice, project, claim and stance," rather than as a bounded group (Brubaker 2005, 13). It could gain from thinking beyond cultural difference as a product of human exceptionalism to engage place-based and ecocultural forms of an extended self in an all-encompassing world that elude possession (Milstein and Castro-Sotomayor 2020, xix). In mainstream diaspora studies, diaspora is often posited as placeless due to an assumed distrust of roots and territories. This reveals a tendency to suppose that diaspora must remain "space" and not "place" to retain its subversive potential. Clifford notes that diasporic space differs from Indigenous people's notion of land sovereignty because "their sense of rootedness in the land is precisely what diasporic people have lost" (1994, 310). Gilroy claims that diaspora's antiessentialist effects register political life more in "space, spatiality, distance, travel, and itinerancy" than the "fixity, rootedness" of place (1994, 207). Indeed, much early diaspora scholarship and its reliance on cultural theories of globalization is now susceptible to criticism for its anthropocentric disregard of materialist and environmental concerns, as well as for overlooking place as a helpful tool for countering the very imperialist, nationalist, and racist systems of modernity that perpetuate diasporic displacement and struggle.

In recent years, ecocritical scholarship has sought to reimagine an inclusive sense of place by calling for literary and cultural forms that connect the local and the global in the context of environmental risks and globalization (Buell 2005; Heise 2008). Ursula Heise's notion of eco-cosmopolitanism explores how cultural theories of diaspora and deterritorialization can be reoriented to cultivate environmental world citizenship, or a sense of planet that understands local cultural and ecological systems as being imbricated in global ones (2008, 61). While these projects have largely displaced parochial localism with a networked understanding of planetary ecology, they also accentuate the formal and conceptual challenges for environmentalist writing and criticism if they are to address the seemingly irreconcilable conflicts between planetary ecological awareness and the persistent return to local senses of places for lived experiences of nature and ethical responsibility. They also highlight the tension between liberal-humanist, Eurocentric tendencies of cosmopolitanism and the "environmentalism of the poor" in the wake of colonialism and neocolonalism (Weik von Mossner 2012, 147).

*The Time of the Peacock* invites readers to consider place as a pertinent concept for rethinking diasporic subjectivity in ecological and embodied terms, and how diaspora facilitates transnational and mobile senses of place. Shifting the focus from place to placemaking, I explore how Abdullah's stories portray the ways diasporic characters reshape culturally hybrid landscapes through practices of ancestral memory, spirituality, and interculturality, which render a rural farm in inland Australia an ecocultural site of local, national, and cosmopolitan modes of belonging. But the book emphasizes not liberal-humanist and globalist moral stewardship so much as the planetarity from below ecologies that I outline in this book, where more-than-human interdependence is depicted as the political substance of diasporic survival, playfulness, and freedom within the cracks of settler colonialism and racism. This is expressed through the fragility of childhood and the vulnerability of wonder, both of which may be considered literary strategies, or cultural forms, that reappropriate the pastoral to pinpoint diasporic ethical ecologies as fields of political stakes and negotiation. Unlike settler colonial land narratives of masculine conquest or modern nationalism, the migrant characters and their interactions with flora, fauna, and earthly forces point to an ethical crossroads where diasporic subjects might unlearn self-possessed modern mastery in favor of inhabiting planetary ethics of alterity and unknowability in relation to human and nonhuman otherness. This ethical orientation provides a counternarrative where diasporic settlers recognize and refuse a colonial hierarchy of race, place, and animality, while initiating a conversation about how diasporic modes of existing in plurality might contribute to ecological awareness and ethics.

## Diasporic Intervention in Settler Pastoralism

*The Time of the Peacock* interrogates settler colonial myths of the Australian landscape to recuperate silenced environmental histories of the South Asian diaspora and their cultural memories and spirituality of place. The family in the stories embodies a nexus of histories that point to transnational mobilities of land and sea. The family comprises a Punjabi Muslim father who first came to Australia as a hawker before settling down as a sheep farmer, a Kashmiri Hindu-Brahmin mother who remains devoted to Krishna and Shiva, their four children—Nimmi, Rashida, Lal, and a newborn—who inherit their parents' ancestral ties in addition to an Indian

Australian consciousness, and the family friend Uncle Seyed, a Pakistani Punjabi Muslim. The family's complex background challenges settler colonial pastoral representations to reclaim the countryside and rurality as what environmentally intersects natural history and human histories of empire, nation, capital, race, and labor migration, with a particular focus on the history of Muslim hawkers. These histories materialize the British Empire's imperial networks that facilitated the global movement of Indians to Australia, settler nation-making on dispossessed Indigenous land in Australia, and racial and territorial anxiety in the white settler imaginary. Through this historicization of land, Abdullah rewrites the pastoral bush landscape as a space that triangulates colonial, intercolonial, and settler colonial mobilities across Britain, Australia, and India in the early twentieth century.

That Abdullah's stories were first published in the Australian periodical *The Bulletin* in the late 1950s makes them a direct intervention into the bush literary tradition and the settler colonial pastoral imaginary. The bush has been one of the most enduring landscapes and national symbols in Australian cultural history. It is central to pioneer legends and frontier myths that are increasingly contested yet remain quintessential in defining white settler senses of belonging to the land. Culminating in the 1880s and 1890s, the bush myth flourished during a formative period when Australia was to become a federated nation to offer a nationalist ideology of land. Canonical writers and poets like Banjo Paterson, Henry Lawson, and Joseph Furphy turned to the pastoral landscape to characterize national distinctiveness, and the then-popular weekly magazine *The Bulletin* provided a platform for this cultural nationalism. It is believed that the bush and the frontier life of nomad pastoral workers express "typical Australian" characters and way of life (Ward 1992). Across diverse settings, the bush is represented almost exclusively as a pastoral landscape, a "*settled* landscape" transformed by European activities of farming, fencing, and livestock (Carter 2017, 44). In other words, the bush myth symbolically expresses how European settlers and pastoralism establish possession and belonging, transforming wilderness into property and emptying it of Indigenous history and labor exploitation. It is a proprietary myth.

Freedom, manliness, egalitarianism, and the conquest of vastly open and sometimes demonic land are common tropes in the bush legend. These tropes are potent in Banjo Paterson's well-known ballad "The Man from the Snowy River" (1890), a poem that celebrates a stockman's heroic mastery of a landscape of rugged hillside, kurrajong trees, and wild horses. As David Carter suggests, the fact that "the Man" is nameless and the poem's setting in a legendary past reveal the symbolic and memory-making function of the pastoral landscape, which gives the land a history of "achieved settlement" and a sense of democratic independence, or even superiority, compared to that of Britain and the old world (Carter 2017, 44–45). Yet the bush pastoral is rife with paradoxes and contradictions. The assertion of national distinctiveness falters because similar narratives of colonial pastoralism and masculinist frontier myths exist in other settler colonial contexts, such as the American West. Critics note that the bush legend is, ironically, an urban myth, with many bush literature writers and artists being city dwellers disillusioned with urbanization and industrialization. They project onto the bush and the outback a yearning for an earlier, lost, and idyllic frontier marked by "egalitarianism, independence, and a higher measure of economic self-sufficiency and security" (Waterhouse 2000, 204). In this nostalgic idealization, there is often a reductive binary between a corrupt urban life and an innocent rural existence. Pastoral aesthetics thus become an eco-optimist instrument to historicize the everyday Australian bushman as embodying liberal democratic ideals of opportunity, mateship, and progress that are problematically founded on settler colonial territorial and capitalist expansion on land as *terra nullius*.

Although in the 1950s the official ideology of assimilation remained a haunting obstacle to culturally diverse environmental imaginations, the appearance of Abdullah's stories in *The Bulletin*, as Thomas Shapcott writes, acknowledges the impact of postwar migration on Australian society and the "secret heritage" of prewar migration patterns (2019, 3). This secret heritage references the submerged history of South Asian migrants and how their mobilities and material cultures reshaped the Australian cultural landscape, outback economy, and pastoral life. This history can be traced back to Bengali seamen and indentured agricultural labor in New South Wales in the 1830s, Afghan and Indian Muslim cameleers and camel trains transporting goods and mail inland from the 1860s to the 1920s, and enterprising Punjabi men who sought economic opportunities in hawking and farming in the 1880s and 1890s (Spennemann 2021, 129–30). Intercolonial mobility facilitated this history, with the empire's shipping routes and imperial networks enabling Indian migrants to travel to Australia legally as British subjects. Once they took up the highly mobile jobs of hawking, many young Punjabi men traveled by foot, horses, and wagons to supply clothing, food, and other goods to outlying farms, establishing daily mobile circuits among Australian rural and agricultural communities before the advent of automobiles.

But as White Australia and anti-Asian sentiments arose, the mobility of colored Indian bodies became a contested issue clashing British liberalism and Australian settler nationalism. In the years leading up to the Immigration Restriction Act of 1901 (also known as the White Australia policy), white settler discourses deployed naturalist rhetoric of biology, diseases, invasion, and animality to racially dehumanize immigrants and nonwhite people. *The Bulletin* published cartoons like *The Mongolian Octopus* (1886), which animalized the Chinese as smallpox and typhoid carriers. Around the same time, economic competition between white settlers and Muslim cameleers led to environmental racism that blamed camels for introducing disease to Australia (Jones 2007, 11). The "turban-clad" mobility of Indian hawkers over land and across oceans was quickly racialized and gendered as a locus of white settler anxiety over stable property, national borders, and protecting domestic women from the perceived sexual threat of mobile Indian masculinity (Rhook 2015, 116). In dominant settler narratives, a dichotomy of white settlement and colored mobility sets up the perception that itinerant hawkers had no real ties to the land, whereas in reality they had a multifaceted relationship to land, including owning land, farming land, and market gardening, with the intent of making Australia their new home (Spennemann 2018, 225–29). Such a dichotomy serves, as Aileen Morton-Robinson has put it, to construct discursively, materially, and morally the prerogative of whiteness as a form of property, white people as property-owning subjects, and the nation as a white possession, with race operationalized to legitimate dispossession and subjugation (2015, xix).

Against this backdrop of settler colonialism and racialization, Abdullah's poetic stories of an Indian family in rural Australia can be interpreted as reimagining, rather than rejecting, the pastoral mode through diasporic mobilities and cultural imaginations of land. Although *The Time of the Peacock* is attributed to the joint authorship of Mena Abdullah and Ray Mathews (who assisted the writing from Abdullah's narrative material) (Malak 1994, 46), the semi-autobiographical style of the stories draws from Abdullah's experience as a second-generation Indian immigrant growing up on her family's pastoral sheep farm. While there is a lack of Indigenous presence, her version of diasporic pastoralism deserves a careful reading, particularly in how it diverges from settler wilderness romanticism to give voice to migrant presence in the rural landscape. Abdallah's stories embed migrant bodies and cultures in the land with a poetics attuned to natural forms, foregrounding an affective sensibility of vulnerability: not as passive victimhood but as "a tool in breaking down barriers of unfamiliarity or difference" (Shapcott 2019, 5). From the child narrator's viewpoint, the bush is intimately connected to diasporic practices of ancestral memories, community building, and religious cosmology. It is beside the burning autumn leaves on the banks of the Gwydir River that Ama, the Hindu mother character, tells "stories of Krishna and the Flute-player and his moving mountains" (Abdullah [1965] 2019, 9). The Muslim father narrates his travels as a hawker and describes turning from the southern stars toward Mecca at night to pray. While the father migrated willingly, the mother moved due to marriage. Her yearning for a lost homeland materializes in the Arcadian garden that is her little India, "the country that she knew" (18). The mother's diasporic nostalgia for a lost homeland might parallel the settler pastoralist's yearning for a bucolic past, but such ideological simplification is subverted when we learn that the garden is also a haven for magpies, singing birds, and a mix of native and Indian animals. The garden becomes a sanctuary where an isolated migrant woman can practice cultural remembrance in a patriarchal, white-dominated landscape. This mixture of agencies—protection and isolation, human and nonhuman, and diasporic and settler—as spatially expressed by the mother's garden, reveals the versatility of the pastoral to contain and seemingly evade multiple tensions and contradictions (Gifford 1999, 11).

Diaspora theorists like William Safran have described homeland return as an earlier defining feature of diasporic collective memory (1991, 83) or as an eschatological utopia that makes life in the host land more bearable (1991, 94). But in *The Time of the Peacock*, the temporal myth of return and its associated cultural nationalism are displaced by the idea that diasporic roots, both imaginary and material, are an evolving formation in shaping culturally hybrid places. In the story "Mirbani," migration composes the ontological primacy of difference, in which remaking the self depends on an affective mode of receptivity and vulnerability to relational becomings with multiple others, human and other than human. When Mirbani, the family's Hindu-Brahmin grandmother, visits from India, Ama is anxious. Having married a Muslim farmer, Ama had once upset her family, and the death of her first son has been interpreted as God's punishment. During the grandmother's visit, Nimmi's brother Lal falls ill with meningitis, and caring for him unites the family across boundaries of religion and caste. A shared emphasis on interdependence emerges as the family members draw on their faith to pray for Lal.

Uncle Seyed prays to the all-merciful Allah whose divine providence, he believes, governs the seasonal and weather changes affecting his sheep farming (Abdullah [1965] 2019, 40). His prayer ruptures settler colonial exceptionalism by underscoring human vulnerability within the pastoral landscape, revealing how diasporic spiritualities can contribute to resacralization and humility before nature's agency. Nimmi's prayer intertwines feminine care and cultural hybridity at the intersection of diasporic and settler senses of places:

> I went into Ama's garden, her Indian world, and I looked out through the squares in the lattice at the paddock and sky, at the five hills that were our hills. Ama gave them to each of us when we were born. As soon as she was well she carried each new one, each Australian, out through the garden with its Indian jasmine and Kashmiri roses and Himalayan violets and out through the lattice-gate where all the Australian world was watching. She held each of us up so that we would see the hills and she told them, and all the Gods that were, that we had come. "This is Nimmi," she had said when she held me. "Nimmi whom the Gods must love."
>
> "Oh, love *him*! Love Lal!" I cried out, whimpered and prayed. (40)

Nimmi's prayer reflects how her diasporic sense of belonging is anchored in place, land, hills, sky, and plants. This place-sensitivity draws from her immigrant mother's strength and the life-sustaining land. Yet her language of ownership, "our hills," echoes an ambivalence in settler place attachment, suggesting both kinship with the nonhuman and a subtle possessiveness. Her identification as "Australian" affirms an Indian diasporic heritage in the landscape, inviting us to ponder the relational depths of place and to what extent diasporic claims to place or cultural pluralism risk reinforcing settler nationalist logics. At the same time, her family's composite history affords her a view of the land as a realm of eco-cosmic abundance blessed by a plurality of "Gods." Notably, this eco-cosmic diversity is expressed not through the divine as an external dominating force but through a spiritual materiality in the everyday lifeworlds of migrants where challenges give birth to ecological care and relationality. An ethics of care becomes vital for addressing histories of injustice, including gender, racial, and environmental subjugation, through the wisdom of relational practices that understand life in embedded and interdependent terms (Whyte and Cuomo 2018, 9). In her caregiving for Lal, the grandmother overcomes separateness and religious prejudice. After nursing Lal day and night, she makes a prayer that appeals to "two Gods in one," invoking "the God of the Brahmins" alongside "the God of the Muslims" to revive Lal (Abdullah [1965] 2019, 41). Lal's recovery celebrates an ethics of care inspired by diasporic collaborative practices of spirituality and reciprocity with the land. The story's focus on sacred nature, care, and cosmic unity posits relational alternatives to a settler masculinist vocabulary of power, land conquest, and individualist enterprise. These affective networks of care underscore ecological interdependence as vital to the strength of diasporic communities in the face of structural alienation and injustice.

A decolonial critique of the pastoral can be detected in two other stories that more explicitly question colonial settlement and Australia's migrant origins. "The Outlaws" is a story that brings the colonized and the bushranger into political alliance through their shared resistance against colonial authority and settler property claims. This intercolonial dialogue is environed when Uncle Seyed takes Nimmi to the Outlaw's Cave, named after an Australian bushranger Captain Thunderbolt, and compares him with Malik Khan, a legendary Pakistani mountain bandit who defied the British Raj. Uncle Seyed commends Malik Khan as a folk hero who embodies antiauthoritarianism and the virtues of camaraderie and kindness. By taking the bushranger legend out of its singular national context, Uncle Seyed's retelling foregrounds the tension between law and outlawry in (settler) colonial formation. Shared during a horse ride with a migrant girl, these cultural folklores allow diasporic children to reinterpret the bush across multiple story traditions and beyond settler masculinity.

"The Singing Man" depicts the shared experience of diasporic nostalgia between the Indian family and the family's Irish accountant, known as Paddy-the-Drunk. The Indian immigrants' yearning for Kashmir or Punjab commingles with the wandering Irishman's anguish and longing for the green meadows of Ireland. The pastoral land is reimagined beyond the unity of settler nationalism, reframing white settlers as migrants themselves. The story is an unhomely reminder that Australia is composed of migrants on Indigenous land and that the term "Anglo-Celtic" is a homogeneous label that glosses over the sectarian pasts within white settler communities. Diaspora, thus, becomes a useful framework to contest white settler claims of indigenization and folds a sense of migrancy or unsettledness back into settler colonial modernity.

Migratory routes and diasporic mobilities fracture the myth of a settler Australian nation territorially predicated. Yet it is through a focus on migrant bodies inhabiting, storying, and walking the land that the cosmopolitanism from below in *The Time of the Peacock* transgresses a globalist fixation on cultural difference to connote how diaspora might give rise to an ontology of planetary conviviality in embodied terms. The book's concluding story, "A Long Way," examines how migrant walking and traveling inspire a world vision of compassionate humanity against insularity. Set in Pakistan, this story follows a village mother walking to give a departing Begum a jumper for her son studying in Australia. During her journey, she encounters kindness from people across religions and social classes. At the wharf, she meets the Begum who will travel to Australia to report on the Colombo Plan, an initiative that has facilitated educational and cultural exchanges between Australia and postcolonial Asia but is now being questioned for its economic value. The mother's son is among the many who have received a scholarship, and the locals view him as a bridge connecting a Pakistani village to the wider world. Upon realizing how the old Muslim mother has walked a long distance with her dusty feet, the Begum feels a renewed commitment to the causes of social justice and interculturality. Tossing prepared lecture notes into the ocean, the Begum resolves to speak from the heart, asserting that "the world is all our people" (103). As the discarded pages swell and sink into oceanic waves, the story questions nationalist borders, capitalist value, and the land-sea dichotomy, framing the walking journey of the Muslim mother in a continuum with the oceanic journey of the Begum. It articulates the importance of continuous movement and alterity, not a linear point of arrival or a politics of assimilation, as central to diasporic lifeways, and considers what these diasporic practices might offer to our collective ways of being in and with the world.

## Unlearning Possession and Decolonizing Wonder

This section seeks to extend an ethics of wonder for decolonial ecocriticism by examining how the poetics and onto-epistemology of wonder interrogate the constitutive tension between alterity and possession, a tension central to the diasporic impasse within and beyond liberal modernity. Just as "racialization is the process by which whiteness operates possessively" to construct its supremacy under settler colonialism (Morton-Robinson 2015, xx), anthropocentrism is the process through which humans commodify land, water, matter, and animals for economic extraction. Both racism and speciesism are invented and reproduced by the modern colonial separation of nature and culture. I argue that diasporic ecologies of wonder in Abdullah's stories flesh out the unsettling conflicts between unknowability and certainty, racial otherness and liberal assimilation, and nonhuman agency and domestication. Her stories illustrate the raced subject's appreciative relationship with the natural world and the vulnerability of such relations to the possessive logics of modern, autonomous, and rational individualism through a discourse of colonial recognition. By demystifying possession as a core contradiction within migrant liberatory resistance, *The Time of the Peacock* can be understood as indexing a decolonial shift away from a politics of liberal inclusion toward an exploration of diasporic ethics and ecological practices that unlearn modern colonial systems of ownership, racialization, and possessive settler culture.

Wonder is often assumed to motivate knowledge and scientific inquiry, but it has an ambivalent relationship with knowledge in Western intellectual history. There have been incommensurate views on wonder's role in relation to the unknown in nature. Philosopher Mary-Jane Rubenstein distinguishes two main approaches to wonder in Western philosophy: the Aristotelian and the Platonic. Aristotelian thinkers like Aristotle, Bacon, and Descartes aim to resolve and neutralize wonder's uncertainty into causality (Rubenstein 2008, 12–15). In this line of thinking, wonder vanishes when humans gain epistemological domination and possession over wondrous objects. By comparison, Platonic thought regards wonder as a primordial uncertainty and a profoundly unsettling ethos that resist full mastery. This kind of wonder opens the possibility for thinking but ultimately eludes "calculation, comprehension, and possession" (Rubenstein 2008, 8). Rubenstein contends that wonder is "an uncanny opening, rift, or wound in the everyday," even though modern consumer culture has decimated and domesticated wonder's capacity to arouse terror, awe, worship, grief, and a destabilizing interruption in the daily course of things (2008, 28). Unlike the modern impulse to epistemologically and materially possess the marvelous, the repressed power of wonder to reveal the uncanny, unthinkable, unassimilable, and terrifying in the mundane remains crucial to its ethical and transformative potential.

One of the few philosophers to connect a poetics of wonder to the task of reimagining human-nonhuman relations through an ethics of alterity is Ronald William Hepburn. In his work on existential wonder, he argues for a close affinity between an attitude of wonder that is "non-exploitative, non-utilitarian" and attitudes that seek to affirm and respect other beings in their intrinsic value and otherness (1984, 145). Wonder acknowledges the forms of personhood and intrinsic value proper to other beings as they are without reducing them to mere human knowledge or utility. To wonder at a vivid blue ocean, a rainbow, or birdsong is to open oneself to their phenomenal irreducibility—light, color, sound, motion, and combined sensory impressions that have immanence, defying a calculative mindset. Literature, art, and music are poetic instruments in exciting a sense of existential wonder by presenting ambiguous and sense-disturbing objects and experiences, whose strangeness, unassailability, and incommensurability invite us to interpret "a field of experience as a 'world in itself'" (Hepburn 1984, 150). Hepburn's conception of wonder facilitates an affective reading of how the contemplative and appreciative poetics of wonder can evoke feelings of compassion, respect, humility, dread, and delight toward nonhuman nature in ways that affirm its otherness. Through affectivity, wonder ecologically and experientially disrupts the discrete boundaries between bodies, texts, and environments.

The relationship between wonder and childhood is a topic of much debate within ecocritical scholarship. Rachel Carson associates wonder with childhood, suggesting that a child's sense of wonder and endless questioning are life-loving antidotes to the disenchantment, alienation, and rationalism of modern life ([1965] 2017, 30). Like Hepburn, Carson emphasizes wonder's affectivity, encouraging parents to nurture in their children the ability to *feel*: "Once the emotions have been aroused—a sense of the beautiful, the excitement of the new and the unknown, a feeling of sympathy, pity, admiration, or love—then we wish for knowledge about the object of our emotional response" ([1965] 2017, 33). For Carson, there is a child in all of us, and wonder helps us reclaim our lost instinct for feeling what is beautiful, awe-inspiring, and strange in everyday nature, which modernity, adulthood, and technological domination have dulled.

For ecocritics like Louise Economides, however, if wonder is to inspire imaginative alternatives to existing norms, artistic expressions that nostalgically confine wonder to childhood amount to a profound "political defeat" (2016, 74). Economides compares the romantic poetry of William Wordsworth, who laments the loss of youthful wonder as something lost in adulthood that can only be aesthetically revived through transcendental sublime imaginations, with that of Samuel Coleridge, whose early work sees wonder's enduring presence in adulthood through "a *pleasurable* decentering of ego boundaries" experienced in moments of awe and nonhuman agency (2016, 52). By associating wonder with an Edenic childhood and an early stage of individual imaginative power, Wordsworth's verses tend to create a dichotomy that opposes wonder and knowledge. In contrast, Coleridge's poetry treats wonder and knowledge as interdependent intellectual projects that need not dwindle with maturity. Whereas Wordsworthian wonder evokes nature to reinforce individual agency, Coleridge's wonder decenters the human with nonhuman agency. A more radical ecopolitics of wonder may emerge only when environmental literature of wonder respects the otherness and agency of nature beyond anthropocentric self-interest.

My approach to ecological wonder in the context of decoloniality expands upon these two main inquiries: wonder's role in ecologizing an ethics of alterity and wonder's contentious relationship with childhood and knowledge. In addition, I propose that while previous scholarship has questioned positivist and anthropocentric perspectives, it has rarely moved beyond an individualistic tradition of human-nature relations to consider a political ecology of wonder. Scholars working on environmental justice have deepened our understanding of how race and nature are terrains of power that animate and haunt the cultural politics of difference, political representation, social hierarchies, and violent exclusions (Moore et al. 2003, 3). Culturally specific knowledge shapes a person's sense of wonder, and a racial politics of place would also inform one's embodied openness and capacity to wonder in the phenomenal world. In *The Time of the Peacock*, where race and nature intersect, the diasporic child's sense of wonder should not be dismissed as a political compromise but must be read as offering a potent ethical and political critique of colonial racism and settler possession. Moreover, it is also wonder's resistance to ideological calculability that moves diasporic liberatory politics beyond a colonial dichotomy of domination and survival to other dimensions of playfulness, creativity, and interspecies ethics within the planetary web of life.

Wonder is a vital ecological relationality through which Abdullah's immigrant characters counter racial isolation. The narrator, Nimmi, is depicted as an inquisitive child who is always asking questions and privy to many secret things. Her incessant questioning sometimes strains her parents' patience. Her questions, such as "Why do peacocks have beautiful tails?" (Abdullah [1965] 2019, 13), display a genuine curiosity to know the nonhuman beings, with whom she cultivates a sense of affinity within a racially alienating environment. Her treasured "secrets" are playful repositories of wonder that appreciate the sentience of plants, animals, rivers, mountains, and sky by noticing the strange within the familiar. Secrets are shared intergenerationally, as Nimmi shows her father "the gum-tree where the wild bees made brown honey" and "the way you touched a trigger-plant and made it jump" (32), while he shares with her "the way the river was deep holes held together by shallow water" and "the way to stand still like a tree and see the fish move across the shallows" (33). These moments of wonder defamiliarize the everyday landscape with what is uncanny and enigmatic. Wondering, sensing, and imitating earthly things are ecological mapping exercises through which the diasporic characters realize that they are not discrete beings but embodied and perceiving selves embedded in nature's inexhaustible and regenerative intelligence.

In *The Time of the Peacock*, wonder is often connected to spiritual and imaginative acts of perceiving nature's abundance or a cosmological respect for nature's power. Abdullah seems to draw a link between nature's agency to inspire awe, primordial religious feelings, and diasporic cultural and spiritual practices. As Hepburn observes, "The presence of wonder marks a distinctive and high-ranking mode of aesthetic, or aesthetic-religious, experience characterizable by that duality of dread and delight" (1984, 151). Wonder's ability to evoke awe and reverence is evident in the story "High Maharajah." The children respectfully ask an eaglehawk, whom they regard as the king of the sky, for permission to fly their kites, whereas a white farmhand derogatorily calls the eagle "mean" and "cunning," threatening to shoot it to protect the farm's lambs (Abdullah [1965] 2019, 54). The children's encounter with the eagle is thrilling yet terrifying due to the uncertainty of the eagle's actions. After the eagle seemingly locates one of the children's missing kite, the children salaam to the eagle with gratitude, associating it with moral kindness.

Cultural hybridity is woven into the composition of the kite, which is crafted from diverse materials: an Indian bamboo reed spine, colored paper from an ethnic Chinese grocer, and flour-and-water paste made in Australia. This blend materializes a meaningful negotiation of an evolving Asian Australian sensibility in which diasporic subjectivity engages with a culture of abundance. In this story, wonder resists a settler capitalist ideology that instrumentalizes land and animals as mere commodities. As Candace Fujikane suggests, mapping abundance is a decolonial act that encourages seeing beyond a settler capitalist mindset of scarcity and resource competition, instead insisting on life and reciprocity with the land (2021, 5). We could further suggest that wonder becomes a practice of mapping nature's abundance and immanence. For example, Nimmi describes how in a state of contemplative wonder she sees the divine Krishna in nature's scared revelations: "The grass was green and gentle and the blue of Krishna was everywhere—in the sky, in the sea, in the puddles after rain, in every drop of water that you held to look at" (Abdullah [1965] 2019, 73). This sacred, place-based poetics of wonder perceives the sky, sea, rain, and water as exuberant of animacy, vitality, and personhood.

The tension between alterity and possession ignited by wonder calls for a different politics of migrant freedom, one that shifts epistemologically from liberal-humanist recognition to an ecological democratization of all life-forms. A decolonial solidarity between migrants and animals within a colonial hierarchy of animacy runs throughout Abdullah's stories. To wonder at, yet not possess, nonhuman creatures presents both a challenge and an opportunity for racialized immigrants to recognize a parallel mechanism of inhuman property relations imposed upon them through colonial racial subjection. In the story "Because of the Rusilla," two sisters find a bird they name Rusilla and place it in a cage. Their lonely younger brother, Lal, befriends the bird, but when Rusilla flies away, Lal is devastated. To console him, they are taken to town where they encounter white children who call them "nigger." Following this racist encounter, they are taken to a white lady's cottage for respite. Lal becomes captivated by the whistle of a boiling kettle, which he interprets as a birdsong and calls it Rusilla. Before they leave, the white lady gifts Lal the kettle, saying, "A friend gives you what is already your own" (24).

This story holds multiple layers of meaning, the overt being the overlap between the possessive logic that imprisons both the animal and the racial other. It also calls for an ethical mode of wonder that perceives the natural world nonpossessively. The bird's regained freedom parallels the immigrant child's access to open-ended wonder, where Lal's ability to hear birdsong in a kettle's whistle renews an ethical bond with the nonhuman world oriented toward reciprocal flourishing rather than utilitarianism. The immigrant child does not need to emulate the liberal-humanist model of property ownership to achieve freedom or recognition. The white lady's parting words imply that wonder can reanimate the inanimate and spark imaginative creativity in racialized migrants, just as the migrant can also perceive the communicative poiesis of the vibrant world. This story provides an ecological counternarrative to settler colonial imperatives of private property and human exceptionalism.

Wonder presents the nonhuman and the unknown as powerful sources of political resistance and renewal for migrant subjectivity. In the story "The Time of the Peacock," attention is drawn to how nonhumans defy human calculation, much as diasporic ecologies exceed the assimilatory confines of the settler nation-state. The family welcomes a white peacock named Shah-Jehan who has traveled from India to Australia. Wondering if the peacock will open his tail, the adults give different speculations ranging from anthropomorphism to ornithology. The mother and father see Shah-Jehan as a fellow migrant unlikely to open his tail in a foreign land, while Uncle Seyed explains scientifically that the peacock needs a hen to display his tail. As the family grows accustomed to the peacock, their anticipation fades, until one night, Nimmi has a miraculous encounter with Shah-Jehan. In a wondrous moment, with the peacock "white as frost in the moonlight," Nimmi begs him to fan his tail (14). In response, the peacock slowly unveils his tail like a fan of lace as white as the moon. Then, as elusively as a mirage, the scene disappears and Shah-Jehan's tail droops as usual. The next day, the family celebrates the birth of the youngest daughter, whom the father names after Uncle Seyed's sister in India. Nimmi recounts her magical encounter with the peacock, but the others dismiss it as a dream. For her, it becomes another cherished secret. This story reveals a political and ethical pull for the diasporic self to cultivate an ecological ethics of wonder. To be open to the displaced animal's indeterminate ways of flourishing is to embrace the multifarious ways that the migrant can make home in a new land. Wonder renews hope in the unknown, the very possibility of the ethical.

"Kumari" is a story that warns against wonder's domestication, a call for interspecies mutuality and decolonial modes of care. Rashida, the family's eldest sister, rescues a young vixen she names Kumari, who becomes her playmate and pet. As time goes by, Kumari grows miserable and pines for freedom beyond the fence. The parents encourage Rashida to free Kumari, but Rashida feels torn between love and ownership: "'She's mine.' . . . 'She knows that I love her'" (29). Rashida eventually respects Kumari's will, but by then the fox has lost the ability to hunt and returns later to die by Rashida's side. This story troubles possessive care by illustrating how ecologies of wonder prompt ethical reflection on the limits of care when nonhuman agency is respected. Although the immigrant child ultimately overcomes ownership, the damage of anthropocentrism proves irreversible.

The "Kumari" story is especially poignant in the context of invasive species discourse in Australia. The red fox (*Vulpes vulpes*), introduced for colonial hunting in the 1850s, is both a threat to native fauna and an unsettling reminder that settlers are not Australian natives. Invasive species management gains symbolic significance as ecological belonging appears to overlap with where social groups (indigene—settler—migrant—refugee) sit on a social hierarchy of cultural belonging (Trigger et al. 2008, 1274).

The frequent mobilization of a native-invasive binary and eco-nationalism in Australian invasive species discourses enable white settlers to assert an Indigenous sense of place against hybrid and diasporic identities, recognizing yet denying settler colonization itself as a form of feral invasion (Smith 1999, 302). The link between settler coloniality, animality, and racial subjection is articulated by Nimmi, who compares the domesticated fox to the racialized self: "She's a nigger" (Abdullah [1965] 2019, 29). This comparison implies that animal domestication is structurally akin to colonial racialization, both reproduced through colonial infrastructures of possession and domestication. The alienated fox and the racialized self are both denied embodied freedom in the full sense. It is through a decolonial ethics of wonder and mutuality, by respecting the nonhuman other's singularity beyond colonial capitalist ownership, that diasporic settlers may begin to properly address their own subjugation and responsibility on unceded Indigenous lands.

In Abdullah's stories, we observe a decolonial ecology of migrant placemaking that rejects a colonial politics of racialization and recognition. Decolonization demystifies the universalist myths and traps of the modern, autonomous, and possessive liberal individual as a progressive ideal into which migrants are expected to assimilate in settler colonial states. Decolonization need not dilute the diasporic politics of alterity, hybridity, and freedom; rather, it can offer pathways for rerouting a diasporic cultural politics of difference and movement toward place-based and interspecies practices that do not center Man as the organizing principle of the planet or privatize cultural differences as global capitalist property. The ongoing challenge for diasporic decolonialization is to keep exploring the praxes, imaginations, and actions through which these nonexploitative relations might be ecologized. The project of antiracism without confronting how racism is possessively reproduced by settler colonial capitalism, along with the alienation of nonhuman and Indigenous bodies from land, remains incomplete.

In this chapter I have proposed diasporic placemaking and ethics of wonder as a decolonial praxis, one that constructs more-than-human modes of migrant belonging through the entanglement of stories and landscapes, receptivity and responsibility, and human and nonhuman relations. Diasporic placemaking responds to a spatial politics of place, race, and animality in settler colonial geographies. The onto-epistemology, poetics, and affects of wonder open up possibilities for diasporic ethical placemaking and multispecies sociality in the context of ongoing racism, settler colonialism, and possessive capitalism. As Glenn Willmott writes, wonder obligates the perceiving self to make an ethical choice: to return to old ways, to not care, or to "care in a new way, for new things, for the precise content of the object and its uncertain life-world" (2018, 46). *The Time of the Peacock* challenges its diasporic characters and readers to seek relational alternatives and human-land relationships that are non-anthropocentric. Nonhuman beings, with their immanent incalculability, are political allies that reveal diasporic characters to a colonial hierarchy of things. At the same time, they open the door to a more-than-human realm of enchanted ecology and collaborative survival, allowing diasporic subjects to belong and become in incalculable ways.

# 2

# Decolonizing Waters

## *Indigeneity, Diaspora, and the Aqueous Commons*

> Molecular & spectacular, water will return what we give it, be that
> arrogance & poison, reverence & light, ambivalence & respect
> let our societies be revived as watersheds.
>
> —**Rita Wong, *Undercurrent***

> My family, migrants, had crossed incredible distances to arrive in this place called Canada, but the place itself never belonged to us. The irony is that the migrant is clamoring for entry into the national space of "Canada," while Indigenous people are automatically excluded from it—have to be excluded for that national space to exist in the first place. The further irony is that people like me and my family have more access to the space called Canada than Indigenous Peoples do because we, for the most part, are willing to buy in, sign up, and accept those naturalization papers and citizenship as if we were entitled to them.
>
> —**Kazim Ali, *Northern Light***

In the poem "Declaration of Intent," Chinese Canadian poet Rita Wong reflects on water's life-giving nature in our everyday lives. She traces its material embeddedness in pumps, cells, breaths, clouds, rain, rivers, aquifers, and oceans. Water is a lively and sensual matter that transforms, yet in our modern urban cultures, we often take it for granted, reducing it to a background resource to be piped, bottled, and governed. "I will learn through immersion, flotation & transformation": Wong attunes us to the fluid rhythms of water, its molecular and ever-becoming responsiveness, and its ambivalent capacity to absorb and dissolve colonial and capitalist modes of containment because "water will return what we give it" (2015, 14). Subjected to anthropocentric logics of progress, privatization, and pollution, water becomes volatile and fearsome, manifesting in floods, cyclones, acid rain, oil spills, toxic tailings, microplastic pollution, dead zones, and ocean garbage patches. Modern water tales are kinship relations turned into discord. At once destructive and redemptive, water relations are "the quiet witnesses to atrocities, greed, mean-spirited hierarchies, hostages of capitalism" yet also reminders of our "shared, fluid vulnerability" (16). Thinking with water implicates terrestrial humans in a reciprocal relationship with the aqueous earth. The poet pledges that "because i am part of the problem i can also become part of the solution" (15).

Wong's pledge enlists not only a poet's positioning of humanity within planetary water ecologies but also her situated resistance as a racialized settler coming to terms with the colonial capitalist violences of the settler state that perpetuate Indigenous erasure, a structure in which immigrants are implicated. She challenges immigrant communities to ask, "What happens if we position Indigenous people's struggles instead of normalized whiteness as the reference point through which we come to articulate our subjectivities? How would such a move radically transform our perceptions of the land on which we live?" (2008, 158). Rita is a second-generation immigrant born and raised in Treaty 7 territory, also known as Calgary, Alberta, Canada. Her family moved from the Pearl River Delta in southern China to Turtle Island, or what is commonly known as North America. She is part of a cohort of Asian Canadian writers and artists, including Larissa Lai, Sky Lee, Fred Wah, and Hiromi Goto, who critically engage with issues of multicultural racialization. They reflect on migrant complicity in settler colonial norms and pay respects to Indigenous knowledge in order to forge decolonial alliances between diaspora and Indigeneity. This growing diasporic-Indigenous dialogue helps create cross-racial ties of justice, care, and decolonial action in response to the ongoing ruination by settler colonialism.

Through her creative and activist work, Wong expresses solidarity with Indigenous community striving for environmental justice and water sovereignty. She has actively participated in various demonstrations at the Peace River, the Columbia River, the Fraser River, the Salish Sea, and within the Arctic Ocean watershed. In 2019, Wong was sentenced to twenty-eight days in prison following her peaceful protest against the Trans Mountain pipeline, a controversial oil expansion project in the Alberta tar sands that would increase toxic sludge, carbon emissions, and petro-nationalism, with devastating consequences for the lands and communities of the Coast

Salish people. Wong brings decolonial hydropoetics to respond to settler capitalist initiatives of damming, industrialization, and extraction that submerge ecological balance, Indigenous knowledge, and cultural memories. She consciously positions herself as a person of color who bears an ethical responsibility to resist the capitalist property system—a system upheld by generations of immigrant ancestors, benefitting them while erasing its dispossessive violence behind liberal promises of freedom.

In examining Wong's water poems and other Asian North American literature such as Kazim Ali's memoir *Northern Light* (2021), this chapter explores the decolonial water commons as a praxis of planetarity from below. I analyze how these narratives ecologize relational ethics and cross-racial alliances by reimagining water commons as aqueous sites of emplaced memories and shared care. These recent diasporic narratives invite a decolonial reading by demonstrating how diverse poetics of water memories, movements, and passages can reorient migrants toward unlearning settler capitalist imaginaries of resource and property. In the previous chapter, I traced placemaking narratives that cultivate ecological wonder and interspecies mutuality through a diasporic lens. I argued that historicizing diasporic mobility enables a critique of the possessive apparatuses of settler territorialism and colonial racialization. By foregrounding wonder's ethical potential to unsettle possession, Abdullah's stories encourage reflection on how antiracist struggles by Asian diasporic subjects might collaborate with nature's alterity and unknowability to collectively counter a politics of colonial assimilation and settler possessive humanism. Continuing with this focus on nature's unknowability, I now turn to water ecologies. Much like wonder's capacity to elude certainty, water has a primordial indeterminacy that defies containment.

This chapter builds on recent work in Asian diaspora studies that challenges the migrant inheritance of settler culture and complicity with (neo) colonial capitalist ideologies that continue to dispossess Indigenous people of land and resources. Migrant and ethnic agendas for justice in settler colonial states have historically been defined in relation to whiteness, without necessarily questioning how antiracist agenda may adopt and uphold normative white settler structures of property ownership. In this context, silence on the part of migrants is complicit with past and present colonial injustices. The racialized conditions framing the entry of migrants and refugees into settler nation-states mark the contradictions and perennial deferral of diasporic senses of belonging to place. These contradictions of liberal political humanism raise a pertinent question: What does it mean for migrants to inhabit land and drink water that are haunted by colonial ghosts?

## Asian-Indigenous Collaborative Ecology: Imagining the Aqueous Commons

Asian diasporic and Indigenous communities in settler colonial states register distinct political and cultural histories and ecological concerns shaped by their asymmetrical relationships with liberal modernity. As Ann Curthoys observes from an Australian perspective, there has been a bifurcation in popular and intellectual discourses between white-Indigenous and white-multicultural relations—the former concerning a history of colonization and the latter focusing on cultural diversity, ethnic politics, and immigration policy (2000, 21). Despite shared experiences of racial oppression in relation to whiteness, immigrants of color and Indigenous people diverge at the level of identification with the nation-state. Immigrant struggles for rights, citizenship, and freedom in Western liberalism have been framed to consolidate the legitimacy of state and capital while perpetuating Indigenous land seizures and disenfranchisement (Lai 100). In *Unsettled Solidarities*, Quynh Nhu Le examines Asian-Indigenous crossings in the Americas, considering how both groups have been unevenly incorporated into the territorial claims, telos, and liberal beneficence of the settler nation (2019, 4). Given their divergent experience with the settler, imperial, and racial logics of nation-building, the justice demands or liberatory resistance of one racialized/colonized community can rest on the very logics that oppress the other (Le 2019, 4). These disparities underscore the tensions and difficulties for building solidarity across the cultural politics of diasporic and Indigenous peoples.

Environmentally, scholars have foregrounded diasporic skepticism toward land and nativism and Indigenous commitments to literal places and lands. Daniel Coleman has noted the distinction between migrant and refugee politics of inclusion and belonging and Indigenous politics of separatism, sovereignty, and decolonization (2016, 62). But absolute differences give way to more entangled threads when we consider the formative roles of land and sea in shaping diasporic mobility and how settler colonialism and extractive capitalism have rendered Indigenous people internal diasporas. Colonialism and racism have historically decoupled nature and culture to obscure the violence of Indigenous displacement and the dehumanization of Asian labor. While postcolonial ecocriticism has resorted to historicization as a method for questioning the progressive narratives of space and time imposed by colonialism, the postcolonial recuperation of place, far from returning to a premodern idyllic wilderness, involves historicizing the violently transformative impact of empire on land and sea (DeLoughrey and Handley 2011, 4). In a similar vein, recent Asian diasporic ecocriticism has turned to historical analysis to renew a sense of place that accounts for racial labor, war histories, and empire's toxic legacies (Fitzsimmons et al. 2014; Suzuki 2021; Santa Ana et al. 2022). From these histories and movements, there is a shared understanding of nature and place in diasporic and Indigenous contexts as what are marked by unequal powers, political negotiations, and instability.

The more significant difference may lie in how diasporic and Indigenous views of land take shape in settler colonial societies, particularly regarding nonhuman agency and Euro-Western ideas of property ownership. Many Indigenous perspectives on land and water are imbued with sacredness and spiritual connection. Listening to the Dene elders at the Keepers of Water gathering in Canada, Radha D'Souza recounts how Indigenous elders describe themselves first and foremost as guardians of water, land, flora, fauna, and the well-being of the earth, and only secondarily as people with rights. These rights, however, are not property rights in a Western legal framework but rather the rights to live by the natural laws of the Creator that sustain the cycles and rhythms of life (D'Souza 2016, 199). Indigenous Canadian author Lee Maracle expresses this idea by asserting that "the water owns itself" and that humans must respectfully seek permission to use it (2016, 37). In comparison, migrants and ethnic communities in settler colonial societies are more divided on nonhuman sentience and are positioned, though not uniformly so, as beneficiaries of a capitalist system that disavows Indigenous ecological worldviews. To be sure, settler capitalist racialization and exploitation of Asian labor have historically limited the environmental agency of Asian immigrants. As Robert Hayashi reminds us, Asian American environmental experiences, whether in Gold Mountain, railroad, agriculture, or fishing, differ from the liberatory white representations of "the Frontier, the Garden, or the Sublime" (2011, 65). Efforts to historicize Asian racialization like Hayashi's, however, must be distinguished from celebratory tales of the diasporic entrepreneurial spirit, Asian industriousness, and transpacific capitalism—developmentalist narratives that glorify the Asian economic subject while overlooking anthropocentrism and Indigenous struggles.

Bringing immigrant and Indigenous ecologies into dialogue while respecting their incommensurability requires a steady commitment to decolonial coalition. This process, as Larissa Lai suggests, is "neither direct nor easy" (2013, 100). By highlighting the racialized subject's inheritance of colonization, scholars such as Rita Wong and Larissa Lai have foregrounded how historical debts and ethical obligations should motivate a diasporic settler solidarity with Indigenous decolonization (Wong 2008; Lai 2013). While historical debt may indeed compel immigrants to recognize their roles as uninvited guests on Indigenous lands, such indebtedness alone is insufficient to redirect Asian diaspora studies toward decoloniality. I call for recognizing the shared entrapment of diaspora and Indigeneity within the racialized possessive logics of settler colonial capitalism—logics that abstract Indigenous place into space and Asian labor into instrumental capital. By understanding this shared subjugation, we can reframe the decolonial alliance between diaspora and Indigeneity not just as a matter of moral duty but as a route for diasporic emancipation. Aboriginal Australian activist Lilla Watson once eloquently stated, "If you have come to help me, you are wasting your time. If you have come because your liberation is bound up with mine, then let us work together" (2004). With this perspective is the realization that, for immigrants and ethnic communities, decolonization is not simply about supporting Indigenous causes but about collaborating and learning *with* others to remake diasporic earthly connections.

The recent turn to a material, immersive, and post-anthropocentric water imaginary in the blue humanities and critical ocean studies expands frameworks for revitalizing an ethics of alterity in diaspora studies against the erasure by abstract global capital. Scholars are moving beyond abstract and flat depictions of watery surfaces and metaphors to consider the representability of water's wet ontologies and voluminous depths (Steinberg and Peters 2015); feminist, posthuman, and Indigenous epistemologies of water (Alaimo 2016; Christian and Wong 2017; Neimanis 2019; Suzuki 2021); and militarism and extractivism at sea (DeLoughrey 2017, 2022). This scholarship recognizes bodies of water as material-discursive sites with mutable and culturally specific relationships to human society. Water and the seas provide an epistemology not only for studying surfaces, depths, and extraterrestrial relations (Blum 2013) but also for deconstructing land-based heterosexual sociality entrenched in stable structures of family, nation, energy, and consumerism.

Thinking with water enables an ecomaterial corrective to the figurative representation of water in diaspora and transnational studies at large. Globalization and diaspora studies of the 1990s turned toward the seas for exploring the fluidity and flow of immigrants, refugees, and cosmopolitans to challenge the terrestrial fixity of nation and ethnicity (Gilroy 1993; Dirlik

1994; Bauman 2000; Hu-DeHart 2000). But this earlier diasporic focus on liquid modernity has theorized water bodies as symbolic and inert surfaces for human mobility, culture, and capital, neglecting water's own materiality and multispecies ecology. As Erin Suzuki and Aimee Bahng aptly point out, "The mobility and fluidity emphasized by transpacific cultural studies are also concepts central to the abstraction and dissemination of global capital" (2020, 9). Suzuki observes how a colonial legacy in Asia Pacific imaginaries or Pacific Rim studies homogenize the Pacific for a market-driven teleology that overwrites diverse Indigenous Pacific epistemologies (2021, 12–14). Ecologizing migratory circuits in a decolonial context, then, raises the question: How can migrant water imaginations cultivate a fluid ethos of alterity and connectivity through ecologically oriented poetics and cultural forms, such that diverse human-water flows resist standardization by capitalist property norms?

To this task, this chapter traces the "watershed consciousness" that renews migrant fluidity in embodied and emplaced poetics. Dorothy Christian and Rita Wong describe watershed consciousness as an awareness of how time, space, and humans are "situated and embodied within micro-and-macro flows" of watershed cycles, with water carrying an intrinsic agency in and of itself beyond modern colonial commodification (2013, 245). The works of Kazim Ali and Rita Wong circulate a relational ethos of watershed consciousness by converging ecomateriality with situated cultural politics. In their works, watersheds and water bodies provide sites of fluid intelligence enabling both authors to connect colonial histories, diasporic memories, embodied intimacies, and environmental change in meaningful dialogue. More specifically, their works call for an Asian-Indigenous decolonial partnership by invoking water-centered stories to disrupt the modern settler colonial regime that seeks to regulate and exploit planetary commons for capitalist and technological mastery.

Ali's *Northern Light: Power, Land, and the Memory of Water* (2021) couples memoir with environmental nonfiction to trace a South Asian immigrant's quest for a lost childhood home and how this leads him to confront his family's involvement in a hydroelectric dam on the Nelson River in Manitoba, Canada—a project that disrupted river ecosystems and the Cross Lake Crees with whom he forms solidarity. Wong's poetry collection *Undercurrent* (2015) invokes relational ways of knowing water, recasting the human body as an aqueous assemblage of the rhythms, flows, and porosity of water bodies, be it the Pacific Ocean, chlorinated drinking water, or toxic tailings. Troubling colonial binaries and discrete individualism, both authors draw on water to reflect on more-than-human interdependency and responsibility, and to explore how Indigenous and diasporic self-determination can be renewed through connection to, by, and with water relations. Water's ambiguity as both environmental commonality and political substance gestates a relationality for decolonial community building, fostering unexpected alliances while allowing one to remain situated in a politics of location. Water's immanent capacity to connect and differentiate allows for the cultivation of an ethical epistemology and a poetics of unknowability among historical differences.

When reimagined from commodity to living flow, water may give us hope for nurturing ethical collectivities toward an otherwise ecology of latent planetarity. The stories by Ali and Wong demonstrate how decolonizing waters through Asian-Indigenous solidarity cultivates what Anna Tsing calls "latent commons" in capitalist ruins. Latent commons is "ubiquitous" yet neglected, "undeveloped" yet resistant to institution, and indeterminate yet bubbling with unrealized possibilities for collective survival (Tsing 2015, 255). Tsing's latent commons resonate with Amy J. Elias and Christian Moraru's vision of planetarity as what presupposes and further stimulates the bioconnective networks of a "world commons" (2015a, xxiv). Rather than monocultural models, planetarity implies interwoven, nested, and nonhierarchical cultural and material ecosystems that honor Earth as a shared habitat (2015, xxiv). Adding to this dialogue, this chapter considers how different epistemologies of the commons—Indigenous, diasporic, and Western scientific knowledge systems—might diverge and collaborate. To put this another way, I explore the potential of "from below" politics for iteratively decolonizing settler colonial practices by attending to water poetics that deromanticize the commons, foreground Indigenous ecological and political struggles, and generate cross-racial coalitions. Specifically, I ask: How might Asian diasporic cultural politics reconnect with water in ways that respect Indigenous decolonization and planetary ecology, moving beyond mere metaphorization, or what Eve Tuck and K. Wayne Yang call "settler claims to innocence" (2012, 17)?

The water stories by Ali and Wong envision a planetary imaginary of what I call an *aqueous commons*, illuminating how collective flourishing and political life can emerge from collaborating with water as a facilitative milieu and lifeblood rather than managing it as property. They emphasize sacred and reciprocal relationships with water in Indigenous cosmologies, suggesting that learning with these ecological alternatives can help reclaim watershed consciousness from global markets. In this way, I interpret Ali's and Wong's works as ecologically engaging *aqueousness* to articulate interconnections among bodies, cultural worlds, and ecosystems in a water commons of ecopoetic care. In doing so, they shift away from the inevitable tragedy of the commons to an aqueous politics that ecologizes an ethics of alterity. This shift reimagines water rights from private ownership to an acknowledgment of the intrinsic right of water itself to "proliferate, flow, gestate, differentiate" (Neimanis 2009, 174). It also expands the political stakes of the water commons to include "multiple others—human and otherwise, past, present, and future" (Chen et al. 2013, 6). Aqueousness directs our attention to how water flows across and sustains diverse material and temporal scales and lifeworlds, from individuals to communities, bodily fluids to hydrological cycles, and historical differences to a planetary ecology.

Why the aqueous commons? The notion of "aqueous," as I theorize it, posits a new materialist poetics against a split between matter and meaning in Western metaphysics. Aqueousness permeates the fecund zone between "of water" and "like water" and thus establishes a metonymic link between narrative form and ecological substance. It might be considered an ecomaterial mode of perception, making visible the obscured coemergence of watery matters and watery poetics. Aqueousness reconceives waterscapes and water bodies not as passive properties but as shaped by intra-acting human and nonhuman agencies in relational becoming, expressing material and discursive dynamics of "narrativity" and "storied matter," to borrow from Iovino and Oppermann's account of material ecocriticism (2014, 7). My argument is that aqueousness reorients us to a diasporic hydropoetics that unmoors colonial epistemic habits and infrastructures. It reveals that answers to the planetary water crisis are cultural, social, and political; reimagines bodies of water as ecocultural archives of the discrepant epistemologies, temporalities, and toxicity submerged by settler colonial capitalism; and offers a responsive poetics to trace the aesthetic and cultural forms that express how migrant and diasporic subjectivities move *through* and *with* waters.

Given the persistence of settler capitalist property institutions and their complex ties with diasporic and Indigenous peoples, the aqueous commons is by no means romantic, coherent, or determinate. Rather than positing reconciliation between diaspora and Indigeneity, the aqueous commons embraces what Donna Haraway calls "staying with the trouble," or the more modest possibilities of "partial recuperation and getting on together" (2016, 10). The works of Ali and Wong resist neat solutions to diasporic and Indigenous senses of home. While Ali writes a personal reflection on learning with water and Indigenous communities to challenge colonial hydropower and diasporic placelessness, Wong composes a haunting poetics of flow that recasts bodies, cities, and landscapes as a liquid matrix of capitalist injustice, petrocultural modernity, and species loss, expanding toward a posthuman ecology of wet connectivity and responsibility. These texts bridge a planetary ethics of unknowability with an aqueous ecopolitics of the decolonial commons, instilling a sense of humility toward water's movements and morphology beyond positivist knowledge and capitalist capture. Yet they remain hopeful in exploring an *aqueous otherwise* through narratives of decolonial solidarity, elemental connectivity, speculative ethics, and multispecies justice. In doing so, they seek to decolonize settler capitalist hegemonies over property and resource, while restorying ethical water ecologies that account for human and more-than-human alterity. Together, their works present the aqueous commons as an ongoing practice of ethical worlding that potentiates planetary alternatives to the global neoliberal imaginary.

## Water, Memory, Community: River Homecoming in Kazim Ali's *Northern Light*

In literary works and cultural theory, it is not uncommon to see an excessive vocabulary of flows, circulations, and mobility used for describing economic and cultural dynamics, especially in discussions on globalization. Such metaphorical uses of water can detach it from the places where it flows, indicating its pervasive role in our conceptual landscape while overlooking its materiality. Diasporic and cosmopolitan theories have mobilized water metaphors to celebrate the "fluidity" and "liquidity" (Bauman 2000, 2) or "ambivalence" and "liminality" (Bhabha 1994, 214) of transnational identities against fixed territories. In his memoir *Northern Light*, Kazim Ali challenges cosmopolitan rootlessness and abstract fluidity. He tells a homecoming story in which a diasporic sense of place is made tangible by folding the self into the thickness and depths of specific lands, watersheds, and ecological communities. Interweaving cultural memories with embodied water intimacies, his memoir can be seen as remapping terrestrial categories of land, place, and belonging with aqueous relations of fluidity, remembering, and community in order to facilitate Asian-Indigenous solidarity and counteract colonial hydropower and amnesia.

Expressing displacement and a sense of unbelonging as a second-generation immigrant moving from place to place, Ali begins his memoir with a stark admission, "I am 'from' nowhere" (2021, 1). During the political and military conflict between India and Pakistan in the 1960s, his parents pursued economic opportunities in London, where Ali was born. When Canada adopted official multiculturalism in the 1970s, they moved to Winnipeg, where Ali's father worked as an electrical engineer with Manitoba Hydro and helped construct a hydroelectric dam on the Nelson River. This project brought workers' families together to create an isolated and temporary town called Jenpeg within the boreal forests and waterways of the Canadian north. It was in Jenpeg that Ali spent his formative years, learning to read, write, and gaze at the starry night, and to which he still feels a sense of belonging after years of living in Ohio in the United States. But this feeling is complicated by the dam. Through online research, Ali realizes the dam's hidden colonial history, including its operation on unceded land, the Cross Lake Cree community's condemnation of the dam, the alarming rates of youth suicide, cultural loss, and intergenerational trauma linked to Canadian residential schools, as well as environmental impacts of flooding, contamination, and wildlife damage inflicted by the dam. Though the town of Jenpeg no longer exists, the Jenpeg dam continues to operate, and the ongoing colonial dispossession of Indigenous communities in Cross Lake haunts Ali. "What had happened there was somehow a part of me, too" (19), he explains. Unsettled by these unfinished pasts, Ali embarks on a northward journey to decolonize his relationship with the Cross Lake Crees, water, and place.

A key theme of water as a force enabling relationality and overcoming isolation underpins Ali's homecoming quest. His memories of Jenpeg are marked by "sensory remembrances" he can still "feel" in the body: the biting cold of winter, the sun's darkening yellow, the thick snow, the crystalline structure of snowflakes, and the melting of snowflakes into vapor upon meeting hot breath. He insists that watery embodiment can transmute across forms and bequeath a repository of memory, stating, "The lake, the snow, the ice, the sky—water cast its spell on me in it many forms" (29). Water's shapeshifting enables Ali to engage his senses in perceiving nature and cultivate ecological bonds through tactile observation of elemental forms. This connection resurfaces years later when a frigid polar vortex, howling down Lake Erie near his Ohio home, inspires him to rediscover the Canadian north. As his plane descends into Cross Lake, he observes the "silver threads" of rivers swirling into a "tarnished gleam" beneath him (35). He likens this homecoming journey to "entering the water" (35). "Entering the water" conveys not only the physical geography of Cross

Lake, where vast expanses of water and river tributaries weave through land, but also the cultural meaning of aqueousness that situates humans within a communicative world of memory, senses, and community across time and place.

Engaging with Indigenous communities, Ali confronts the historical debt owed by settlers and the Western epistemologies of land and property. When he reaches out to the Cross Lake Chief, he is invited to visit the community. As the son of an immigrant engineer who contributed to the Jenpeg Generating Station, a Canadian nation-building project that exploited First Nations people, Ali is uneasy, "How could I account for that?" (27). He feels like a diplomat and ambassador for his immigrant family, sent to atone for their colonial debt to Indigenous people. During his stay, an Indigenous council member, Lee Roy, welcomes him to a sweat lodge ceremony, a purification ritual to ensure this curious visitor's intention is not political or capitalist, but about "the soil, the rocks, the river" (23). This gesture underscores the common ground for an Asian-Indigenous coalition built on ecological connectivity. Throughout the memoir, Indigenous inhabitants express a land philosophy different from a bordered nation, advocating for the intrinsic rights of land, trees, stones, and water to exist in place. "It is not just our own communities we are trying to protect, it is the whole of the planet," a Cree elder asserts (47). This worldview implies that Indigenous ecological care contributes to a diverse and richly textured notion of life, where humans are an integral part of an interconnected ecosystem.

Ali's awareness of the elemental connectivity between body and water grounds his shift from capitalist relations to ecological reciprocity. In Cross Lake Cree cosmology, water is sacred and the sweat lodge stands as a gift for Ali to understand water as a spiritual life force. He participates in the traditional practice of bringing an offering to the ritual, which expresses Indigenous reciprocal relations with water through respect, gratitude, and giving back. For Indigenous Canadian elders, the sweat lodge is a cleansing ritual, "returning the body and spirit to its purest state, akin to its emergence from the womb" (Blackstock 2001, 6). During the ceremony, water embodiments of thirst, drinking, perspiration, sweating, and breathing exchange with elemental forces of water, fire, heat, steam, rocks, and herbs, intermingling internal and external atmospheres and dissolving the boundary between self and environment. Ali feels dizzy and experiences a flux of multisensory memories from childhood, including visual images, feelings of touch and speed, people's voices, and bird calls, as if he were embedded back in the very land of Jenpeg. Ancestral memories of his maternal grandfather surface, adrift in the songs of Indigenous companions. The watery ceremony erodes stable categories of racial differences, individual bodies, and the five senses to entangle bodies in common porosity and liquid materiality.

*Northern Light* intertwines cultural memory and water's ecomateriality and unveils how both depend upon moving flows to stay lively. This liveliness entails relinquishing humanist modes of isolation and enclosure. Despite his initial frustration over diasporic placelessness, Ali gradually realizes that water archives memory and facilitates diasporic bodies to become, evolve, and forge new relations. His portrayal of the pulse and flow among water, body, memory, and community in the sweat lodge shows how bodies of water enact a relational ontology challenging the Enlightenment version of isolated, atomized, and self-sufficient individuals. Water troubles liberal individualism because humans are bodies of water that drink, sweat, weep, and constantly exchange with a more-than-human hydrocommons (Neimanis 2017, 2). For the immigrant subject, aqueous becoming helps restore a materialist imagination to a diasporic sense of place, allowing meaningful exchanges across past, present, and future. In this way, Ali's return is a material and metaphorical journey of "entering the water," a call into connectivity. He draws a parallel between the hydrological cycle to his quest for home, reflecting on how the rhythmic fall of rain, or the return of water from sky to earth, symbolizes the diasporic self's return from colonial to relational ways of knowing. He contemplates Toni Morrison's words: "All water has a perfect memory and is forever trying to get back to where it was," finding a resonance with his own journey (Ali 2021, 36). Rather than a return to a fixed origin or static past, water homecoming buoys the migrant self's becoming by building new conduits for past tribulations to undergo transformation.

Ali's personal history and water imaginations do not drift in the abstract. They are intertwined with the collective memory and environmental justice issues faced by the Cross Lake Crees, embedded in and through the materiality of water that encodes inequality, trauma, and deluge incurred by settler capitalist resource hegemony. Morrison's insights on water memory originally critiqued projects to straighten and modify the Mississippi River for housing and farming, which have increased flooding. Rejecting the objective term "flooding," Morrison instead frames it as water's agency of remembering and haunting (1995, 99). Bodies of water are sites of memory. Water's tempestuous forms of extreme weather and climate upheaval testify to the environment-making processes of colonialism and capitalism. Upon talking with Indigenous locals, Ali learns about the multiple dams obstructing, diverting, and harnessing the powers of rivers in northern Manitoba, creating erosion, siltation, undrinkable water, flooding, and biodiversity loss that disproportionately affect Indigenous communities. The dam's hydraulic regime establishes hierarchical and oppressive water relations, with benefits accruing to the energy companies and urban dwellers in southern Canada and northern US cities, while Indigenous peoples bear the environmental and social consequences. According to Indigenous oral stories, water's agency manifests in the specters of river "spiders," or floating roots of dead trees from soil erosion, that interfere with boat motors and cause them to capsize and drown people (Ali 2021, 62). Overpowering water and unknown rivers fracture a universal myth of hydroelectric development and human technological mastery over nature, but the "anger" of rivers is felt unevenly.

The hydroelectric dam and resulting inundation undermine capitalist resource imaginaries and temporal-spatial narratives of modern progress. Ali notes that the construction of the Jenpeg dam in the 1970s reflects a historical era fixated on grandiose projects, when local river systems all across the Canadian north were diverted into larger rivers for dam building (4). Dams are material monuments that not only regulate water systems but also concretize dominant geopolitical imaginaries and epistemes of meaning-making. Marcus Nüsser and Ravi Baghel observe a global rise in "technological hydroscapes" that embody developmental paradigms, evident in the modern history of big dams as symbols of national progress, from the 1930s Hoover Dam in the United States to the middle mountains of Germany, to post–World War II Soviet transformation of nature, and to the association between megadams and national ascension in Global South countries like India and China (2017, 292). The suffix "-scape" conceptualizes the geography of social imaginaries and networked political, economic, cultural, and ecological relations that shape hydrosocial spaces like dams. The hydroscapes are built on technologies of displacement that enclose the water commons and racialize Indigenous people as expendable to national development and technological prowess.

Writing on megadams and developmental refugees, Rob Nixon discusses the invention of "surplus people" by national resource development projects of water, oil, gas, minerals, and forests (2011, 151). Nixon explains that surplus people are often ecosystem people made dispensable through both imagined and physical eviction, "evacuated from place and time and thus uncoupled from the idea of both national future and a national memory" (2011, 151). Sometimes surplus people are not physically removed but become downgraded from inhabitants to "uninhabitants," existing in a kind of "vaporized dwelling" (Nixon 2011, 153). In Ali's memoir, the dispossession of Crees reflects how the rational structure of dams concretizes a colonial logic of disposability, submerging Indigenous water knowledges and ecosystems under capitalism. Racialized as obstacles to capitalist modernity and national progress, Indigenous communities and their homelands become superfluous in the neoliberal extractivist imaginary.

Through conversation with local Crees, Ali learns that the dam submerges not only river ecosystems but also Indigenous knowledge, culture, and multispecies lifeways dependent upon water ecology. Indigenous water sovereignty is pivotal for self-determination and cultural preservation. Max Haiven argues that dams are artificial edifices that not only manifest cultures but also transform local and Indigenous cultures through the spread of "consumer capitalism, possessive individualism, social drift, and Westernized/colonial forms of modernization" (2013, 216). This transformation can be seen in the challenges faced by Cree traditions in the wake of the Jenpeg dam. Cross Lake Crees, known as the *Pimicikamak,* or "otter people," in Cree, historically relied on "the abundance of fishing, hunting, and trapping" and fertile agriculture provided by the water-rich region (Ali 2021, 69).

The construction of the dam has drastically restructured this multispecies reliance on the water commons, leading to cascading consequences like altered fish spawning patterns, reduced fish populations, the disappearance of muskrats, bears, beavers, deer, and moose, decreased hunting opportunities, and the erosion of both ecological and cultural heritage—all exacerbating mental health issues within the community. Furthermore, the gains of capitalist development are unequally distributed, with Manitoba Hydro extracting energy from traditional lands and selling it back to the community at rates above the provincial average. The local Crees view this water and land dispossession as part of a broader continuum of settler colonialism and racial disposability, linked to the legacy of residential schools that aimed to assimilate Indigenous children into white Canadian culture, and substandard local healthcare and education infrastructures. Taking on this integrated picture means understanding the rising rates of youth suicide and substance abuse in the Indigenous community as symptoms of intersecting social and environmental injustices.

"So what does it mean to be 'from' a place?" ponders Ali (3). His book diverges from the memoir's conventional focus on the individual to imbricate a diasporic self's renewed sense of place with a semi-ethnographic account of Indigenous oral histories. It unearths the layered meanings of place to resist settler capitalist amnesia and abstraction. Appealing to an interconnected sense of place, Ali argues that all those who receive power from the dam, including distant urban consumers, partake in the responsibility for its effects. When shown a former residential school now turned into a parking lot, he is dismayed by how the settler capitalist property system alters landscapes and erases place memories. He reflects on how engaging with place can become a decolonial act if people work to recuperate personal, intergenerational, and collective memories. The intergenerational trauma resulting from the residential schools troubles official narratives of closure and forgetting, such as those presented by the Canadian government's state apology and dispute resolution plan.

Ali posits that the nation-state, by erasing important place memories, is as much a geopolitical container as a fabricated story, an abstract homogenous space where immigrants like his family clamor for entry, while Indigenous people "*have to be* excluded" to exist in the first place (99). Ali's critique triangulates the relations among migrants, Indigenous people, and the settler state by complicating simplistic ideas of inclusion and exclusion. This tension reveals a key distinction: whereas migrant struggles often seek inclusion within the nation-state, Indigenous struggles demand a politics of sovereignty. Ali's experiences, however, illustrate how both migrants and Indigenous people are not simply included or excluded but are differentially positioned in a racialized economy of settler capitalism, an economy sustained through the intertwined governance of social differences and markets. He notes that the Canadian state mythologizes the "wilderness" of the "true north" in its national anthem while simultaneously suppressing Indigenous culture through residential schools and capitalist resource extraction. Migrants, in pursuit of citizenship and multicultural inclusion, solidify colonial land use, yet the uneven distribution of liberal recognition and the land's colonial legacy haunt migrant claims to place-based belonging. Ali writes, "Jenpeg . . . never belonged to us and there was nothing there to be found. The real story, I realize, the real reason I came, is in Cross Lake. Not in Manitoba, not in Canada. Right here. In Pimicikamak" (122). Still, the profound connection to place he felt in childhood remains genuine and continues to inform his evolving sense of place: "The little Indian boy . . . he's still me, still *with* me" (22).

Clearly, Ali's water imagination does not advocate replacing solid land with liquid flows. It may be tempting, indeed, to romanticize ceaseless water as the antithesis to discrete land. Instead, his memoir collapses the land-water dichotomy to envision an aqueous sense of place. This perspective unmoors rigid identities by acknowledging the fluid and lively character of place, its ability to affect and revitalize the self. "Places do not belong to us. We belong to them" (167), Ali writes. His idea resonates with Philip Steinberg and Kimberley Peters's call for a "wet ontology," a materialist perspective that reconsiders traditional practices of territory to reveal "a world of fluidity where place is forever in formation and where power is simultaneously projected on, through, in, and about space" (261). Ali's effort at a decolonial ecology expresses this wet ontology, which emphasizes the embedded dynamism of place and a political commitment "not just to visit but to *see*" (120). Apart from seeing ecocultural contexts, he also stresses the need for attentive listening to foster humility and respect for Asian-Indigenous dialogue. "I'm back here to listen to you," he states at a Cree community gathering. Ali eschews romanticization of Indigeneity, portraying the heterogeneity within the Cree community, including Indigenous workers' involvement in the dam project, the fragmentation caused by developmentalism, divisions about spirituality, varied responses to cultural revival, and the attempts by Indigenous leaders to integrate traditional practices with settler European political manners.

Ali's narrative pinpoints the significance of emplaced and embedded knowledge to cross-racial environmentalism and decolonial modes of learning *with*. Embedded practices of sensing, seeing, and listening exemplify a decolonial ethos for engaging with the aqueous commons, which are relevant for building ecological collectives across diverse political landscapes beyond the immediate Asian-Indigenous context. To Ali's surprise, the Cross Lake community warmly welcomes intercultural exchanges, as shown by their greeting, "*You've come back at last! We've been waiting for you*" (168). Chief Merrick conveys the Pimicikamak's pluralistic, inclusive worldview: "We are a part of you now. . . . We will always have a place for you here" (163). Plurality sets the stage for dynamic encounters between Indigenous and settler cultures. Reflecting on his ancestral roots and the growing Muslim community in Winnipeg, Ali reaffirms a migrant sense of place: "We [migrants] are not landless people. We will always belong to the place we buried our ancestors . . . where we first . . . looked up at the infinite sky" (166). Migrants, having crossed oceans to this continent, to this place where rivers meet and waters merge, find themselves subject to settler capitalist infrastructures of racialization, evaluation, and regulation, which they have limited power to alter. And yet migration remains this generative process where disparate cultures and people meet to create new eddies, relations, and communities. Could these generative currents now be channeled into decolonial and post-anthropocentric modes of migrant belonging?

"And what is a place anyhow? We are from bodies, from land and landscape—they shape us and accompany us" (Ali 167). When humans alter elemental cycles, watery places become unstable. When objectified as property, elements are rendered placeless. Toward the end of his trip, Ali begins an ecological practice of elemental intimacy to denaturalize the capitalist commodification of water. Decolonization is an ongoing trek. Will the Asian migrant, upon leaving lands marked by colonial wrongs, forget history and his part in it? Upon returning to the motel and flicking on the plastic switch of light, Ali imagines a fire drawn from the northern river's rushing currents and sparkling an everyday material entity like electricity (168). Decolonizing capitalist energy consumption is one way migrant settlers can acknowledge and respect the water and ecosystems upon which their comfort depends. Before his departure from Cross Lake, Ali releases a talisman paper crane with his prayers for the Pimicikamak community into the river, where "the water takes it in" (145). "You're plugged in," an Indigenous boy tells him after the sweat lodge. Plugging into water's memory and connectivity is a starting point from where the Asian settler can form more ecologically oriented practices and dialogues for the decolonial commons.

## "Water Will Return What We Give It": Rita Wong's Aqueous Dissolve and Otherwise

Kazim Ali's framing of decolonial ecology within embedded watersheds and cultural memories affirms the relevance of situated knowledge for historicizing place and counteracting settler capitalist extraction and erasure. In comparison, in her poetry collection *Undercurrent*, Rita Wong composes planetary poems of water cycles, swirling molecules, organisms, humans, animals, plants, fossil fuels, plastics, products, cities, lifestyles, and colonial histories into a wet network of toxicity, accountability, and regeneration that troubles the world ecology of capitalism. Water in Wong's poetry is not confined to specific sites of ocean currents, rain clouds, or underground aquifers; instead it saturates and infiltrates multiple scales and bodies, connecting the micro and macro, land and sea, and human and more-than-human. By reassembling the wet materiality of terrestrial bodies, Wong dissolves the bounded individual and shows that we do not just rely on water in our environment, but are water from within: "hypersea is a story of how we rearrange our oceanic selves on land" (2015, 11). Water replenishes ecological foundations of elements, sustenance, and ecosystems, while also gestating milieu, spirituality, and worldview. Wong's water poetics highlights the aqueous inseparability of matter and meaning, a co-constitutive relationship she traces in *Undercurrent*, where water shapes and emerges from human embodiments and cultural imaginaries.

I argue that Wong's liquid matrix interweaves two ethical hydro-imaginaries of the aqueous commons. The first is the *aqueous dissolve*, an ecomaterialist figuration of water bodies as transcorporeal conduits of life and toxicity within anthropocentric capitalism. The second is the *aqueous otherwise*, a planetary call for kinship, care, and the irrepressible commons that crack open settler capitalism to exude alternatives in the here and now. Wong intertwines these two visions in "Declaration of Intent," where she writes, "water will return what we give it," be that "arrogance & poison, reverence & light, ambivalence & respect" (2015, 14). The aqueous dissolve and aqueous otherwise converge in Wong's concerns for environmental justice and her imagination of the latent commons. Together, they encapsulate the contradictory and incalculable "undercurrents," as her book's title suggests, of the Anthropocene present, marked by lost equilibrium, ubiquitous risks, and ethical potentials.

These hydro-visions also braid two decolonial praxes: differentiation and collaboration. In an article on Asian-Indigenous relationality, Wong outlines the simultaneous tasks of confronting the immigrant inheritance of capitalist private property system "in the realm of the partial, the fragmented, the ruptured, the torn" (2008, 1), and undertaking cultural labor that aligns migrant allegiances with Indigenous values of earth guardianship and ecological interdependence (2008, 2). In *Downstream: Reimagining Water*, Wong and Dorothy Christian make a case for the creative commons as essential to supporting a healthy water ecology and cultivating courageous, democratic practices that foster solidarity and respectful relationships (2017, 15). Wong's hydropoetics is exemplary of these creative efforts, which combine a situated dissolving of settler capitalist infrastructures with a planetary reimagining of aqueous ways of knowing, being, feeling, and commoning toward the hopeful renewal of worlds in ruins.

My interpretation of Wong's aqueous dissolve places her work within critical dialogues that trouble the modern capitalist imaginary of water as an abstract, homogenous, and quantifiable entity. In *What Is Water? The History of a Modern Abstraction*, Jamie Linton contends that the current water crisis stems from a modern construction of water in a reductive scientific discourse that alienates water from its wider ecological, social, and cultural dimensions. This modern abstraction treats water as an infinite resource and frames solutions predominantly in "technical and hydrological terms" (2010, 7). Yet how we relate to water is shaped by our ideas of water. The global water crisis compels us to acknowledge the unsustainability of modern water to allow alternative, neglected hydrosocial realities to spring to life (Linton 2010, 13). Besides scientific rationality, capitalism further abstracts water. Understanding capitalism as a world ecology of organizing nature, Jason Moore proposes the concept of the Capitalocene to describe how modern capitalism dominates, exploits, and cheapens of the web of life for endless capital accumulation (2015). While the fluid materiality of water bodies defies land-based sovereignty, capitalism seeks to flatten the land-water distinction through "terraqueous territoriality" to enclose water resources and spaces for the commodity market (Campling and Colás 2021, 3). From a posthuman ecology of wet connectivity, however, the modern capitalist making of water is also remaking human existence in unpredictable ways. Wong's poetics critiques global capitalist fantasies of mastering and controlling water. Her verses persistently dissolve and recompose the human through wet and unknown interchanges between body and material environment, thereby dismantling the discrete individualism that underpins the myth of commodity capitalism.

In Wong's poetry, water bodies are transcorporeal vessels and transits that underline the human body as permeated by the vibrant matters and sociocultural practices of consumerism, fossil fuel reliance, and waste pollution. Her aqueous dissolve echoes Stacy Alaimo's concept of "transcorporeality," a posthumanist epistemology of understanding human bodies as perpetually interconnected with material agencies and substances of the environment (2010, 2). Transcorporeality addresses the porosity of the human and challenges a convenient myth of discrete consumers and benign products advertised by global capitalism and the medical-industrial complex (Alaimo 2012, 477). In her poem "bisphenol ache," Wong writes that "kindred water is a secret player reflecting industrial flaws back to us, naming the chemical creep is the first step in returning to our responsibilities" (2015, 46). Toxic intimacies between industrial waste and the human body reveal how water registers the insidious transcorporeality of global petrochemical economies.

One of the industrial toxins that Wong portrays is Bisphenol A (BPA), a chemical compound used in the mass manufacturing of polycarbonate plastics to make beverage bottles, tableware, synthetic resins, and other consumer products. As a highly moldable material, plastic depends on BPA to achieve its durability and adaptability, which epitomizes the modern desire to manipulate passive matter to human will. Yet the pliability of plastic matter also reveals the undoing of techno-utopian promises of protection, with plastic offering both a convenient, sanitary, and sterilized life, and paradoxically, piles of cheap, clingy, and toxic materiality (Davis 2022, 8). The purported hygienic benefits of disposable plastics obscure a false separation between nature and culture. Global capitalism conceals the link between the gleaming plastic products in shopping malls and the fossil fuel infrastructure of global plastic engineering and the haunting afterlife of plastic waste in the world's waterways and oceans. In "bisphenol ache," Wong depicts transcorporeal seepage to expose the pervasive reach of everyday oil infrastructures,

> corporate cancer embedded in diets . . . gradually accumulated illnesses blossom in our bellies, breasts, bladders, intestines testify to trace amounts hoarded in blood & bitumen, brimming with slow malignant release, remind us that biology is determined by chemistry cartels infiltrating our shampoos & synthetic textiles, room deodorizers & tin can linings & receipt paper coatings & hand sanitizers sing a slow song of poison by a thousand exposures (2015, 46)

This passage describes the body's entanglement with petrochemical plastics, emphasizing both corporeal interconnections between inside and outside and complicity with global industrial and consumer systems. Wong marks the insidious nature of toxic exposure with phrases such as "gradually accumulated," "hoarded," "slow malignant release," and "slow song of poison." These expressions convey the chronic infiltration of pollutants into human bodies through water transits beyond the certainty of knowledge, as these toxins "seep intimately, expertly, into the creases we didn't know we had" (Wong 2015, 46). The unforeseen and unwanted health risks of our petrocultural reliance reveal that incalculable material agencies transgress modern techno-triumph and containment, orchestrating a planetary unraveling that Wong terms "consumed while consuming" (41).

The risky fluidity across blood, bitumen, and deodorizer in Wong's poetry attends to the aqueous transits by which "'progress' extracts / from our bodies' immune systems" (52) and traps us in "massive ghost nets" that eventually engineer "our own disposal" (12).

In "Body Burden," Wong describes how environmental illnesses like "eczema" and "rashes, scars, bruises, faint scratches" signal the body's "porous / ongoing experiment / rich in nurdles / poor in ecological literacy" (40). What does it mean to develop an ecological literacy of the self in a risk society of chemical toxicity? This requires the average human consumer not only to understand the often unmappable molecular circulations of atrazine, PCBs, furans, and dioxins, but also to interrogate the economic, political, and sociocultural practices of the automobile, agricultural, and pharmaceutical industries that manufacture a toxic landscape of ever-emergent risks that reconfigure the more-than-human world. Microplastics are now found in the human body, alongside the known death of marine animals like turtles, seabirds, and fish from ingesting plastic debris. In "North Shore Sewage Story," Wong describes urban drains pumping out chemical discharges and birth control pills, "morphing fish anatomy / decreasing sperm counts" and "transgendering water & children" (50–51). Here she highlights the queer effect of endocrine-disrupting chemicals (EDCs) on human and animal bodies. Heather Davis considers plastic a queer matter that denaturalizes heteronormative reproductivity as the ultimate signifier of hope, politicizing the emergent flows of chemical toxicity to open up trans-species empathy beyond normative family kinship and to hold chemical companies accountable for the vast harms they enact (2022, 83). Like Davis, Wong's poem politicizes the excess of wastewater discharge and rebellious toxins. She makes visible the flush-and-forget infrastructure of urban pipelines that implicate chemical companies and human consumers in networked toxic responsibility beyond one's immediate biological kin.

Wong's aqueous disturbance of toxic infrastructures invites readers to understand the coemergent trajectories of matters and discourses across bodily natures in a storied world. In our era of sensational media, public sentiment grows numb to the incremental ecological violence of toxic buildup, greenhouse gases, and species loss. In his discussion of "slow violence," Rob Nixon centers the question of representation, "how to devise arresting stories, images, and symbols adequate to the pervasive but elusive violence of delayed effects" (2011, 3). Wong's poetics meets this representational challenge by expanding aesthetics to fossil fuel infrastructures.

Although fossil fuels shape contemporary lives, oil infrastructures remain largely hidden in our modern visual and cultural representations (Wilson et al. 2017, 5). But Wong is careful not to paralyze action through individual blame. Instead, she situates personal responsibility within broader life narratives, social norms, and cultural habits of consumerist modernity. In "A Magic Dictionary from Bitumen to Sunlight," she traces how petrocultural narratives are created and sustained through affective desires for automobiles that refigure eons of mineral wealth into a "vintage car more retro than we know" (2015, 28). In "Borrowed Waters," she remaps the Great Pacific Garbage Patch as "a manmade network" branching into our "bathrooms with its plastic shampoo bottles & toothbrushes" and "plastic beverage bottles belched out by nestle, coca-cola, pepsi, visible tip of the corporeal iceberg" (10). Oceanic waste is not ahistorical but forms a physical and conceptual archive of global consumerism; its biosemiotics emerges through the discursive practices of transnational brands, neoliberal globalization, and "the good life" fueled by plastics.

Through her portrayal of the coemergence of substance and significance, Wong illustrates the narrative agency of water. She writes that water "has a syntax," extending beyond mere flow to compose a polyphonic lexicon of "tidal rhythm," "choppy waves," "dissonant grammars," and "hazardous passages" (9). These aqueous expressions "pivot," "punctuate," "sing," "roll," "churn," and "gurgle," creating a rich tapestry of water's textuality (9). This poetics counters the modern tendency to abstract water, instead giving voice to an aqueous ontology in which water is storied matter, full of patterns, cultures, and dynamism. Wong suggests that a watershed teaches us "climate fluency," a literacy to interpret the sea's rising voice (2015, 14). Her poems of the aqueous dissolve are firmly ecomaterialist because nature and culture and inside and outside are inextricably fused, constituting life and the world in their continuous becoming.

By questioning how the toxic infrastructures of extractive capitalism compound settler colonial histories of dispossession, Wong's aqueous dissolve aligns with decolonial and anticapitalist politics. She exposes the resource theft and colonial technologies imposed on Indigenous peoples and geographies by the Canadian settler state and its neoliberal partners, through "hydro dam construction, tar sands, uranium mines, global warming" (66). In "Dispatches from Water's Journey," Wong writes, "i live at the west entrance of a haunted house called Canada" whose "hungry ghosts, windborn spirit, call us to conscience" (64). These spectral presences are residues of the petro-state's cancerous terraforming and violent reorganization of social and ecological life. A rhetorical pairing between extractive capitalism and nation-building is evident in the Canadian petroleum industry's framing of resource operations like the tar sands as "'ethical' economic opportunities for all" (Preston 2013, 43) and "equity offers" for Indigenous self-determination through employment and technological training (Preston 2013, 48). Wong demasks the neocolonial logic in these developmentalist promises that continue to alter Indigenous lands and waterways for "the greater good," insisting that "reconciliation needs land restoration to ground / itself & grow" (2015, 64). She fractures the seamless continuum of national history by underscoring submerged undercurrents, suggesting that Indigenous "healing time" from the traumas of residential schools and environmental contamination does not align with the official timelines of "the truth & reconciliation commission" (64). Moreover, she reminds us that the river itself is in danger from petroleum.

In "Lupus, a Doubled Being," the reader is invited to witness the eerie spectacle of Alberta tar sands: "Disney-manufactured in white wilderness, alberta / fiction is flashier than truth, a plastic-signed detour / exported by pipelines, tankers, digital propaganda / that forgets & even sells the ground holding it up" (52). The modern state's developmentalist fiction of infinite resources is rooted in a white settler colonial ideology of discovering and conquering wilderness as resource frontiers. This ideology resurfaces in bituminous horrors of oil sands megaprojects that poison the Athabasca River ecosystems and produce increased cancer rates in Indigenous communities. Downstream from the Athabasca River, Chipewyan, Cree, Dene, and Métis Indigenous communities face threats to their right to clean water from the toxic sludge of tar sands mines. Under neoliberal globalization, the Alberta bitumen supply chains extend beyond the local region to implicate international buyers such as the United States and China in a complex web of transnational accountability.

In "Dada-thay," named after the Dene word for "death rock," Wong critiques uranium mining in Saskatchewan, which leaks silent radioactive waste that poses formidable harms to Indigenous water and food sovereignty. She walks around Wollaston Lake "lightly, gratefully," comparing the Dene's reverence for land and the destructive actions of governments and corporations who "desecrate the water for the mines" (70). The poem links uranium's local harms in Canada to global events of military and imperialist violence. According to the Saskatchewan Environmental Society, long-term radioactive contamination of mining sites is one issue, while Saskatchewan's uranium exports have fueled the global spread of nuclear weapons, from sales to the US Atomic Energy Commission in the 1950s and 1960s to current transactions with India (2015). Wong references the Sahtu Dene's historic journey to Hiroshima and Nagasaki, depicting a "village of widows" who apologize to survivors for the "death rock" mined on their land and used in atomic bombs. The Dene's apology embodies an ethical stance of remorse and accountability that Western governments avoid. This poem calls for transnational solidarity, demanding an awareness of the interconnected local and global impacts of environmental degradation, colonialism, and militarism, while connecting Indigenous communities and ecologies in Canada with peoples worldwide who share decolonial concerns for peace, justice, and ecological responsibility.

Literary critics have remarked that Wong's poetic style diverges from conventional expectations of poetic language, which is typically characterized as figurative, ambiguous, or obscure (Bradley 2021, xx). Nicolas Bradley observes that Wong's poetry emphasizes "clarity and intelligibility," using straightforward vocabulary alongside technical terms, political discourse, and pop-cultural references (2021, xx). While I concur that Wong's poetry extends beyond tradition, it is important to recognize her formal innovations that evoke the material textures and rhythms of capitalist ecology and transcorporeality. For instance, "Borrowed Waters" is arranged into one chunky paragraph that expresses the physical mass of the Great Pacific Garbage Patch and its indiscriminate gathering of miscellaneous consumer debris. The poem "immersed" deploys anaphora, repeating "immersed in" at the start of each line, to establish the rhythms of saturation, accumulation, and atmospheric intimacies between the body and material agencies of "chlorinated water," "car exhaust," and "barbecue aroma" (Wong 2015, 32). Additionally, *Undercurrent* collects quotes from many writers and critics that are formatted into wavy shapes at the bottom of pages. This choreographs water's capacity for circulating knowledge and generating dialogue across time and space. Wong's deliberate avoidance of capital letters, except for names of people and places, presents a break from colonial hierarchies, egocentric capitalism, and the authority of the English language.

We can notice stylistic experiments in "For Gregoire Lake," in which Wong (2015, 68) draws on her experience of the Tar Sands Healing Walk, hosted by local Indigenous groups, to contemplate two onto-epistemologies of water:

| | |
|---|---|
| in the fresh morning | *hexavalent chromium* |
| i dip my hands into you | *arsenic* |
| tentatively | |
| thankful to camp on your shores | *alumium* |
| amidst mosquitos, mud & grass | *zinc* |
| knowing you hold airborne | *thallium* |
| toxins | |
| from the tar sands | *nickel* |

The poem emphasizes the value of collaboration across plural and shifting knowledge traditions for cultivating a planetary ethics that respects alterity. Stylistically, it combines personal reflection with a stark acknowledgment of chemical pollutants, juxtaposing different ways of knowing and being—spiritual and scientific, experiential and laboratory, Indigenous and settler—in a dynamic of collision and collaboration. This approach questions the epistemic dominance of Western science and encourages relational dialogues. In the left column, the poet expresses gratitude and respect for the lake, while in the right column, a sobering list of toxic contaminants reveals that the lake is sick from tar sands pollution. This juxtaposition opens the door to a decolonial dialogue between Indigenous wisdom and Euro-Western knowledge, suggesting they could jointly contribute to exposing corporate greed and safeguarding water's well-being for collective survival. But this potential partnership is fraught, as the poet's connection to the life-giving lake is compromised by her scientific knowledge of its contamination. The poem thus raises pressing ethical questions: How can we engage with science without reinforcing epistemic mastery so that water's alterity keeps flowing? How might ecological vulnerability translate into transformative justice instead of fearful division? And how can we envision an otherwise as the current world crumbles?

The poem above also reveals the fraught ground from which the poet speaks, reiterating her pursuit of a decolonial commons across multiple localities, cultures, and knowledges from the position of a diasporic settler, or "unsettler." Wong describes her learning with water as "a journey of becoming worthy to live as a guest" on the sacred lands of Indigenous people (2015, 22). In "Journey to the West 西遊記," she decolonizes the conventional migrant dream, asserting that the descendants of millions who migrate to Turtle Island with hopes of securing a better future may instead face a foreclosed future: a land and coast altered by corporate greed, where "fresh sea urchin breakfast" turn into "wretched carcinogen" (20). *Journey to the West* is a classic sixteenth-century Chinese novel about the pilgrimage of four characters, Monk, Monkey, Pig, and Sandy, who travel west to India, facing trials and tribulations, in search of Buddhist sutras. Wong draws from this mythological tale to recalibrate the migrant journey westward not as a quest for assimilation and success but as an eco-spiritual responsibility to protect and sustain, to take part in a collective guardianship over a "costal home" ancient as stone and vulnerable to settler colonial capitalism.

In "Night Gift," Wong continues to reorient diasporic subjectivity beyond capitalist abstraction toward the ocean's material ecology, writing that "the humble migrants who've travelled the ocean have felt its wisdom more deeply than an arrogant elite who doesn't heed the world's necessary stories" (23). Given that seas and oceans provide vital conduits for migration history and culture, and that Asian diaspora studies have historically mobilized transoceanic fluidity for emancipatory politics, why is there a lack of migrant voices in the blue humanities? Wong explores migration through oceanic imaginations to emphasize water's facilitative capacity for enabling hybridity and mobility, both are central to migrant and diasporic politics. By foregrounding a felt respect for the ocean's wisdom, she proposes a new oceanic imaginary for migrant agendas that ecologically and affectively interprets how water bodies encode and enliven migratory movements. The poem uses night as a space of solidarity among the marginalized, when the "ragged," "dispossessed," and "wrongly imprisoned" unite for hopeful visions of insurgency, "fueled by a love more immense than the injustices we've inherited" (23). Wong envisions an alternative future grounded in eco-activism and cross-cultural alliances, where migrants mobilize for a livable world through community, music, lake gatherings, forests, and guerrilla gardening.

Although water may be polluted by colonial and capitalist management, it remains a vessel of decolonial hope in Wong's imagination of an aqueous otherwise. Dissolving and dwelling in water's fecundity helps fissure existing structures of containment and potentiate the latent commons in capitalist ruins. Aqueousness creates an ethical milieu immanently open to the rearrangement and indeterminacy of existence. Mielle Chandler and Astrida Neimanis elaborate on water's gestational role in cultivating ethics, noting that water facilitates "the inception, repetition, and proliferation of life in its potentially infinite plurality" (2013, 62). Water stories like Wong's open up an aqueous commons by defying the objectification, privatization, and atomization of life that underpin the capitalist property system, taking emergent and toxic naturecultures as an ethical opportunity for systemic change and more-than-human modes of care. This emphasis on worldmaking and revitalization of life differentiates Wong's poetics from apolitical interpretations of material entanglement, a tendency that has been raised in debates around new materialism.

For Wong, an aqueous otherwise is already circulating in the here and now. She declares that "another world is not only possible, she is already here, carrying on underneath our feet" and "reconstituting us with each new sip of ancient water" (2015, 26). She imagines a collective "we" that is not yet, invoking a sense of speculative or anticipatory planetarity: "we need to live in the world that is possible even as we navigate through war" (23). In "For Gregoire Lake," she posits a hopeful politics of repair, remarking, "i wish I had met you [lake] in better times / but i am grateful to meet you at all / even in our compromised states / we remember why we are here" (68). Here Wong expresses a modest reparation of relations in the middle of ruins and calls forth a planetary commons that arises from a refusal to despair. She turns to water memory as a shaper of ecological patterns, asserting that "kindred spirit, autonomous water remembers forest before rubble / revives the forest before the terror is reined in" (27). This remembrance is not a return to a premodern wilderness, but an opening up to the participatory continuity of water flows as a way of anticipating a new ecological equilibrium of abundance and renewal.

The poet proclaims, "Who are we? We are the beings who need clean water in order to live a life of dignity, joy and good relations" (16). Water makes possible a planetary collective of more-than-human interdependency. She invites readers to participate in the aqueous commons, "Maybe you are part of 'us' without even knowing that you are" (16). Envisioning an aqueous otherwise means contesting the modern template of "the good life" based on possessive individualism, and redefining what is good in light of earthly obligations, where "dignity and meaning comes from keeping the earth healthy for future generations" (19). This otherwise involves transspecies care, where "tree care is self-care" (34), and unfolds through storied worlds brought to life via truth telling from below: "jail the stories & storytellers, but they will keep speaking the night, until empire expires" (23). Wong stands for reviving societies as watersheds, an endeavor necessitating "not *tar* but *tears*," where the added *e* inserts "a listening, witnessing, quickening eye" (15). The shift from polluted tar sands to empathetic tears for water's suffering signals a departure from capitalist resource imaginaries. Instead, it gestures toward symbiotic interactions with water, attentive to its signs, safety, and ethical orientations.

Imagining an aqueous otherwise directs our attention toward multispecies justice, decentering human superiority to honor species and elements as emerging from and sustained within multispecies communities. Wong depicts animals, plants, microbes, and a multitude of life-forms that share water with humans not as mere victims to capitalist exploitation, but as witnesses, kin, hospitable providers, wonder makers, and vigilant survivors. In "Unsung Service," Wong invokes strategic anthropomorphism to give voice to a nonhuman chorus, "We are tardigrade and tawny owls, river dolphins and rockhopper penguins, slow sloths and fast elk" who are "your relatives," who "precede and supersede" your "patriarchal mind games," and who "call upon you to remember your ancient oaths, your debts to all realm that enable your existence, your obligations as earth-dwellers" (35). By considering water life-forms as persons of justice, the poem engages with multispecies justice—raising questions about expanding justice beyond the human, decolonizing its practice, and heeding the risks of ventriloquism when humans speak "for" and "of" nonhumans across species differences (Kirksey and Chao 2022, 4). Wong's approach decolonizes species hierarchies by allowing the creativity, persistence, and dignity of water animals to speak for themselves. She depicts beavers who have "built dams you can see from outer space" (2015, 18), "implacable" sturgeons that carry on in hazardous opaque rivers (34), and "a wild swimming wolf" quietly watching human damage, a presence of untameable spirit (52).

In Wong's poetry, we can also locate a poetics of "the irrepressible commons," a more radical vision of planetarity from below. It embeds decolonial ethics and politics in water's immanent persistence and unstoppable potential to eventually crack open unjust systems and reclaim the commons. In "Take a St.and," Wong describes wastewater bursting open urban pipelines at "the corner of fifth and st. george," where "water shoots exuberant into sky," prompting the poet to wonder: Is it "coincidence, haunting, or the stubborn stream's refusal to be confined?" (60). Urban water grids and pipes conceal groundwater and pollution, until wastewater's uncanny resurgence demands visibility. This moment also reflects Wong's use of fragmentation as a poetic technique. The visual stop in "st.and" disrupts the flow of the phrase much like urban water systems disrupt natural streams. Wong's visual enjambment reflects this rupture, revealing how capitalist infrastructures attempt, but ultimately fail, to contain the water commons.

The irresistible return of the water commons can potentially manifest in unruly climate forms: "We are wet premonitions, ferocious spirit waiting for the master's dams to crack, the inexorable and unrepentant rain, the tidal waves taller than tankers, the vigilant survivors of neoliberal snakepits and slimy advertorials" (Wong 53). This resurgence embodies a multispecies undercommons within and beyond capitalist manipulation, representing those "who cannot be bought, the ones who will not sell out, the ones who refuse to be bullied" (53). It brings forth suppressed excess, unlocking the potential for intercultural, intergenerational, and interspecies alliances: "we are the thunderstorms that precipitate when too much has been repressed, the weeds that refuse to stop, the coyotes, the grandmothers, the yet unborn" (16). This planetary resurgence embodies the nonlinearity and shadow ecologies of capitalist ruination, signaled by indelible traces of reclamation: "the machine's gears rust in rain, moss & lichen slowly creep life back" (15). Moss, lichen, and weeds are endurant, adaptive, and unsung life-forms that thrive in inhospitable environments, capable of regenerating worlds for new cycles of life.

If the irrepressible commons are bound to return, it is because they follow ancient pulses of water, life, and ecological patterns, even in distorted forms. In "Sunset," Wong connects alternative futures with ancestral wisdom, proposing that "channels of return" follow "the paths of dreamtime" (58). The poem's speaker, displaced from her ancestral rice paddies, juxtaposes the industrial "sick roses & smokestacks" and the memory of "guava harvest" and "pomelo promise." Her solastalgia, or homesickness caused by environmental change (Albrecht 2007), manifests as an embodied sense of loss and unresolved longing, expressed in "the throat's fullness, the heart's hesitation" (Wong 2015, 58). This feeling is not merely nostalgia for a past but a place-based distress and an embodied grief for vanishing ecological knowledge and the body's own microcosmic connections. She envisions underwater "meridians abound underneath linking foot, ear, heart, liver in the body's complex orchestra," "accompanied by & enabled by spirochetes & microflora" (58). When she hears that "wild rice used to grow where chinatown is now," she invokes its return, imagining a reclaiming of lost multispecies and playful connections. Yet "the channels of return are unpredictable / they follow the paths of dreamtime that evaporate with sunrise" (58). These reconnections to ancestral memory and symbiotic continuity are fragile yet persistent, accessible in fleeting, lucid, and ritualistic moments that demand attentiveness.

With the irrepressible commons, Wong expresses how decolonial ecology could upend the linguistic and property hierarchies of settler colonialism. In "Q'élstexw," she writes, "the city paved with ~~cement~~ english cracks open, stubborn Halq'eméylem springs up" (59). The word *q'élstexw*, meaning "bring back; return things," is from the Halq'eméylem dialect of the Stó:lō Indigenous people of the lower Fraser River in British Columbia (FirstVoices, n.d.). The poem envisages Halq'eméylem names for trees, ferns, and ravens springing up unpredictably in urban spaces, on sidewalks, newspaper stands, and supermarkets overflowing with imported foods (59). The poet connects Indigenous linguistic diversity with an ecotopian vision of a cityscape where ferns sprout from any available crevice. In this eco-linguistic merging, water metonymically links Indigenous worldviews to a future ecoculture that might burst open the rigid cement of capitalist world economy. Wong underscores that the resurgence of the commons, channeled by persistent, weedy growth, is inevitable—its eruption offering a speculative opening into an immanent planetarity from below: "we're not going to shut up, we're water bodies" (74).

The concluding poem of the book, "Holders," instills hope by embedding ethics in the everyday acts of cultivating and sustaining a more-than-human web of life within unjust systems. This poem anchors collective change in a feminist ethics of care, portraying women as guardians and gardeners, like trees with unseen roots. Such a stance could initially draw criticism for seemingly essentializing nature and the feminine as idealized caregivers. Yet we are invited to challenge a monolithic concept of care by redefining it as situated political commitments and ethical doings that must be constantly reclaimed from hegemonic ethics exploiting care to perpetuate social inequalities (Puig de la Bellacasa 2017, 7). The poem articulates a processual ethos of care through depictions of women standing united against "army trucks & policemen, uniforms & riot gear," bound by kinship with mothers, daughters, and grannies as they strive to "crack open the ugly pavement of unjust laws" (Wong 2015, 80). Their sacred commitment to all life is cultivated in soil practices of planting trees, foraging mushrooms, and composting. In this way, Wong imagines the decolonial commons as a collective of caretakers, where regenerative futures emerge from the everyday labor, preservation, cultivation, play, and kinmaking of those who care with thick webs of life. As Wong encapsulates this ethos, "[The women] find ways to laugh even when life isn't funny. the women remain" (80). Alternative worlds and systemic change will unfold from the ongoing ethicality of invoking, virtualizing, and composing in our hearts and actions this planetary collective of ecopoetic care and multispecies democracy. In the epilogue, set in the year 2115, Wong imagines a future world where "people live & watch water's journey the way they used to watch the dow jones" (87). The water is to return; so is the worlding of an otherwise.

This chapter is bathed in an immersive journey of decolonial water narratives in Asian North American literature. It hopes to open up a new migrant ecology that disinherits capitalist property relations and redefines unsettler responsibilities through decolonial water alliances and ecopoetic care. This engagement critiques private property as central to Indigenous displacement, resource exploitation, and planetary water crises. I have traced the water movements and stories of Kazim Ali and Rita Wong, who insist on learning *with* Indigenous ecological knowledge and water's materiality. This decolonial journey begins with Ali's quest for an embedded sense of place by refusing settler capitalist hydropower and ends with Wong's ecomaterialist dissolution of water bodies, matters, and cultures to seed a planetary resurgence in global capitalist ruins. I develop the concept of the *aqueous commons* in order to characterize latent ethical and political collectives that emerge from reimagining water's planetary alterity and its connective milieu, as these networked streams are charted by writers like Ali and Wong. The commons become aqueous in two senses: They connect and differentiate in ways that are shared and situated, and they pulse and flow through matters and meanings in coemergence. The aqueous commons are subversive undercurrents from the margins that do not tally with property ownership, individual atomization, and rationalist control. They are feral effects and weedy hope whose uncanny return erupts and haunts. They are messy, lively, asymmetrical, and collaborative. They are irrepressible, unstoppable, bottom-up, and more-than-human. They hold open past futures and future pasts of symbiotic abundance and planetary renewal in the here and now.

In Part II of this book, we will explore how the irrepressible commons, in motion with refugees and migrant workers, articulates the entangled mobility that often gets abstracted in modern humanist bio- and necropolitics. Thinking with oceans, extinction, climate change, and technological waste, the following chapters examine ways of "thickening" migrant agency, freedom, and mobility from state and capitalist reductions to more-than-human emergence. They invite us to encounter residual ecologies with an ethics of subsistence, alterity, and exposure, telling thick relational accounts of collaborative survival from below and pushing back against the victimhood imposed by a colonial hierarchy of life and animacy. A planetary poetics calls forth alternative cosmopolitics by ecologizing the subterranean excess of mobility and the kinetic materiality of cosmic energy, whose transversal, unruly, and open-ended interplay implodes colonial capitalist geology and its rational economies of extraction. Following thick mobility, migration literature and film attempt to ground planetarity in the irrepressible commons that move through the affective and geosocial intimacies of global neoliberal biopolitics, shining light on the new assemblages, collectivities, and ethics of coexistence in the movement and continuation of life.

# Part II

# Thick Mobility

Freedom is the negotiation of ghosts on a haunted landscape; it does not exorcise the haunting, but works to survive and negotiate it with flair.

**—Anna Tsing, *Mushroom at the End of the World***

We are called to consider others not as passive bodies but rather as thinking subjects inhabiting their own worlds of action and meaning. A world, in this thick account, includes the body, the self, the relevant environment, and the interweaving matrix that holds these elements in the dynamism of ongoing life.

**—Deborah Bird Rose, *Shimmer***

# 3

# Refugee Thick Mobility

## *More-Than-Human Emergence at Oceanic Borders*

In the documentary film *Island of the Hungry Ghosts* (2018), director Gabrielle Brady explores a more-than-human poetics of refugee mobility. On Christmas Island in the Indian Ocean, sixty million red crabs undertake their annual migration from rainforest burrows to coastal breeding grounds, swarming across roads and disrupting traffic. Poh Lin Lee, a trauma therapist, works with asylum seekers held indefinitely in a walled detention center. Under a full moon, Chinese islanders perform hungry ghost rituals for wandering spirits caught between worlds. These seemingly disparate storylines converge to unfold the island's social and environmental histories. Beneath the beauty of nature lie ghostly histories, where resource extraction, migrant labor, and refugee detention have shaped eco-social geographies of violence. Human settlement on Christmas Island began relatively recently, in 1888, following the British discovery of its phosphate deposits (Woinarski 2018, 16). This led to the development of a mining industry that relied on indentured laborers, or "coolies," from British Malay, Singapore, and China, who toiled under atrocious conditions. More recently, Christmas Island became the site of high-security immigration detention camps, established by the Australian border force to process asylum seekers arriving by boat.

Juxtaposing the natural wonder of red crab migration with the enforced immobility of asylum seekers, *Island of the Hungry Ghosts* intersects species diversity with human diversity, and seasonal changes with biopolitical borders. This clash lends environmental weight to the asylum seeker as a ghostly figure who denaturalizes the idyllic image of Christmas Island as a tropical paradise for privileged tourists. The disturbed wildlife due to mining activities and the past and present racial ghosts make Christmas Island more than a territory on the map. It is a haunted landscape, with borders that cannot preclude exchanges between inside and outside and past residues that continue to leave material traces. The film's cinematic techniques, depicting surreal imagery, strange bird calls, overcast skies, and sparse narration, evoke an eerie sadness and a somber mood that spectralize Christmas Island. Instead of inundating viewers with facts on refugee and environmental politics, the film immerses its audience in atmospheric intensity, amplifying moments of feeling. This affective texture and opaque aesthetics convey the tension and uncertainty of refugee life—a state of existence caught in limbo, where transience turns into permanence.

Analyzing *Island of the Hungry Ghosts* alongside Behrouz Boochani's memoir *No Friend but the Mountains* (2018), this chapter introduces *thick mobility* as a method for reimagining refugee migration in the context of extinction. This method shifts the focus from modern humanist discourses of mobility to ecological and posthuman representations that narrate migration in more-than-human entanglements. More-than-human relations provide both an explanatory tool and a transformative site for refugee agency and belonging delimited by contemporary bio- and necropolitics: state and capitalist practices of racialization, bordering, and governance that reproduce the epistemic coloniality of migration rooted in Eurocentric humanism. Against universalist abstract knowledge, thick mobility asks how the excess of mobility emerges from contingent, affective, and residual ecologies of sustaining life and movement in precarity. It opens up the possibility of a planetary ethos, one that relies less on biopolitical moral norms than on attunement to the affective ambiguity and corporeal porosity of life in more-than-human emergence.

Refugee cinema and literature like Brady's film and Boochani's memoir invite audiences into a "poetics of thickening," an interpretive process of witnessing the conjoined displacement of humans and nonhumans in more-than-human biopolitics. They explore interspecies kinship as shared vulnerability, grievability, and solidarity in the face of planetary ecological crises, colonial capitalist divisions of life, and the delimited borders of settler colonial states. In what follows, I place thick mobility in dialogue with existing scholarship on migration and refugee biopolitics, before illustrating some aesthetic and poetic forms of "thickening," including haunting and affective atmospheres, in the selected texts. These aesthetic and poetic forms posit a thick ethos of reimagining refugee existence beyond the biopolitical life-or-death binary. They invoke residual ecologies of state and capital, of excess, opacity, and decolonial truth-telling that account for the irresolvable tensions between presence and absence, movement and stasis, and land and sea—contingent formations of refugee ecologies contesting a politics of closure. By rejecting the life-or-death dichotomy imposed by sovereign borders, thickening allies refugees with the wider cosmos and animates ecologically expansive networks of mobility and freedom that create fissures in carceral colonial systems.

## Thick Mobility

The seasonal migration of red crabs underscores an ecological imperative, yet the detention of asylum seekers exposes the inequitable distribution of mobility in a world of man-made borders. The ocean is a material-discursive field for examining this hierarchical mobility, its grammar of fluidity and flow encoded with histories of colonial empire building, globalization, and capitalism. The politicization, militarization, and globalization of oceanic spaces have been fundamental to European colonial and neocolonial world dominance. This colonial vision of the ocean not only controlled trade and migration but also produced cultural myths of mastery at sea, where a habitual pairing of the boundless ocean with the white male voyager upholds the idealized subject of the Euro-American individual. Suvendrini Perera traces the liberal subject's oceanic prerogative in Western culture, observing that "from Homer to Conrad" and "from the biblical Jonah to Melville's Ishmael," the sea represents a vast and unknowable domain where white masculine heroes project "the moral attributes of imperial racial virtue, to end by making for themselves new homes and new worlds" (2013, 103). While popular tales like *Robinson Crusoe* (1719) and *Titanic* (1997) reproduce seafaring images of white, masculine, and settler colonial adventures, they simultaneously obscure the violent histories of racialized bodies at sea—bodies displaced by slavery, indentured labor, and convict ships. Today, alternative stories at sea unfold with the precarious journeys of refugees and asylum seekers navigating treacherous waters like the Mediterranean Sea. Their stories are counternarratives to neoliberal freedom, constantly framed by Global North media as a "refugee crisis" through images of rickety boats, anguished faces, and first-world rescue operations. These stories remake oceanic spaces through impure crossings, uneven grievability, and precarious lifeways.

The term (im)mobility has emerged in recent migration and critical refugee studies to address the mutually constitutive relationship between mobility and immobility, and how cross-border movements are delimited by regulations, inequalities, and biopolitical technologies in our current world, where xenophobia is on the rise (Bélanger and Silvey 2019, 3424). In the era of securitization, sovereign nation-states politicize certain geographies, like oceans and islands, as territorial borders for racial exclusion. Australia's Christmas Island gained geopolitical focus after the 2001 Tampa affair, when the Howard government barred a Norwegian ship carrying four hundred asylum seekers from docking. This event, alongside the subsequent "children overboard" affair, where officials falsely accused asylum seekers of endangering children to pressure authorities under duress, ushered in a harsher chapter in Australia's border policy, encapsulated by John Howard's federal election speech: "We will decide who comes to this country and the circumstances in which they come." In the post-9/11 time, Australia has excluded Christmas Island from its migration zone, organized armed interceptions to "turn back boats," relocated asylum seekers to offshore detention camps in Nauru and Manus Island, and has been contracting multinational companies in servicing the border-industrial complex. The government's rhetoric criminalizes and objectifies asylum seekers with labels such as "people trafficking," "queue jumpers," "disease carriers," and "illegal immigrants," while downplaying human rights concerns (Perera 2002, 28). Australian media tends to visually frames asylum seekers as faceless masses behind barbed wires, perpetuating themes of "illegality, invasion, and potential guilt" (Bleiker et al. 2013, 408). Consequently, a dehumanizing narrative pervades public policy and media, reducing asylum seekers to abstract figures of security threat, racial fear, or humanitarian rescue.

When engaging refugee (im)mobility and border politics, it is difficult to miss the analytical relevance of biopolitics. Scholars have drawn on key concepts of biopolitics (Foucault 1978) and necropolitics (Mbembe 2019) to examine refugee studies, bordering practices, and camp politics in relation to the politicization of human life. These frameworks emphasize the ways modern sovereign states measure, discipline, and exterminate lives based on assigned value and worth. Foucault's analytic of biopolitics, for instance, reveals how liberal sovereign governance exercises power not only through specific technologies of knowledge, such as statistical categories, but also a political economy of freedom predicated on critiquing state reason to enhance "the quasi-natural/autonomous characteristics" of economy and society (Means 2022, 1969). This draws attention to how (un)freedom is itself a biopolitical tool of liberal governmentality. Examining the dark biopolitics of war and colonial occupation, Achille Mbembe formulates necropolitics to explain how sovereignty dictates "who is able to live and who must die" (2019, 66). Necropolitics considers the ways in which life is instrumentalized into desirable and disposable categories, where vast populations are subjected to the social existence of "the *living dead*" and where standing up to death equates to freedom (Mbembe 2019, 92). Necropolitics is particularly pertinent to refugee politics, as it interrogates a sacrificial economy structured by a colonial hierarchy of subjection. At the top is the rational, autonomous, liberal humanist individual, deemed a full political subject capable of moral agency, self-awareness, and the good life. At the bottom are the dehumanized "others," including war victims and refugees whose racialized bodies are marked as unwanted, superfluous, and killable. Necropolitics thus names the contradictions of liberal freedom.

Bio- and necropolitics offer valuable frameworks for investigating how colonial hierarchies of "life" and "human" reproduce refugee struggles and the contradictions of liberal freedom. Yet these concepts also inadvertently reinforce anthropocentric structures of Life, naturalizing bodily integrity, securitization, and liberal humanist norms while foreclosing ecological possibilities for refugee political mobility. In posthuman and more-than-human frames, biological life moves through and is recomposed by permeable interchanges with everyday environmental substances of air, water, nutrients, and pollutants, undoing the bounded body and individual subject in favor of transversal understandings of body, self, and environment. In Karen Barad's account of "intra-activity," subject, object, and agency are not discrete things but arise from relationships and entangled intra-actions (2007). In this light, a humanist ethics will not suffice because the very boundaries of the human are continually being reconfigured and the human subject is not an externalized rational being or the locus of knowing (Barad 2007, 393). This differs from a political rationality of biopolitics by opening ethicality to the self's responsiveness and participation in the world's ongoing becoming, or emergence. For instance, how might humanist biopolitics account and compensate for a refugee's life when hunger, hygiene, violence, and trauma and their accumulated and combined effects on the body take months and years to manifest? How might we restory refugee agency, freedom, and mobility in the Anthropocene when considering that air, water, food, and energy always already play a constitutive role in refugee displacement and survival?

Recent critical theories have begun to engage a posthuman biopolitics animated by affects, objects, and environments that perform or subvert a colonial order of things (Bennett 2009; Chen 2012; Povinelli 2016; Puig de la Bellacasa 2016; Pugliese 2020). One example of this shift is Elizabeth Povinelli's concept of "geontopower," which examines how liberal governance moves the biopolitical focus from the life-death binary to a distinction between life and nonlife (2016). This perspective articulates how settler liberalism combines a cultural politics of recognition (the governance of difference) with a neoliberal economy of extraction (the governance of markets) through a colonial hierarchy of animacy, dividing life (the lively) and nonlife (the inert) (Povinelli 2016, 169). Geontology is relevant to my analysis because it recognizes how a racialized discourse of animacy within the liberal imaginary constructs the refugee as either an inanimate figure stripped of agency and mobility or as an overanimated subject imbued with anger and threat. This operation of biopoliticized animacy is visible on the aforementioned Christmas Island where governance and justice regimes assign differential animacy and value to humans, nonhuman species, mineral deposits, and oceanic environments. In more-than-human biopolitics, Mel Chen notes, animacy has become a political grammar of mobility in racial, sexual, and disability environments, as it reveals how the so-called "insensate, immobile, deathly, or otherwise 'wrong'" matter could animate cultural life in affective and embodied ways that queer the biopolitical integrity of the enclosed and heterosexual body (2012, 2). Building on this, a more-than-human perspective seeks to transgress the colonial division between life and nonlife by allowing nonlife to make demands on the existing biopolitical order, bringing forth inhuman and nonhuman materialities that always already shape who we are as humans.

In order to broaden ecological modes of mobility and freedom in migration biopolitics, I propose a method of *thick mobility* to account for the entangled, contingent, and more-than-human emergence of migrant and refugee lifeways against biopolitical abstraction. Thick mobility provides a hybrid environmental imagination for holding together the seeming opposites of mobility and immobility, situatedness and fluidity, and human and nonhuman. It explores the ambiguity of motion and stasis, considering not just fluidity and flow, but also the blockage and stagnation of cross-border movements, thus directing ethical attention to the slow violence and slow death rendered invisible by bio- and necropolitical structures imbuing borderlands with fear and death. But thickness also attunes us to the slow hope found within the fissures of biopolitical orders and the everyday, messy, and subsistence practices of migrant and refugee worldmaking. It illuminates how life moves through and becomes with others and places in concrete materiality and dense intersubjective relationships that express yet exceed biopolitical capture. Thickening mobility in relational terms foregrounds an ethics of alterity, of being humble to the unknowable subjectivity and nonpresent history accompanying the other's arrival. It considers others not as "passive bodies" but as feeling and "thinking subjects inhabiting their own worlds of action and meaning" (Rose 2022, 55). What is more, thickness challenges linear time and the biopolitical bifurcation of life versus death to embrace intergenerational and interspecies cosmologies where deaths are knots in the ongoing dynamism of life, plural temporalities saturate the "now," and life is always in motion with others. This perspective engages with a relational ontology of moving-with as emergent naturecultures in storied landscapes. It shows how close attention to entangled bodies, places, affects, temporalities, stories, humans, and nonhumans reveal new biopolitical formations, alongside new assemblages of feelings and animacy that ecologize planetary collectives of re-existence and coexistence.

Thickening refugee mobility in more-than-human worlds posits a decolonial critique of what counts as freedom in migrant struggles for justice, as we bear in mind colonial legacies of modern (un)freedom: the subjugation of the dehumanized and the contradictions of liberal humanist freedom. The neoliberalization of Western democracies in the late twentieth century has emphasized individual choice and reinvented freedom as an economic principle organizing all aspects of earth life in light of capitalist market value. As we confront the crisis of this hegemonic neoliberal freedom, our political present is plagued by a decline in collective justice, ecological balance, and openness toward the other.

What, then, constitutes freedom? Is it a status of being, a practice, a measure of individual autonomy, or social activism? As I unpack the layered meanings of freedom in refugee worldmaking, I find resonance with Anna Tsing's study of matsutake mushroom forgers and her interpretation of their freedom not as an individual rational choice but something that emerges from "open-ended cultural interplay" that is "irregular and outside rationalization" (2015, 76). Freedom has to do with a contingent mobilization of a political and multispecies collective outside of American liberal politics and industrial capitalism, where invisible refugees, war veterans, and Indigenous and migrant mushroom pickers "pursue a commons haunted by the possibility of their own exclusion": a ghost-ridden freedom (Tsing 2015, 79).

When researching refugee ecology, I repeatedly encounter a ghost-ridden freedom. I follow artists and writers who appeal to a just, shared, and cosmic planetary commons, a yet-to-come haunted by carceral colonialism and neoliberal capitalism. Ghosts show us the suppressed pasts that are to come. My analysis of refugee ecological worldmaking reveals how freedom tends to emerge from affective, communal, and small-scale experiments of collaborating with the natural environment for material interdependence. In this context, reimagining refugee freedom in naturecultural thought could benefit from engaging with posthumanist notions of "distributed agency," which decenters human exceptionalism to consider the nonhumans in the production of sociality and ethicality (Puig de la Bellacasa 2017, 141). Reading refugee narratives with a thickening method attends to distributed agency, affective opacity, and more-than-human ghosts that may not always bring revolutionary freedom, but nonetheless embed refugees as feeling and thinking selves within intersubjective ecological terrains and contingent forces where entangled potentials and dangers emerge. I am drawn to a poetics of thickening while heeding Yen Le Espiritu's warning that some epistemological critiques risk rendering the refugee "only as a lack" (2014, 13). As she puts it, engaged critical refugee studies should be aware of the pitfalls of romanticizing and reifying marginalized subjects through critiques of modern nation-states; instead they need to integrate critique with the everyday concerns of real refugees as they navigate social worlds as complex and multiple subjects (2014, 13).

Thickness articulates freedom as life's innate creative poiesis to bring forth presence within absence, animacy among extinction, and movement against confinement. Freedom exists in the contingent and continuing processes of commoning and preforming "as if." The conjuring of planetarity by incarcerated asylum seekers calls upon our ability to imagine a democracy of all forms of existence. I invoke this vision along the verses of Behrouz Boochani, who perceives freedom not in terms of assimilating into a political community structured by unjust humanism, but in finding communion with the cosmos: the stars, the trees, the mountain, the ocean, and the jungle. The natural world evokes a sense of wonder, abundance, and spaciousness, a reminder of the freedom and vitality denied, yet latent in the imprisoned. Freedom is cultivated in reciprocity and mutualism by witnessing in the other the dignity we seek for ourselves. It is a sustained struggle against oppression, with a persistent demeanor like the "dignified coconut trees" that stand upright despite harsh conditions. In Boochani's words,

> Defence against the fences /
> Defence against the prison guards /
> Defence against the other prisoners /
> Until the death /
> And the feeling of freedom /
> Standing face to face with the awe of the boundless heavens /
> The freedom of standing face to face with the stars /
> The freedom of standing face to face with the immensity of the ocean /
> The freedom of standing face to face with the splendour of the jungle /
> The freedom of the dignified coconut trees. (2018, 298–99)

In the following discussion, I will explore an ecopoetics of thickening through analyses of two texts, *Island of the Hungry Ghosts* (*Island* hereafter) and *No Friend but the Mountains* (*Friend* hereafter). *Island* draws on an affective atmosphere of "haunting" to direct ethical weight to the slow death incurred by liberal capitalist governance over biodiversity and human diversity at migration borders. It evokes interspecies spectrality to explore a hybrid environmental imagination in which land and sea, humans and animals, and stories and places are not individuated forces but intra-act to create materialities in flux that resist linear territorial and biopolitical boundaries. Boochani's memoir presents an affective ecology of (im)mobility in which the author's anxiety, fear, hope, and wonder intertwine with the migration border regime. These affective intensities shed situated insights into refugee biopolitical regimes, while also deepening a more-than-human understanding of refugee mobility as embodied and affective emergence. Such emergence materializes as affective impurity and ambivalence that refuses state-sanctioned fear and stasis.

## Negotiating Ghosts on Haunted Landscapes: On More-Than-Human Necropolitics in the Age of Extinction

Ecologies of land, sea, and migration converge in *Island of the Hungry Ghosts*. The film places refugee (im)mobility within thick networks of colonial, racial, species, and mining histories, enfolding refugee stories into ecosocial webs of entanglement that have been silenced or segregated by a modern necropolitics of extinction. This planetary interweaving of social and ecological justice across past and present, living and nonliving, and presence and absence delineates a more-than-human biopolitics through which refugee ecology emerges at oceanic borderlands. Confined in a detention center that runs as a high-security military camp, with iron-and-metal fences, asylum seekers on Christmas Island face criminal control, uncertain futures, inadequate mental health care, threats of violence, and extreme isolation. These dire conditions of refugeehood press upon the meanings of mobility. Mobility comes to encompass not just freedom of movement, but also the continuation of life, animacy, and the capacity to feel in the face of forces that relentlessly seek to obliterate them.

A sandbox in the film serves as a portal to past, present, and future stories for detained refugees. This sandbox is central to the sandplay narrative therapy that Poh Lin Lee employs to interact with traumatized refugees and asylum seekers. It includes delicate white sand and figurines that refugee clients can freely arrange to facilitate self-expression. Lee has previously written about how sandplay therapy can help clients counter the effects of restriction, limited choice, and curtailment of agency and movement (2018, 1). Her practices explore embodiment and environment to offer "a holistic framework" that communicates narrative ideas beyond the spoken and written word (Lee 2013, 2). The sandbox facilitates refugees' agency by allowing them to create worlds and stories of their choosing, thus reclaiming a sense of self and mobility from the dehumanizing confines of detention. It also fosters a reconnection to preferred values, memories, dreams, and legacies to establish the therapeutic environment as an emotional counterpoint to the detention environment (Lee 2013, 3). In one scene, a female refugee arranges figures to depict a person carrying a baby in the ocean, a rescue boat, a sniper, a bomb, and a police car, a scene she describes as "the life that we left behind." In another scene, a male refugee constructs a "peaceful" homeland with "no fight," replete with natural beauty. Yet this narrative act of imagining the otherwise also highlights the painful gap between hope and reality, conveying the violent disconnection of refugees from society and nature. Disentanglement is expressed by a refugee's testimony of self-harm, sewing his lips to "block the air" in a desperate protest against captivity.

With the sandbox, *Island* invokes the Indian Ocean, it militarization, and interactions with racialized refugee bodies. The film portrays the ocean as a ghostly space of lost possibilities. Sand materializes the fluid sedimentation of geologic deposits and mineral dust. As mobile matter, sand is constantly drifting with wind and waves, flowing from land to ocean, washing ashore, resting on beaches, and riding deep into submarine canyons. However, in the film it also presents a material archive of the refugee's ecological unbecoming. This idea is articulated during a dialogue between Lee and a female refugee client, when they discuss the sensory experience of sand (Brady 2018, 04:50):

> LEE: The sand that we use in the boxes is what we consider to be the smallest particles of earth. You imagine that every grain of sand that we see, you know, used to part of rocks, mountains, formations, and now they are down into their finest form. How does the sand feel? Is it cool or warm?
> CLIENT: Yeah. I think, it's like cold.
> LEE: Cold, yeah? Does it feel soft, or hard, or sharp, or gentle?
> CLIENT: It feels . . . I like the sound, you know.
> LEE: The sound?
> CLIENT: Yeah, coz I guess the sound, you know, it reminds me of the waves.

The client's response shows an appreciation of the acoustic quality of sand and waves in living ecosystems, a reminder of natural rhythms and elemental connections different from the ecological impoverishment and multisensory alienation of refugee experience. In another conversation, a male refugee client is curious about the sand's origin (Brady 2018, 20:35):

> CLIENT: What sort of sand it is?
> LEE: This is sand from the beach.
> CLIENT: Oh, sand from the beach.
> LEE: Yes, sand that I collected. I don't know if you've ever been out on Christmas Island. But this is from Merrial Beach. Have you been to Merrial Beach before?
> CLIENT: No.
> LEE: No. It is a very, very small beach. You can only get to it when the tide is out. When the water is out.
> CLIENT: Oh okay. Is this on Christmas Island, Merrial Beach?
> LEE: Yeah, yeah.
> CLIENT: Yeah [awkward laugh].

The sandbox materializes absence. It becomes a vessel of refugee immobility, alluding to the inaccessible natural beauty of Christmas Island—

its picturesque beaches, lush jungles, and striking coastlines—denied to refugees who also live there. As where land greets the sea, and migration meets borders, the sandy beach is a physical and conceptual borderland. It enforces the liberal humanist hierarchies that separate freedom from captivity, legality from illegality, and citizen from refugee. Lee's therapy practice challenges the biopolitical territorialism of oceanic borders by attending to the singularity of refugee life. Her sandbox archives submerged refugee life stories and bears witness to their unresolved traumas, dreams, and feelings that are personal and multiple.

The sand therapy exemplifies the film's spatially diffused poetics, which evokes an affective atmosphere of heaviness, slow waiting, subtropical heat, and inner struggle to attune to an emotional charge permeating individual bodies and social structures. In "Affective Atmosphere," Ben Anderson asks, "How does an atmosphere 'envelope' and 'press' upon life? How, put differently, to attend to the collective affects 'in which we live'?" (2009, 77). Brady's film explores this question by tracing how collective atmospheres circulate, accumulate, and perturb personal affective experiences around and beyond biopolitical structures of the nation-state. Lee's therapeutic practice operates under the shadow of shifting government policies. The film poignantly reflects on the 2013 policy changes announced by then Australian Prime Minister Kevin Rudd, aimed at bolstering border security and reducing costs, which mandated that asylum seekers who arrived by boat would no longer be resettled as refugees in Australia. This stringent policy weighs heavily on the mental well-being of refugees and social workers alike. In one scene, we see Lee, in emotional turmoil, slash through dense rainforest thickets, eventually reaching a hilltop overlooking the regimented layout of detention camps. This scene expresses her battle against the immobilizing force of sovereign power. In the film's ending, Lee slowly pours the sand from the sandbox into the ocean, merging refugee stories with rhythmic waves, linking the personal with the planetary. In this glimpse of possibility, static borders and island edges are redefined by the continual motion of water. The heterogeneous histories, animated matter, and diasporic flows archived in the palimpsest of the sand are reimagined as the ocean's ongoing articulation and diffractive waves.

Caribbean poet Kamau Brathwaite destabilizes fixed territorial identities with the tidal movement of the sea. Whereas Western philosophy had traditionally interpreted human existence through dialectics, Brathwaite puts forward "tidalectics," an oceanic worldview to describe a life constituted in movement, performed by the rise and fall of tides and the connectivity and locality of water (1999, 32). A tidalectic worldview collapses the land-sea binary to conceive a fluid ontology open to the regenerative potential of hybridization and diaspora, where islands and oceanic spaces are contact zones for the mutual becomings between local and planetary, geography and history, and humans and nonhumans. Tidalectics is provocative for thinking with islands in the context of climate uncertainty, as Jonathan Pugh argues that global environmental insecurity tends to paint a reductive and romanticized picture of islands and Indigenous islander communities as "being saturated with vulnerability, adaptation and resilience ethics," externalizing Western projections and anxieties of the Anthropocene onto islands (2018, 104). If islands exceed modern rationalist frameworks—due to their fluid relationality and situated climate vulnerability—this excess is further compounded by the excess of refugee mobility. In Brady's film, a tidalectics of refugee migration encourages a thick ethos of alterity and unknowability, pointing to the multiple potentials and vulnerabilities of oceanic movements beyond stable boundaries and epistemic certainty. The excesses of islands and refugee mobility are conveyed in the film through an affective atmosphere of absence and haunting, as incongruous racial and species ghosts continue to leave material vestiges in the present.

*Island* makes a case for an interspecies ethics of shared vulnerability in contemporary refugee ecologies. The film considers race and species together to offer comparative insights into human diversity and biodiversity governance in the era of extinction, highlighting their parallels and disparities to call for multispecies justice. It draws attention to Christmas Island's unique biodiversity, which, due to prolonged isolation and evolution, is known to have over 250 endemic species of flora and fauna, encompassing wetlands, breeding seabirds, subterranean fauna, mammal fauna, and an abundance of crab species (Woinarski 2018, 48–49). This biodiversity is both rich and vulnerable to natural and human disturbances. The human settlement of Christmas Island is marked by modern colonial histories of industrial promise and ruin, particularly from phosphate mining, which is notorious for causing irreversible ecological harm. Phosphate mining disrupts ecosystems through topsoil bulldozing, on-site dumping, air and water pollution, and exposure of underground limestone compromising revegetation. These activities have led to substantial habitat loss for various species, including the red crab, Abbott's booby, frigatebird, goshawk, and other endangered creatures. From here, considering the plights of displaced humans and nonhumans in a joint framework of migrant ecocriticism compels a planetary perspective of shared vulnerability and solidarity in the face of extinction and extraction.

The red crab (*Gecarcoidea natalis*) is a linchpin species in Christmas Island's biotic community. It dwells on rainforest floors, eats saplings and fallen vegetation, recycles nutrients, shapes the composition of native flora, and sustains the island's unique ecological equilibrium. Evolutionary biologists have raised concerns about the potential impact of irregular rainfall caused by climate change, which could threaten the survival of migratory species like the red crab that depend on precise dry and wet seasons (Shaw and Kelly 2013, 3288). *Island* spotlights this keystone species, showcasing its annual migration from the jungle to the shoreline during the wet season around November. Millions of crabs turn parts of the island into moving crimson carpets, reminding viewers that human habitation is only a recent addition to the island's deep ecology. An epic natural wonder, the red crab migration has become a global tourist attraction, pulling in visitors from around the world and adding revenue to Christmas Island's tourism industry. The film shows park rangers engaging in conservation activities, such as building funnel bridges and redirecting traffic, to support the crabs' journey. In one scene, a ranger remarks, "You gotta give them [the red crabs] a chance to walk away. . . . Give them a chance to migrate and do what they wanna do, you know" (Brady 2018, 12:01)

The ranger's comment and the national park's efforts reflect a commitment to preserving the red crab migration. At first glance, this contrasts sharply with the nation's stringent stance on refugee migration. However, a closer look at biodiversity conservation and species extinction on Christmas Island reveals a parallel mechanism of biocontrol across the governance of wildlife and human life, both subject to liberal capitalist taxonomies of value and worth. Australian ecologist John Woinarski examines the tension between conservation and mining on Christmas Island, especially during the environmental movement of the 1970s, when scientists fought to protect the endangered Abbott's booby seabird and its rainforest habitats from mining bulldozers. His research exposes how the Australian government made incremental but reactive measures that prioritized short-term capitalist gains over long-term intangible environmental conservation. Political inertia and mining capital have resulted in the extinction of many rare and inconspicuous species, such as the Pipistrelle bat, whose disappearance remains largely unnoticed and unmourned in the shadow of spotlight species like the red crab that garners significant media attention and conservation funding. As media focus and conservation efforts concentrate on eye-catching and charismatic species, the silent loss of many smaller species goes ungrieved.

The unmourned death of smaller species questions the very concept of extinction. The quiet sacrifice of species "others" to industrial progress raises doubts about the effectiveness of the supposedly objective term "extinction" in holding humans accountable. As Woinarski aptly claims,

> "Extinction" itself is an odd and inadequate word, whose grammatical passivity distracts from its immediacy and totality. Species "become extinct," as if that is an abstraction, a progression, or a fate long reserved for them. The sometimes used alternative "disappear" is perhaps worse, suggesting a conjuring trick, and the vague promise of return. The death of (human) individuals is not so neutered: we "die," or are "killed": sharper words that speak of directness and loss. (2018, 1)

Extinction is thus not merely a biological event; it is a social, cultural, and systemic issue. Woinarski's argument can be extended to rethink the slow violence inflicted on refugee lives. Judith Butler, in her study of the differential allocation of grievability that upholds exclusionary norms about what counts as a livable life, asserts that "some lives are grievable, and others are not" (2009, xv). An uneven distribution of grievability extends to the nonhuman realm, as the slow, systemic, and unnoticed death of many refugee migrants parallels the inconsequential fate of nonhuman species made to "disappear." Placing extinction at the ethical crossroads between species and race, we can see how the settler colonial state's biopolitics prioritizes capitalist instrumental value. Under this hegemonic valuation, the loss of certain human and nonhuman lives is not only inevitable but also justifiable. This logic sustains the slow violence of more-than-human necropolitics, making it challenging to assign accountability and feelings to quiet losses. Through themes of haunting and absence, *Island*'s grimly slow cinematography and its affective aesthetics attach emotional thickness to this silent loss. The ghosts of the present urge us to imagine what has been and what is to come. They invite us into remembrance and mourning, through which death may continue to inform life.

Although *Island* does not directly portray phosphate mining or species extinction, it entangles species and race through the motif of "hungry ghosts." The film's title pays homage to the Chinese ancestors who arrived as indentured laborers during the colonial mining period. In 1888, the British phosphate company on Christmas Island sourced two thousand four hundred indentured laborers from war-torn China, who endured horrible housing conditions, poor hygiene, ravaging beriberi, low wages, and grueling labor demands that stretched human limits (Dennis 2008, 30–31). In the film, ethnic Chinese islanders burn joss paper during the Hungry Ghost Festival (*zhong yuan jie*) to the sound of gong bells and prepare ritual offerings for immigrant ancestors who died without proper burial. In one scene, a couple venture through a dense jungle to offer respects at the tombs of Chinese miners. These acts of public mourning acknowledge previously ungrievable lives. In the ensuing scene, the camera shifts to a lone coconut crab scuttling across the rainforest floor beside haunting relics of abandoned houses. This juxtaposition locates the film's reflection on species loss within a shared ethical framework that also grapples with the disposability of racial and refugee lives.

*Island*'s interspecies spectrality provides a theme to link biodiversity with cultural diversity and to retell species stories in ways that account for racial and migratory struggles. This extends our discussion in Chapter One, which examines how invasive species discourse is entangled with colonial racist ideologies, to ongoing debates around the environmental imaginations and affects toward invasive species. Ideas of "nativeness" and "invasiveness" take on heightened symbolic weight in the liminal geography of migration borderlands like Christmas Island, where residents face political and economic uncertainty. In anthropologist Simone Dennis's ethnography, for instance, the metaphor of invasive species is mobilized by multiethnic residents (Anglo Europeans, Malaysians, and Chinese) who use the binary between "red-crab-us" and "yellow-ant-other" to articulate anxieties over the arrival of "boat people" (2009, 219). The yellow crazy ants were inadvertently introduced to Christmas Island on human boats in the early 1900s and have wreaked havoc on local ecosystems by forming supercolonies and spraying formic acid, which kills the island's endemic red crabs. These ants are vilified in media as the culprits behind the "Christmas Crab Massacre" (Bittel 2015).

The entanglement of species discourse with anxieties about refugee migration must also be understood within Christmas Island's broader precarity as an oceanic territory on the fringes of the Australian nation-state, an outpost shaped by declining phosphate mining, detention economy, and dwindling state investment. As uncertain future looms, fears of invasive species and asylum seekers intertwine to fuel a defensive eco-nationalism. In this scenario, personal, natural, and national bodies converge in an opposition between besieged islanders and red crabs versus the clandestine arrival of asylum seekers and yellow ants by boat. Insect invasion fuses with refugee invasion to form a larger eco-nationalist narrative of crisis that casts the island as endangered. "Who wants to come to an island where there are no more crabs and a prison right smack in the middle?" bemoans one of Dennis's interviewee, a resident of Christmas Island (2009, 224). Invasive species rhetoric becomes a powerful device amplifying xenophobic sentiments, enabling settler communities to naturalize their sense of place vis-à-vis refugees who are seen as outsiders. The island ecology of Christmas Island adds a distinct layer to this crucible, raising questions as to how species storytelling might perpetuate insular views of the island.

In weaving together the seemingly disparate storylines of Christmas Island, its rich biodiversity, colonial labor history, and secretive detention operation, *Island* urges ethical and political engagement with past and present ghosts at migration borderlands. The film explores the affective and ethical affordances of absence and ghosts to address a multispecies necropolitics, suggesting that refugees and more-than-human environments share vulnerability and resistance in the face of modern colonial extinction. This interspecies hauntology forms part of a larger ethical dialogue about how nature and species have been instrumentalized for biopolitical bordering, and how they also constitute transformative sites for reimagining nonexclusive forms of collectivity that disrupt the biopolitical spectralization of human and nonhuman lives. This ethical agenda is also prominent in *Friend*. While the affective kinship between race and ecology in *Island* is characterized by a ghostly alliance, it assumes more entangled forms of embodied and abolitionist crossings in Behrouz Boochani's memoir, in which he critiques a colonial hierarchy of life and animacy through the affective ecologies of refugee (im)mobility and searches for a sense of unyielding freedom in places of confinement.

## Ecologies of Affective (Im)mobility

The flight to freedom is long for Behrouz Boochani, the Kurdish Iranian asylum seeker, journalist, and writer. After escaping Iran in 2013, he reached Christmas Island on a leaky boat, only to be exiled by the Australian border force to an offshore detention camp on Manus Island, where he was imprisoned for six years until he finally attained refugee status in New Zealand in 2020. His memoir, *No Friend but the Mountains: Writing from Manus Prison* (2018), expresses the power of literature to testify against brutal systems. Although the Australian border regime barred Boochani, his memoir has won multiple Australian literary awards and international acclaim. This contradiction illustrates how literature can empathetically affect people and support dialogue on refugee migration. The memoir's political and literary dimensions reveal Boochani's skill in addressing diverse audiences, with its harrowing cover portrait, promise of "truthful first-hand experiences" of offshore detention, and sophisticated blend of poetry, prose, dreams, philosophy, and life narratives. Some critics argue that reading the memoir enables Australian readers to express solidarity with refugees and participate in ethical witnessing, confronting "a causal responsibility for the suffering imposed in their name" (Whitlock 2020, 709). Indeed, Boochani's self-representation exposes how the sovereign border regime, what he calls "the kyriarchal system," imposes colonial logics of domination and exploitation in immigration detention often in the name of Australian citizenship. This nationalist rhetoric obscures the settler-state's (neo)colonial agendas, particularly its control over land use and its policies toward Indigenous peoples and Pacific Islanders on Nauru and Manus Islands.

Nature holds a significant place in Boochani's memoir and creative philosophy. In the introduction to this book, I have quoted an interview where he asserts, "I am a stateless person, but I am a free man because the Earth is for me, I belong to nature, belong to mountains, oceans, seasons, jungles, deserts" (2020). The memoir's title, *No Friend but the Mountains*, echoes a Kurdish saying, "the Kurdish people don't have any friends in the world but the mountains" and Boochani's belief that he "will never be alone in this world because everywhere I go there will be mountains for me" (2020). This cosmic view recuperates a feeling of rightful belonging to the universe for refugees, gesturing toward a borderless world free from the carceral colonialism that dehumanizes them as illegal, disposable, or exploitable. What interests me more is the collaboration, or asymmetry, between this poetic sense of planetary conviviality and the political mobility evident in Boochani's life trajectory. Through literature, film, scholarly essays, and human rights activism both during and after imprisonment, Boochani has been a tenacious voice for refugee dignity and justice. This incongruity between his ecopoetic tenderness and political resilience is particularly intriguing. It plays out the planetarity-from-below thesis I put forward in this book. Planetary conviviality does not need to be a romantic abstraction that everything on Earth is interconnected; rather, it can emerge from, and in turn support, the thick politics of marginalized communities in their emancipatory struggles against systemic oppression.

Taking a deeper dive into Boochani's memoir, we see a complex and inconsistent partnership between the refugee characters and the environment. This inconsistency reveals the affective, corporeal, and temporal-spatial technologies of Australia's military-industrial-prison complex that criminalizes asylum seekers. We can observe this inconsistency in various aspects, including the memoir's stream-of-consciousness style and its composition process, both "contingent on specific events and dynamics in the prison and Australia's border politics" (Tofighian 2018, xvi). The memoir is characterized by a fragmented style embedding the author's streams of consciousness within immediate narrative surroundings, which articulates refugee (im)mobility as being shaped by environmental constraints and responsiveness. Remarkably, Boochani composed the memoir by thumbing thousands of text messages on a smuggled mobile phone hid from the authorities and sending them to his translator for compilation. The appearance of the memoir itself stands as a powerful testament to refugee world-making, a collaborative assemblage involving the author, camp politics, internet access, and communities inside and outside the prison. These contingencies demonstrate how the planetary conviviality in Boochani's earthly statement is not a given but a result of political negotiation. For Boochani, writing is both a way to endure and resist: "Resistance and fighting through my writing are my most important tools. . . . on one hand, I can be friends with a beautiful flower beyond the fences, and friends with the birds or sky in a poetic way, with the softest feeling; on the other hand, I must be a strong fighter to fight this system" (2020). This duality—a tender connection with nature and a determinedness to battle injustice—composes a refugee ecopoetics of finding beauty under duress, where nature becomes the refugee's political ally, solace, and strength. Freedom is the ability to see beauty in desolation.

To further explore this refugee ecopoetics, I focus on affect as an ecological device of refugee thick mobility. This approach is important because refugees are seldom portrayed as emotionally complex, if not stereotypically angry and miserable, people in dominant representations. Boochani's memoir blurs the boundary between body and place, whereby an array of affects, like anxiety, fear, joy, and wonder, shape and are shaped by the contingent assemblages of refugee bodies, state biopower, and the more-than-human world. By locating the refugee body at the affective nexus of relations intersecting body, nation, and nature, I suggest reimagining this body through indeterminate materiality to expand the scope of decolonial politics and ecological animacy beyond bio- and necropolitical certainty. I invoke refugee ecologies of *affective (im)mobility* to examine the relational movements between the affective intensity of refugee bodies and the biopolitical regimes of sovereign states during forced migration. Refugee affective ecology holds overlooked ethical and political potential for reimagining refugee agency as a networked intra-activity between human bodies and more-than-human nature in the dynamics of power.

In their introduction to *Affective Ecocriticism*, Kyle Bladow and Jennifer Ladino argue that affect is "ecological 'by nature'" because it operates at the intersection of environments, texts, and bodies, disrupting discrete notions of embodied selfhood and static environment, and inviting us to trace transcorporeal encounters that are intricate and dynamic (2018, 8). This ecological view of affects should be complemented by the idea that refugee body-place relations are ambivalent and express both flow and blockage. In Gregory Seigworth and Melissa Gregg's definition, affect is the vital force that accumulates across "relatedness and interruptions," "bindings and unbindings, becomings and un-becomings, jarring disorientations and rhythmic attunements," marking a body's "*belonging* and *non-belonging* to a world of encounters" (2010, 2). Such a perspective is apt for interpreting refugee ecologies of (im)mobility. The dual focus on relatedness and interruption emerges because sovereign biopower politicizes certain spaces, like oceanic borders and detention camps, into landscapes of fear and terror. Refugee bodies have to negotiate these emotionally charged terrains that impact their perceptions and feelings about the natural environment. This manifests in Boochani's poetic descriptions of experiencing an ambivalent mixture of fear and hope, entanglement and alienation, and movement and stasis: a paradigm that uniquely characterizes refugee affective ecologies of (im)mobility.

As the contested zone between sovereign necropolitics and refugee dreams, the ocean is one space where refugee affective ecologies are expressed. Boochani portrays how the oceanic borderland becomes a survival space where asylum seekers negotiate life and mobility through corporeal encounters with earthly extremes. He begins his memoir with these verses: "Under moonlight / An unknown route / A sky the colour of intense anxiety" (2018, 1). The fear of drowning alters the contours of the ocean, turning it into an ominous landscape, an existential battle against overpowering watery forces: "The dimensions of a boat / Unfamiliar waves / Waves of a foreign ocean" (15). The asylum seekers' bodies literally become part of the ocean when Boochani's boat starts to leak and the oceanscape feels like a motionless hell: "A caravan of weary bodies / Stooped and in motionless sleep / Deep in the expanse of the ocean / Swept away by those giant waves / I smell the scent of death" (21). Watery forces become animated, shapeshifting into "bitter ocean" (37) and "oppressive waves" (42) that gain "confidence" (22) and demand "sacrifice" (44). In these scenarios, embracing nature becomes deadly, and life depends on fighting against the ocean and its necropolitical inscriptions that expose asylum seekers to death.

Apart from fear and terror, Boochani also feels wonder, comfort, and protection in relation to oceanic environments. In one scenario, he experiences both hope and loss, his feelings triggered by the moon shining over the sea. After days of sailing within the boundless ocean on a ship and feeling afflicted by a blurred sense of time and direction, Boochani muses: "Only the sky is reliable; one can trust the sky, the fixed stars, trust the position of the moon" (61). Yet the moon seems to play with his hope, suggesting that they are traveling in circles, leading to his frustration: "I hate the moon. It tells me we are lost, that we are wandering displaced" (61). At the same time, he acknowledges that the moon is "truth-telling," its presence restoring a sense of safety and cosmic order: "The moon appears / Rhythmic waves, majestic ocean / Protection" (62). Upon being rescued by a military vessel to take them to Christmas Island, Boochani and his fellow asylum seekers embrace joy and excitement. In those moments, the moon is "more beautiful than before" and "watching over us," no longer a "deranged moon" and "brutal moon" (64). Oceanic forces reassume benevolent forms of "admirable" waves and "enchanting" sea "caressing us with care" (68). The moon and the ocean embody a paradox of cosmic stability and unknown forces, infusing with the author's hope and despair as an asylum seeker.

The fraught bond between Boochani and the moon is diagnostic of the biopolitical infrastructures that impact refugee mobility and affective capacity. The asylum seeker's conflicted experiences of the natural world go beyond an individual's projections of feelings onto nature to express how refugee affects anticipate and intensify the self's interaction with migration border institutions and perceived ideas of belonging and unbelonging in the world. Oscillating between hope and despair, between the promise of the good life and feeling stuck, is a common affective paradigm found in forced migration narratives (Glaveanu and Womersley 2021, 634). Boochani's tortured emotions are embedded within the ecosocial landscapes of forced migration, influencing the body's potential and shaping imaginations of what is (im)possible. Refugee ecologies reveal affective rhythms of connection and interruption, which exposes how sovereign biopower engineers oceanic environments as terrains of invasion and terror and how these environments also present ethical sites for imagining nonhierarchical forms of collectivity. By reclaiming the affective agency of asylum seekers and presenting them as feeling selves, Boochani's memoir challenges nationalist biopolitics of emotions and directs us to witness the ambiguous and diverse affective encounters between refugees and nonhuman bodies.

Refugee sea crossings thicken the ocean's existential depths, inviting us to historicize it as a material cartography of migrant survival, hope, and solidarity. Boochani depicts one admirable female asylum seeker, Our Golshifteh, whose care and kindness to other passengers' children and during food distribution offers a stark contrast to the emotionless Australian soldiers. Her presence carries an intimate exposure to oceanic elements and embodies both the collective ordeal and the dignity of human spirit, as "her clothes are torn and her body smells like the other distressed people there / Smelling like the sea" (2018, 66). The ocean in Boochani's narrative is thus not merely a perilous route of death and suffering, but also a storied repository of "all our [refugees'] dreams, all our fears, all our brave souls" (37). He negotiates a more complex image of the refugee and the oceanscape by refusing narrow biopolitical categories to reclaim the tension and flow between singularity and collectivity. In doing so, he reimagines the ocean as a palimpsest of countless individual refugee life trajectories and a material transit of ethical reckoning in the face of heartless borders.

At a near-death moment when the first boat is sinking, Boochani's dream visions meld the waves with the Kurdish landscape, transforming the sea into mountains and invoking an eagle's flight through a surreal vision where chestnut valleys intertwine with oceanic depths. He writes, "I am an eagle flying through a frightening dreamlike scene / Through the beauty of the waves / The chestnuts are being swallowed into the depth of the valley / Into the river, into the waves" (33). This surreal vision corresponds with his later reflection in the camp that mountains and forests are nonhuman shelters and witnesses to Kurdistan villagers fleeing war. He was born into statelessness, homelessness, and placelessness, where warfare leaves lingering marks, where "the waste, the smoke, the dust, the smog, the shockwaves, the heat, the multi-coloured sparks . . . the volume of its all" ran deep within the bones (264). His dreamy metamorphosis into an eagle offers a reflective distance from nationalistic ideologies. It evokes a dream of flight for freedom that soars above the confines of imposed borders and the scars of war toward a planetary allegiance to the boundless cosmos. As he writes, "Life for me always emerges from within desolation" (264).

In other places of the memoir, Boochani portrays how the detention camp mobilizes the colonial human-animal distinction to subject asylum seekers to the existence of "caged animals," thereby justifying the slaughtering act. He describes the transfer to Manus Island prison as involving a dehumanizing and affectively charged security apparatus that circulates a politics of fear by dragging asylum seekers onto the plane and stripping them of their individuality. He compares the media and journalists at the airport to voyeuristic "vultures" preying on the wretched without considering their traumatic sea crossings (91). The guards dehumanize the detainees by reducing them to numbers, converting individuals into quantifiable data for border control. Boochani also emphasizes how detention management uses time as a biopolitical and affective control mechanism. Temporal strategies of prolonged waiting, queuing up, starvation, unsanitary conditions, delayed medical care, and monotony are employed to regulate refugees bodies and emotions into what the human is not. This "weaponization of time" functions as systematic torture to infantilize and grind asylum seekers into submission, forcing them to perish, return to where they come from, or pose negative examples to scare future comers (Tofighian and Boochani 2021, 65–66). These punitive tactics result in poor health and bare-life existence and instill debilitating emotions such as dread, hopelessness, competition, internal animosity, dependence, and complicity with the oppressive system.

Camp biopolitics promotes a colonial survival mindset that dissects refugee ties with both human and nonhuman others. This reflects the capitalist property system imposed by sovereign border regimes, where private firms join settler colonial states to commodify refugee detention. The United Nations High Commissioner for Refugees has repeatedly condemned human rights violations in privatized immigration detention facilities and security services in the Americas, Europe, and Oceania (2019). In Australia, the government outsources detention operations to private companies like Paladin, Canstruct, and Serco, notorious for alleged abuses, to maximize efficiency and offload responsibility. Boochani poignantly illustrates how prison conditions pit detainees against each another, describing food queues where extreme hunger causes individuals to act dishonestly for resources. This shapes a neoliberal environment where individualism, competition, and scarcity override communal bonds, further disempowering and isolating refugees. By exposing this tension between relational and atomistic approaches to refugee subjectivity, Boochani challenges readers to reconsider what it means to be human. His critique of neoliberal norms, which reduce individuals to "atomistic, essentially economic units" (Surma 2018, 521), ultimately questions society's capitalist structure that prioritizes instrumental values at the expense of the collective good.

Animality provides a political tool of resistance in Boochani's interrogation of the prison's colonial and penal genealogy. His memoir employs animal metaphors to scrutinize how the detention system disciplines refugees through the species hierarchies of human and animal. He compares exiled refugees to "sheep" tossed into a "slaughterhouse" (2018, 121), refugees in imprisonment to "bats in a dark cave" (125), and refugees reacting to water deprivation to swarming "killer bees" whose hive has been hit with a stick (174). These metaphors culminate in the imagery of refugees as "wolves" on the threshold of a bloody battle (174), agitated by a system designed to produce "primitivism, barbarism, and cannibalism" (168). This violent landscape incites aggressiveness among refugees, who are met with unnecessary discipline by prison guards, who use the occasion to punish refugees like caged animals and fuel stereotypes of them as angry, immoral, and animalistic. Boochani's narrative portrays the refugee body as embodying dispositions that transcend humanity, morphing into "walking apparition[s]" (93), "piece[s] of meat" (131), and "dangerous beast[s]" (177). Incarceration, in this framing, is a beastly machine.

While the colonial carceral logic imposes animality as a mode of dehumanization, Boochani also depicts a different model of strategic animality, one that resists fixed human-animal distinction through trans-species subjectivity. Meat presents not merely a site of victimhood but a transgressive grammar of mobility through which marginalized bodies challenge traditional humanism and express their incalculable multiplicity. Gilles Deleuze writes, "Every man who suffers is a piece of meat. Meat is the common zone of man and the beast, their zone of indiscernibility" (2003, 23). Inspired by Francis Bacon's art, which paints distorted bodies beyond recognizable human form, Deleuze identifies in "meat" a raw potential to morph beyond dominant political orders. As he notes, "Meat is not dead flesh; it retains all the sufferings and assumes all the colours of living flesh. It manifests such convulsive pain and vulnerability, but also such delightful invention, colour, and acrobatics" (2003, 23). This transformative potential of flesh is embodied in Boochani's depiction of a boisterous asylum seeker, Maysam the Whore, who performs nightly circus shows and theatrical acrobatics to elicit joy and camaraderie among detainees. Through costumes fashioned from bedsheets or underwear, flamboyant dances, and near-naked performances, Maysam channels a spectrum of affects, "joy, fear, hatred, envy, revenge, spite, and even kindness" (Boochani 2018, 137). His mimicry ridicules the prison system, provoking "a mixture of abhorrence, envy and barbarism" from guards (136), while detainees find in his performance "the essence of life" (141). In Maysam's performances, the imposed human-animal divide becomes a subversive site of becoming-animal, where refugees use mimicry, theatricality, and affect to create fugitive forms of survival. This duality demonstrates that even in contexts of extreme dehumanization, the materiality of the body retains a latent potential for subversion and reinvention. As other refugees join Maysam in clapping and cheering, they stage a collective utterance of becoming animal and assert the unruly agency of refugee bodies against the biopolitical logic that reduces them to bare life.

An ecological praxis manifests in the multispecies kinmaking between refugees and plants, the jungle, and the wider ecosystems that tells alternative stories about the detention camp as a site of emergent ecology. Boochani poetically honors the vegetal agency of a chamomile-like flower growing in the camp's violent environment, writing, "I love those flowers / A zeal for resistance / A tremendous will for life bursting out from the coils and curves of the stems / Bodies stretching out to reveal themselves for all to witness" (293). He connects the flower's blossoms to the smile of a fellow asylum seeker who carefully avoids trampling them and finds grace and sublimity in nature, in whatever meager portion. This ecological kinmaking is a political response to the shared ways in which carceral colonialism displaces both refugees and rainforest flora and fauna. Boochani reflects, "The prison is like an enormous cage deep in the heart of the jungle" (111). The image of a prison cage within the jungle juxtaposes ecological interconnectivity with artificial borders, creating a visual and conceptual disjuncture that underscores the ethical imperative to dismantle the carceral shackle on refugee and nonhuman lives.

In more audacious acts, Boochani escapes to the beach at night. He associates the transgressive act of jumping over prison fences to the "glorious sensation of mountain climbing," enabling him to flourish in "the space between life and death" (300). Once beyond the fence, he experiences a multispecies connection with the natural world: "I am now part of the jungle. I am the jungle, like the snakes, like the frogs, like the insects, like the birds. I am the jungle itself" (301). Walking barefoot on the beach, he describes the sensation of toes tasting greatest freedom and embracing oceanic waves on voluntary terms. The jungle and ocean gift him reserves of strength and remind him of life's intrinsic right to freedom and movement.

The memoir's final chapter envisions a radical ecological democracy and abolitionist insurgence. Boochani recounts the 2014 Manus riot, which left one asylum seeker dead and many injured. After days of futile peaceful protest, the asylum seekers declare war on sovereign power. There is a feeling among the detainees that the protest is a collective performance of resistance through which refugees, by chanting "Freedom!" assert an alternative self, forge solidarity, and unmask the carceral colonialism structuring the migration border regime. There is also an awareness that the rebellion, seen by some as futile theater, is destined to face brutal retaliation from the security force. Boochani invokes a more-than-human collective, describing how the protesters' democratic singing gains life by merging with the jungle landscape: "The sound that vibrated through the landscape was the sound of the entire prison compound at once" (338). This planetary chorus expresses how the protesters' struggle for freedom is witnessed and amplified by nonhuman forces in a shared cry against anthropocentric, colonial, and nationalist oppression. As Boochani concludes, all the birds on Manus Island are in symphony, lamenting, wailing, their cries fusing with those of the displaced: "The chant of a bird and the chant of a man / Both chants blend into one" (356). This multispecies elegy mourns the lives, time, and freedom stifled by bio- and necropolitics. It also signals a new planetary itinerary for refugee agency and political mobility through ecological alliance with the cosmos.

### Poetics of Thickening

In refugee narratives like *Island of the Hungry Ghosts* and *No Friend but the Mountains*, ecologies of mobility, entanglement, and presence intermesh with those of immobility, disconnection, and absence that also materialize across bodies, affects, and landscapes. Refugee ecologies provoke questions of contingent and precarious survival, where more-than-human relations shape biopolitical governance and the very situated substance of collaborative survival. Rather than presenting inherently progressive networks or romantic unity, the more-than-human offers an ambiguous analytic for ecologically interpreting refugee (im)mobility. By introducing a theoretical framework of thick mobility, I have shown how refugee bio- and necropolitics entangles with oceans, mountains, biodiversity, minerals, islands, ghosts, and other nonhuman elements that are regulated under but ultimately exceed anthropocentric and colonial hierarchies of life and animacy. Thickening enlarges a planetary sense of refugee subjectivity in more-than-human-worlds, across histories, cultures, atmospheres, and geographies.

From a relational viewpoint, the affective atmospherics of haunting and (im)mobility in these narratives can be understood as residual cultural forms or as part of a "poetics of thickening." A poetics of thickening contributes to an ecological ethos of irresolution, precarity, and ambiguity against a modern necropolitical system of extinction. Poetics, I argue, can enable affective attunement to impure phenomena and generate new subjectivity in felt ecological fields. In its nonlinear and untimely qualities, poetics holds the known and unknown in a relation of tension, allowing a humble passage into the opacity, singularity, and density of more-than-human encounters. By moving beyond a monolithic model of global neoliberal mobility, a poetics of thick mobility opens up ecological and affective ways of understanding refugee life beyond the humanitarian gaze that often sentimentalizes them and the biopolitical gaze that reduces them to disciplinary subjects. Ecological makings by oceanic waves, animal migration, and rainforest growth are an indictment of a modern colonial biopolitics of securitization where linear borders racialize refugees as invasive threats, capitalist properties, or caged animals.

In Brady's film and Boochani's memoir, affective poetics is at once an environmental aesthetics, a mode of resistance, a thickened temporality, and a praxis of relational world-making that confounds national borders, disciplinary enclosures, and species distinctions. Through an affective poetics of interspecies mourning, kinship, and solidarity, Brady's film and Boochani's memoir ecologize refugee mobility as practical yet uncontainable assemblages. These assemblages persevere in cracks, pulsate in scarred tissues, and move with nonhuman agency from the margins despite territorial confinement. This attention to the incalculable multiplicity of refugee affects and body-place relations challenges the discrete boundaries of the liberal human and insular notions of citizenship and belonging. New political mobilities for refugee life emerge from more-than-human collaborations that transgress the liberal capitalist policing of markets, differences, and life itself for imagining an inclusive politics of multispecies survival and ecological freedom. An ecologically expansive notion of life and freedom unfolds through refugee coalitions with the cosmos, resisting an exceptional model of humanist subjectivity and its binary demand for either assimilation or abjection.

# 4

# Climate Migration, Carbon Specters, and Planetarity from Below

I couldn't bear the strain. I burst and caught fire.

—Merlinda Bobis, *Locust Girl*

## Implosion: A New Climate Imaginary

If the earth's climate system is a heat engine, as posited by scientists (Becker 1915), it is currently running overheated due to an excess of kinetic energy. Human activities of burning fossil fuels, deforestation, industrial agriculture, and capitalist globalization have accelerated movement, increased heat-trapping greenhouse gases, and disrupted the earth's carbon cycle to the point of climate change. Catastrophic storms, melting glaciers, rising sea levels, wildfires, and droughts are symptoms of human geomorphic agency that are entangled with the mobility of earth systems on an unpredictable and planetary scale. More specifically, the climate crisis materializes the implosion of accumulated entropy and contradictions inherent in the dominant form of being human—a Eurocentric and exceptional model of human subjectivity that structurally and culturally emerged with European imperialism, colonial resource extraction, and the invention of global racial order in the sixteenth century. The entropic excess of carbon that once fueled colonial expropriation of land, labor, and resources continues today under neoliberal capitalism and manifests in forms of climate injustice that unevenly expose the lives and habitats of Indigenous people, people of color, and working-class communities to climate risks and displacement.

In this chapter, I undertake a kinetic thought experiment of reconceiving climate change from explosion to implosion. Implosion recasts current climate phenomena not as "natural," explosive, and sudden disasters but as intensified, cumulative, and entropic symptoms of the structural deformation of our ecosocial environments that are collapsing inwardly. They are collapsing due to unsustainable practices such as carbon-energy-waste overload, colonial racial capitalism, and economies of extraction. Implosion highlights the social and natural dynamics of climate change to mark what Bernard Stiegler, Paolo Vignola, and Mitra Azar term "an Entropocene era," a refiguration of the Anthropocene through the massive increase of entropy across various forms: "(1) thermodynamic entropy, as the dissipation of energy, (2) biological entropy, as the reduction of biodiversity, and (3) informational entropy, as the reduction of knowledge to data and computation" (2021, 28). While entropy typically implies disorder and breakdown, it can also signal the disruption of existing systems to make possible new ways of organizing. Consequently, we are called to collectively engage with entropy and develop geosocial methods that interrogate the geomorphic impacts of humanity together with a reconceptualization of the modes of subjectification tied to fossil fuels, the matter-energy that gives rise to the biopolitical formations of late capitalism (Yusoff 2013, 780).

Implosive thinking directs our attention to the mutual worlding between humanity and Earth, and how geologic and nonhuman matters implode human subjectivity and corporeality, rendering climate change not only palpable in everyday life but also a reflective moment for composing ecologically expansive futures. My argument is that dominant climate change discourses tend to fail to present climate impacts as structural implosions rather than explosive externalities. This conceptual failure hinders the shift from abstract data, neoliberal techno-fixes, or apocalyptic pessimism to a mobilized collective cultural imagination that moves beyond human exceptionalism. In this sense, implosion offers a language and imaginary to describe systemic transformations and a brewing planetarity that cannot be brought forth by a modern biopolitics of control and externality. Instead, more just and collective planetary futures-to-come must be rebuilt from within, by recuperating the excess of mobility and restorying humans as ecologically response-able subjects in a world composed by geomorphic agencies. This unfolding human subjectivity demands climate storytelling that reckons with rupture while cultivating an embodied openness to be affected by the environment, attending to the unruly, entropic, and generative ways in which human and earthly forces co-create and co-become.

Nowhere is the discourse of externality more vehemently at play than in contemporary debates about climate migration. The figure of the climate migrant, or climate refugee, has become emblematic of our era. From Central American migrant caravans heading toward the US-Mexico border to Pacific Islanders facing rising sea levels, from Syrian refugees affected by water and crop crises to Afghans enduring droughts and hunger, the climate migrant has become the human face of climate change in the twenty-first century. However, public media, Western policymakers, and NGOs tend to reproduce narratives that portray climate change as an exceptional and external driver of human migration. This was evident during the so-called "2015 European migrant crisis," when many media outlets and policymakers framed migration from the Middle East and North Africa as a sudden emergency and attributed it primarily to war and drought as significant contributory factors (Cottier and Salehyan 2021). European Commission President Jean-Claude Juncker, for example, invoked the Syria-climate link to identify climate change as one of the "root causes" of new migration patterns, warning that "climate refugees will become a new challenge—if we do not act swiftly" (2015). While recognizing climate change as a threat multiplier for instability, such statements risk reinforcing a crisis discourse that externalizes climate migration as an unexpected catastrophe that disrupts otherwise stable societies. This framing neglects the ways that migration is embedded in longer and ongoing histories of colonialism, resource extraction, and geopolitical instability.

Much research contests the misleading use of the term "climate refugee," which overstates the role of ecological and natural disasters in human mobility while obscuring structural economic and political factors like neoliberal capitalism in exacerbating climate vulnerability (Selby et al. 2017, 239). Some, like Neel Ahujia, analyze how the figure of the climate migrant as a border-crossing threat in public policy reports reinforces a security rhetoric that fits into racialized assumptions of climate change held by Global North states and militarized logics (2021, 38). In dominant media representations, climate refugees are often racialized as victims devoid of political agency, threats to the current geopolitical order, or abstract "stinking strangers" representing a global yet distant problem (Høeg and Tulloch 2019, 233). Others, like Andrew Baldwin, argue that at the core of such racialized discourses is an attempt to deploy the liminal figure of the climate migrant/refugee for the convenient purpose of resolving an ontological crisis of Western humanism, despite various masquerades in the language of progressive liberalism (2022, 4). Still others fear that pathologizing climate migration as a problem to be solved and stabilized by the capitalist-territorial-sovereign nexus overlooks the ontological primacy of mobility in constituting social life in the Anthropocene (Bettini 2019, 337; Nail 2019, 377).

In this chapter, I model an implosive reading of climate migration dynamics—weather symptoms and carbon matters, the bodies and places enmeshed in it, the capitalist-national-bordering complex, and the crisis of humanism—to reimagine climate futures beyond externalized framings that rely on militarized borders, racial catastrophes, and technocratic solutions. From this vantage, the climate migrant/refugee becomes a figure through which the implosive workings of climate change are made visible. Instead of simply a dramatic manifestation of climate crisis, this figure emerges as a pivotal actor in a decolonial and integrated understanding of the historical roots of displacement and environmental degradation. These historical roots include the inequalities, anxieties, and crises of modern humanism and its persistent grip on ideas of the good life. Indeed, the climate crisis is also a cultural crisis, a failure of narrative imagination to divest from the exceptionalism of human subjectivity. Amitav Ghosh traces how climate change challenges the literary imagination, arguing that the dominance of the realist novel privileges bourgeois life and individual moral growth while concealing its reliance on histories of imperialism, consumer capitalism, and the carbon economy (2016, 10). This individualist tendency extends beyond literature to a public politics that privatizes climate action as an individual moral concern or weaponizes green xenophobia. The trend of green xenophobia is exemplified by US, Australian, and European politicians framing climate migrants as resource competitors threatening white possession and privileged "ways of life." As climate imaginations shape climate futures, these narratives reliant on the individual morality of the modern subject or the biopolitics of securitization hinder the imagining of climate futures that are more collective and just.

An implosive reading of climate change thus opens up questions about what forms of geosocial subjectivity and narrative imagination can better describe humanity's planetary capacities, responsibilities, and mobilities in ways that avoid rendering climate change a universal, abstract, and external phenomenon. How can climate migration be understood as an implosive moment for decolonization? While anthropogenic climate change highlights humanity's planetary power, it also foregrounds mineralogical, atmospheric, and nonhuman forces that puncture human agency and sharpen awareness of differentiation and vulnerability. Contemporary climate storytelling calls on writers and scholars to critique anthropocentric hubris while reasserting human agency in favor of a more ethical partnership with nature's agency, demanding stories that shift away from quick techno-fixes toward long-term social-fixes (Johns-Putra and Sultzbach 2022, 8). Climate change entails a constant translation between earth history (deep time and geological events) and world history (empire, capital, and technology) (Chakrabarty 2009, 2021). Such translation is a central concern of ethnic, diasporic, and postcolonial climate fiction (cli-fi) that plays a crucial role in provincializing universal discourses of climate change. This literature abounds with decolonial potential for disturbing a white individualist perspective with social and environmental justice concerns and broadening speculative and futuristic literary forms with worldviews "from below" that have been shadowed by Eurocentric narratives of reason, masculinity, and techno-progress.

It is from this understanding of climate imagination as a material-discursive praxis for shaping climate futures that I develop an implosive method to examine the emergent thick mobility of climate migration beyond the paralyzing logic of threat and victimhood to advance new possibilities for planetary social thought. I argue that the figure of the climate migrant carries the ambiguity, excess, and haunting materiality of carbon as the beginning of, the becoming of, and the responsibility for composing humans as geobodies of the earthly commons. Specifically, I explore how futuristic imaginative poetics can perform an implosive critique of fossil capitalism by ethically engaging the past and present specters of carbon that are bound to return. This chapter turns to Filipina Australian writer Merlinda Bobis's climate fiction *Locust Girl* (2015), a speculative novel that reimagines climate migration as a consequence of colonial geologics of inhuman subjection and capitalist extraction that reproduce inequalities. The novel allegorizes a climate future as a past-to-come, where the repressed specters of colonialism, racism, sexism, and fossil capitalism return to haunt humanity through residual forms of desertification, displacement, and securitized borders.

Set in a post-apocalyptic future, *Locust Girl* depicts a climate-changed world polarized between a refugee community named the Strays, who dwell in a desert with numbered tents, and the last remaining oasis state, the Five Kingdoms, which is home to pious citizens and tyrannical caretakers. After the Kingdoms bomb her village, nine-year-old Amedea sleeps underground for ten years, then wakes up with a locust embedded in her brow. Against the Kingdoms' border control and amnesiac propaganda, and extreme fear and hunger, Amedea ventures on a journey to the Kingdoms, with her locust acting as a sensory compass that predicts, copies, and creates songs to direct her border crossing. Amedea's locust reorients her embodied subjectivity to become in and of the environment: "A stray gust of wind, a rolling pebble, dust from a rock, and my brow itched in response, sometimes into full melody copying what it heard" (Bobis 2015a, 36). In her nomadic openness to alterity and more-than-human becoming, the locust girl suggests the horizon of a planetary future. As the blurb on the novel's back cover explains, "This political fable is a girl's magical journey through the border. The border has cut the human heart. Can she repair it with the story of a small life?" How are we to understand the political possibilities of Bobis's novel, and the imaginative poetics that she deploys, in planetary terms?

*Locust Girl* can be interpreted as a futuristic allegory about Australia's refugee policies, racialized migration management, and climate vulnerability (Herrero 2017), as well as the "War on Terror" in the post-9/11 era (Bobis 2015b). However, the novel's scope extends beyond national boundaries, deliberately avoiding specific national or racial identifiers to address global migration politics and climate change. I read *Locust Girl* as an Asian diasporic writer's response to planetary crisis in a decolonial speculative act, outside of the nation. It participates in a growing body of antiracist, diasporic, and people-of-color speculative fiction that disrupts the genre's conventional association with Euro-Western notions of progress, modernity, and futurity at the cost of alternative modernities and postcolonial histories. The novel explores colonial pasts in a dystopic future of environmental ruin, even as ecological disasters bind humanity globally. Jacques Derrida's concept of the "specter" can help explain the novel's apocalyptic future as the "'experience' of the past as to come" (1994, xix). Climate events such as natural resources depletion, drought and fire, species extinction, and desertification in the novel function as temporal devices that fracture linear progress, while positing generative possibilities to reorient human subjectivity, corporeality, and political collectivity through multispecies entanglement. By portraying the female protagonist whose embodied subjectivity negotiates affective, sensory, and trans-species intimacies, the novel offers an ethical corrective to anthropocentric and rationalist worldviews that racialize her as impure and monstrous.

Through an implosive analytic, I examine how Bobis's novel reclaims the planet as an ethical figure of relationality, demonstrating how planetary imaginations can help to recuperate differences, localities, and subjectivities that have been disavowed by modern temporal geographies of colonialism, racism, extractivism, and militarism. My analysis focuses on climate migration as one of the novel's key sites for reclaiming planetary relationality, attending to how it speculates the implosive worldings of the planet through an ambivalent poetics of futurity: the spectral future predicted from ecological ruins and the future opened by the alternative political life from the margins. These dual futures highlight two implosive understandings of climate change: as the dystopic return of carbon specters and as the iterative mobilization of planetarity from below. By comparing these carbon futures and how they complicate dominant climate discourses, I place *Locust Girl* in conversation with Derrida's deconstructive spectrality and Gilles Deleuze's nomadic ethics, tracing the novel's shift in representing climate migration from a focus on blame and damage to a nomadic praxis of planetarity. The perspective on spectrality problematizes a "universal humanity" premised on endangered environmental futures. But the perspective on nomadic ethics allows us to see that in order to dislodge the colonial racial structures of extractive capitalism that continue to displace and fossilize life, planetary subjectivity needs to ecologize an ethics of alterity beyond the discursive domain into creating new immanent experiences of more-than-human existence.

Pushing back against pathological discourses that project the migratory uncertainties of climate change as threat and crisis, a nomadic praxis of planetarity attests to the transformative and worldmaking potential of migration to social life. "Mobility, then, is a crisis only if we assume that there was or should be stasis in the first place," Thomas Nail writes, resounding how "migrant movements are constitutive and even transformative to nature, human, and society, rather than exceptional" (2019, 377). *Locust Girl* exemplifies a kinopolitics of migration by linking one refugee woman's nomadic becoming to a planetary cosmopolitics of earthly multitude that is genuinely open to the inhuman and nonhuman dimensions of human subjectivity. As the novel connects the migrant woman's metamorphosis to the recuperation of cultural memory and affectivity of the postcolonial subaltern, a micropolitics of planetary becoming connects local space-time-matter to ecosocial change. This metamorphosis across species and borders implodes dominant anthropocentric frameworks, allowing a decolonial recalibration of alternative futures beyond extractive and racialized scripts. In this way, Bobis's speculative fabulation makes a case for placing the diasporic writer's response to the Anthropocene at the heart of a situated practice of planetarity. The situated imagination calls for a generative planetarity centered on movement, multiplicity, and nomadic praxis for cultivating vibrant and transformative encounters with alterity that remake worlds to open postcarbon futures.

## Nomadizing Futurity: Imagining the Planetary Impossible

How climate futures are imagined shapes how they are made. The current climate chaos is rooted in modern narratives of futurity that prioritize unlimited growth and techno-scientific advances through a mechanistic worldview of the earth as exploitable resources. Speculative finance and global capitalism seek to trade future uncertainties into calculated risks for monetary gain (Banhg 2018, 12). Today's climate scientists use computer models to predict future climate for scenario building, risk management, and policy guidance. While scientific knowledge reveals much about the earth system's complex agency, this complexity tends to become oversimplified when science is translated as empirical evidence in public and policy discourses. The future, like the past and present, is fragmented and open. Despite industrial-capitalist societies' attempts to empty and tame the future to make social life more secure, the "embedded, embodied, and contextual" qualities of the future elude the modern habits of mind that extrapolate it for exploitation, calculation, and control (Adam and Groves 2007, 2). To keep climate futures open, we must rely on approaches that are not only characterized by calculability and risk, but also mobilize imaginative and creative acts to strength the cultural resilience of living with uncertain futures, alongside opening alternatives to neoliberal capitalism (Yusoff and Gabrys 2011, 518). Imagination and the arts broaden our capacity to engage climate futures as generative spaces of the unknown and possibilities to become otherwise.

It is from the unknowability of the future that we may make sense of cli-fi as a political act, one that invites us to witness whose imaginations, histories, and futures are taken seriously, and whether and how speculative fiction can expand imaginative methods for alternative planetary inhabitation. In her call for an imperative to reimagine the planet, Spivak suggests the planet offers an ethical corrective to the anthropocentric and capitalist drive to control and commodify the earth because it exceeds human calculation (Spivak 2003, 73). She is careful not to set planetarity as unexamined environmentalism, or in a neat contrast with capitalist globalization, instead positing the planet as a countertext to the idea of city/nation, placing history in nature itself and away from a politics of fear and hostility (2003, 94). Planetarity as such involves the ongoing imagination of a future-to-come and an "experience of the impossible" (Spivak 2003, 98). Following Spivak, I suggest that calling forth planetarity generates an iterative politics of imaginative poiesis, recognizing the future as a praxis of ethical reckoning where the human subject is recomposed through ongoing obligations to others and otherness.

A planetary call sets an ethical agenda for remapping world systems in speculative storytelling, but executing such imaginative worlding proves challenging. Contemporary representations of the future in fiction, film, media, and activism tend to adopt the motif of environmental apocalypse and doomsday hero, despite critiques that such imaginings normalize environmental crisis as part of ordinary life (F. Buell 2003, xiv), reproduce the Christian myth of the apocalypse and modern Western linear time (Keller 1996), and spread fears of racialized others taking over the planet and the Anthropocene as white decline (Smith and Vasudevan 2020, 91). If the Anthropocene proclaims a sudden dystopic future lamenting the end of the world for white liberal communities, it does so while overlooking histories in which environmental collapse has been knowingly exported to people of color in the name of progress, freedom, and modernization (Yusoff 2018, xiii). Indigenous people and communities of color have long survived apocalyptic conditions wrought by imperialism and settler colonialism, processes that continue to cast nature/culture boundaries along racialized lines. The liberal white anxieties over climate futures are evident in the racial futurism that anticipates the figure of the climate refugee as a threat yet-to-come (Baldwin 2022). Through the dehumanization of this racial other, white humanism seek to reassert dominance over world history and revitalizes itself for the future.

Colonial racial legacies haunt climate future imaginings, echoing Frederic Jameson's remark that it appears easier to imagine the end of the world today than to imagine the breakdown of late capitalism, "due to some weakness in our imaginations" (1994, xii). Through techniques of wonder and estrangement, the uncanny, and posthuman hybrids, fantastic and speculative fiction can immerse us in otherworldly futures that shine new perspectives on our existing world, give shape to unimaginable challenges, inspire climate action, and amplify marginalized voices, including Indigenous and diasporic perspectives. The strategies of antiracist, postcolonial, and decolonial speculative fiction allow planetary alternatives to be localized within the uneven geographies shaped by empire and capital. Decolonial speculative fiction such as *Locust Girl* considers the promise of the planet not as a redemptive solution but as a productive analytic for unearthing unrealized historical possibilities and alternative futures that resist universal modern time. The novel deploys nonlinear temporality to explore discrepant futures—one depicting a post-apocalypse haunted by climate specters and the other a nomadic future of planetary regeneration—revealing how life is intimately related to death, the past is unfinished business, and the future is already in and part of our reality.

Bobis's novel and similar texts can be read alongside my proposition of planetarity from below, connoting a collective yet differentiated relational ethics, which requires speculative labor to address the capacious task of charting a planetary commons while remaining attentive to the world's divergent localities. The risk of planetarity becoming yet another unifying trope of abstract environmentalism can be effectively avoided by engaging with literature, for example, from the Global South and Indigenous authors, whose activist planetary perspectives offer local understandings of the planet's trajectory as "always in earthly orbit" (Giles 2015, 145). Métis scholar Zoe Todd suggests that locally informed responses to global environmental crises cannot be constructed without first deconstructing the universalist and Eurocentric framing of the Anthropocene that often sidesteps questions of race, colonialism, and slavery and blunts distinctions between peoples, nations, and collectives whose experiences of human-environment relations have developed differently (2015, 244). In other words, the universalizing tendency of planetarity can and should be revised through a politics of differentiation that takes seriously the local cultures and knowledges that have long been negotiating strategies of multispecies coexistence and co-constitutive relations.

In its creative refusal of anthropocentric futurity, *Locust Girl* cultivates a nomadic praxis that reclaims speculative fiction as what can keep the "not yet" open. The climate futures in the novel might be understood as the implosive build-ups of ethico-onto-epistemological excess due to modern colonial knowledges that foreclose histories, futures, and loving relations with more-than-human kin. Speculative fiction allows the author to openly dramatize these implosive scenarios in performative worldmaking and refract the future as a break from anthropocentric logics, an uncertain space where social relations can be reassembled. In this light, nomadic thought provides not just a framework to describe migrant and refugee experiences, but also an ethical orientation toward non-anthropocentric ecology. As Rosi Braidotti explains, "To 'nomadize' categories of thought means to dislodge them from their often implicit attachment to the humanistic vision concerning the autonomous, liberal individual so as to open them towards other modes of thinking about the structures of the self and the inter-relation to others" (2003, 196). In other words, the process of nomadizing futurity allows a decolonial poetics that engages in speculative worldmaking as an ongoing practice and the exploration of alternative ways of being outside of modern progress and anthropocentric worldviews. Through open-ended speculative ethics, grassroots insurgence, and emplaced storytelling, an imaginative poetics of planetarity keeps materializing the impossible. To nomadize futurity means to divest the future from its singular programming by capital, the performative act of which would summon unknown ghosts, matters, subjects, and political life with the potential to counter the Anthropocene.

## "Climate Refugees" on a Spectral Planet

*Locust Girl*, as Herrero argues, is a desperate call for "an ethics of alterity" and "a politics of care" against the deadly enforcement of borders in our globalized world (2017, 953). A planetary fable that interrogates climate geopolitics in order to explore the shared survival of the human species, *Locust Girl* is set in an allegorical future. Bobis has expressed that she wrote the novel to be about all of us, to be "owned by anybody" (2015b). The names of the novel's characters exemplify this concern of plurality, ranging from A to Z: "Amedea," "Beenabe," "Cho-choli," "Daninen," "Espra," "Fa-us," "Gurimar," "Hara-haran" . . . "Wilidimus," "Xuqik," "Ycasa," "Zacarem." These characters are crafted to embody a multitude of human archetypes, including heroes, villains, perpetrators, victims, and the in-betweens. The borders explored in the novel are both tangible and conceptual, referring not only to physical demarcations but also to fear, hatred, and a lack of love within the human heart. Specifically, Bobis depicts how ecological catastrophes exacerbate existing inequalities and borders, thereby challenging the notion of a unifying planetarity. Through the motif of the specter, the novel invokes the material residue of subaltern and cosmic others and their becoming-withs, whose entropic excess implodes hegemonic temporality.

With the allegorical landscape of the novel divided between the powerful and the powerless, *Locust Girl* is comparable to George Orwell's *1984* (1949). Echoing Orwell's concept of "thoughtcrime," which depicts tyrannical repression of independent thought, Bobis introduces "singingcrime" to expose the silencing of minority voices by authoritarian political regimes. The protagonist Amedea lives with her father Abarama and other Strays, or climate refugees, in numbered tents in the desert. In this desert, life is marred by extreme hunger and relentless sandstorms; resources such as water, seeds, oil, and even colors are rationed sparingly by the Five Kingdoms. When rations fail to arrive, locusts become the only source of food. Each household is allocated a broadcasting box that plays only one tune, "The Songs" by the Minister of Mouths, designed to regiment people mentally and physically to their assigned patches of sky: "*No one should look / No one should walk beyond the horizon*" (Bobis 2015a, 10). Otherwise, a punishment fire from the Kingdoms bombs and burns those daring to cross the border or those who speak out against the Kingdoms' political message.

In stark contrast, in the Five Kingdoms—the Kingdom of "Waters," "Seeds," "Oils," "Colors," and "Fires"—there are "green trees everywhere" and "fields of grain and fruit and flowers" (119). In this lush landscape, the ministers greenwash extractive practices and cloak them under a humanitarian savior rhetoric to foster capitalist monopoly over the planet's dwindling resources. At the yearly festival, the Honourable Head preaches to the applause of his fellow citizens the "ideal for preservation": "Piety comes with the strict observance of caring values that preserves the human race and its home: the Five Kingdoms" (121). Such obfuscating environmentalist claims, however, are predicated on unequal distributions of subjectivity and resources, defining the Kingdoms' citizens as rightful humans and "carers of the natural world" vis-à-vis the Strays as less-than-human "wasters" who have "dried up nature with their profligate ways long ago" and "have no place in this new order" (121). This ironic interplay between environmental justice, environmental racism, and environmental humanitarianism constitutes a key process in constructing the climate refugee as an abstract figure of misery, irresponsibility, and national security threat.

As we can see, the ecological post-apocalypse that Bobis envisages is enmeshed in the politics of climate injustice. The Five Kingdoms' governance displays a colonial ideology that organizes planetary life according to rational ends and human dominance over nature. Their fabrication of a colonial historiography as universal truth is encapsulated in the collective singing of the Kingdoms' citizens, "*Lest we forget / There is only one story / There is only one song / That we take home*" (120). Such a totalizing narrative legitimates exclusive belonging by racializing and dehumanizing climate refugees at a time of existential crisis. Upon her arrival in the Kingdoms, Amedea perceives the fearmongering among its citizens. The Kingdoms' fantasy of a global racial order is betrayed by the creeping exhaustion, fear, and anger of its own people, who are forced to watch war footage as a reminder that only the Kingdoms' lives are valuable and worthy of grief. The ministers enforce this practice out of fear "that they'll forget and . . . stop guarding the border" (158). Simultaneously, the Kingdoms' rulers feed the Strays with "forgetting seeds" so they will forget their memories, their stories, and their desire to cross the border (157). Through this selective remembering, the Five Kingdoms concoct a reductive historical meaning that criminalizes migrants and justifies resource extraction, border militarization, and settler-state governance of land, water, and oil.

Climate events in the novel, such as deforestation, drought, and water scarcity, disrupt colonial and anthropocentric history. These ecological disasters are implosive cracks that reveal the haunting afterlives of empire and extraction. Their uncanniness can be interpreted through Jacques Derrida's deconstructive materialism. In *Specters of Marx*, Derrida resists Francis Fukuyama's claim that we have reached the "end of history" with the triumph of market economy and liberal democracy. Instead, Derrida recenters the alterity to which history fails to do justice. The promise of change and the future, or "the messianic," lies in "the coming of the other, the absolute and unpredictable singularity of the *arrivant as justice*" (Derrida 1994, 33), as opposed to a justice reduced to "rules, norms, or representations, with an inevitable totalizing horizon" (1994, 34). Alterity and otherness cannot be appropriated or assimilated by history because they are fundamentally non-appropriable. Materiality is always in excess of meaning. As telos of progress, claims such as Fukuyama's declaration of the end of history endorse the totality of an ideal finality that represses the inequalities and heterogeneity within historical conditions.

Climate change will lead to the recharging of economic and cultural imperialism by capitalist competition for resources, which further widens the divide between the prioritized and the expendable (Mansfield 2008). As a result, the political economies of climate change are likely to create historical disjunctures in which unresolved past atrocities return to haunt future politics in material forms: scarred nature, economic instability, mass dislocation, and war. In this context, Bobis demonstrates how narratives of climate migration mobilize a discourse of nature to reproduce colonial racial hierarchies. Specifically, racism abstracts and homogenizes historically produced vulnerabilities, differences, and colonial violence into the timeless language of nature, thereby naturalizing structures of domination under capitalism (Hall 1980, 342; Baldwin 2022, 6). The novel depicts this through the Kingdoms' dishonest externalization of climate change as a racial issue of migration and border security, instead of the Kingdoms acknowledging climate devastations as the cumulative implosion of colonial, patriarchal, and extractivist ironies.

In *Locust Girl*, extractive greenwashing operates as a capitalist tactic through which the Kingdoms legitimize resource theft from marginalized communities under the guise of liberal environmentalism. While the Kingdoms blame the Strays as impure, unassimilable people who deserve nature's punishment, the truth, as revealed by Cho-choli, a weeping woman whom Amedea encounters in a cave, is that the Kingdoms' resources once belonged to the Strays: "They came to tell us that we had too much water and we were wasteful. We had to save water for the future. So they built pipes into our well and our water disappeared" (Bobis 2015a, 42). By appropriating water conservation as a discourse of collective survival, the Five Kingdoms deceptively fabricate a sense of planetary "us," which then disguises their ecologically ruinous cultures of occupation. This act of taking water under the pretense of saving it for the future addresses broader patterns of resource plunder in the real world, where powerful nations from the Global North use the language of sustainability and humanitarian rescue to mask exploitative violence. Such practices erase the histories of dispossession and displacement of Global South communities from which resources are taken, while painting the resource takers as noble saviors.

Environmental events in the novel set the stage for planetary alterity to become the ethical center, commanding the need to listen to the neglected trauma of the displaced others and their emplaced stories of loss and survival. Like generations of women before her, Cho-choli weeps out the memory of Indigenous dispossession. Years of sobbing turn her tears into a pool and her eyes into empty sockets. Her grief is not merely personal but also collective, speaking the loss suffered by entire communities over generations. Compared to the Kingdoms' official recorded memory, Cho-choli chants stories of "once upon a time" that evoke Indigenous oral storytelling: "We had a well once upon a time. Our whole village could drink once upon a time, even our animals. It was green once upon a time" (42). Embedded throughout the novel, forms of Indigenous oral storytelling, such as Cho-choli's weeping and Amedea's singing, create gaps in the Kingdoms' imperialist historiography. These acts of storytelling and remembrance carve out a space where suppressed histories and environmental imaginations can surface and offer a counternarrative to colonial erasure.

The uncanny is a useful concept for unpacking how *Locust Girl* destabilizes the Kingdoms' coherent history to articulate extinctions and survivals born from inhuman becomings. Specter-like characters in the novel epitomize a dissociation of history, as their ghostly return gives corporeality to unresolved historical injustices and entropic excesses in a climate future. Strays such as Karitase, a female "creature" who is "afflicted with sores" (84), and Cho-choli are human others in their violated physicality. The narrative's spooky atmosphere intensifies at the burial ground of Strays killed by the Kingdoms' firebombs. Here, Amedea witnesses the "unrested spirits": "white bodies with no face! The skulls and bones are alive, the dead were walking!" (24). In a baffling scene, two white-clad figures are seen cremating a child's tiny skull into white powder while reverently uttering the word "Blessed." Later revealed as workers sampling the earth's richness at the Strays' burial ground, these figures use the ashes of the Strays to fertilize the Kingdoms' trees. These trees, in turn, are repurposed as border watchtowers that signal more firebombing of Strays, perpetuating a cycle of implosive combustion and further drying up the climate-parched landscape.

This surreal moment portrays that even in death, the bones and remains of the Strays are desecrated and capitalized upon as fossils to fuel the Kingdoms' privileged way of life. In the circulation of climate injustice (fires → bones → fertilizers → trees → fires), the material residue of the dispossessed reincarnates and returns incalculably. This cycle is an entropic feedback loop where climate injustice functions as a dissipative structure converting matter and energy in ways that amplify degradation and disparity. The cyclical violence depicted in the novel gives speculative imagination to Kathryn Yusoff's argument that "the geochemistry of fossil fuels underpins the geopolitical life of the subject of late capitalism (now the new geological subject of the Anthropocene)" (2013, 781). The Kingdoms exemplify the geopolitical life of capitalization that depends on the extraction and mineralization of fossils, while the Strays' bones foreshadow the "human fossils to come" that anticipate a future geology of human corporeality sedimented in the earth's strata. This scene by Bobis is a thoughtful speculative experiment because it explores how fossil fuels, assumed to be nonliving and dead matter, implode human corporeality. As Yusoff observes, "The work of fossil fuels is everywhere evident, and yet there is a strange absence in the conceptualization of the agency and historicity of fossil fuels within corporeality" due to their externalization as a commodity seemingly "mute" within the earth (2013, 789). In the Kingdoms' violent unearthing, human fossils return to differentiate life and animate the fires of combustion. Colonial capitalist powers disrupt the organic cycles of fossilized materiality to reproduce structural inequality and climate disorder, but in doing so, they also engineer the entropic breakdown of socio-ecological processes and the irreversible fossilization of humanity.

The residue of the subaltern other is a specter haunting the novel's post-apocalypse. Its return is bodily and physical. Derrida sees the specter as "a paradoxical incorporation, the becoming-body," whose flesh and phenomenality are both present and nonpresent, living and dead, thus collapsing any absolute knowledge (1994, 5). Bobis's portrayal of the specter evokes the minority's remnants by recuperating the many bodies and phantoms that cannot be subsumed into colonial historical meaning, such as the tiny skull that used to carry a young life that has not yet been properly lived. "Haunting belongs to the structure of every hegemony," Derrida writes, because hegemony organizes repression and thus confirms "the future-to-come and the coming-back of a specter" (1994, 46). In its irrepressible return, the Strays' bone powder is the *différance* that suspends hegemonic telos of the world. It comprises the "bodiliness of death" that restores to otherness the materiality irreducible to historical or political valuation (Mansfield 2008). The specter alters the linear ordering of time—the way we separate the past, present, and future—warning that what appears to have been concealed and invisible is very much alive and present (Gordon 2008, xvi). The specter's return recasts the novel's climate future as being saturated with past and present ghosts and differences, the non-appropriability of which aligns the marginalized climate refugee with a damaged planet.

Specters in *Locust Girl* rupture anthropocentric time and restore back to temporality its planetary dimension. In a deconstructive account, time is not proper to human design because it is given by "the absolutely or nonhuman other" whose coming both tears and suspends temporalization (Cheah 2016, 161). For Derrida, the planet would be textually undecidable, consisting of endless *différance* in the name of the real—that is, the infinite attempts to capture meaning with words, while never getting there. This constitutive inability of language is also the realm of literary imagination. The writer is engaged in a repetitive ordeal of returning to the beginning of their task and discovering again the proximity to authenticity from which they "could not make an abode" (Blanchot 1989, 23). Literature is "the gift of time" through which we are given any determinable reality, as Pheng Cheah suggests, because it does not simply represent material reality but generates "a passage, an experience" that fashions a new world while imparting meaning to the existing one (2016, 186). This iterative process enables us to see how fantasy and speculative fiction can be imaginative poetics that remake worlds. Bobis's speculative worldmaking exposes the constructed nature of modern progressive time, and in doing so opens the reader to a temporal reflexivity that negotiates relational alterity between literature's referential exterior and its imaginative and interpretive interiority.

Bobis's imaginative play with planetary alterity, however, goes beyond the textual domain. Derrida's deconstruction conceives materiality in terms of "permanent linguistic reflexivity" (Jameson 1995, 84), figuring the world as always to-come and elsewhere but never present in the relations between subjects. This deconstructive account offers a provocative frame through which to characterize *Locust Girl*'s depiction of the cultural politics of haunting under climate change. But configuring planetarity solely in the sense of textuality lacks a revolutionary edge. It is politically insufficient to dislodge the anthropocentric and sovereign machine that persists in our challenging times. As Emilie Cameron cautions, postcolonial haunting tropes can also "write out" the bodies and voices of living, politically active Indigenous and minority people by translating the specific experience of ghostliness into generalized metaphors of a contested colonial past and rendering postcolonial redress equally a fantasy (2008, 388). Beyond ghosts, damage, and the vestiges of the world's many previous endings, we must also notice the weeds, "the small, partial, and wild stories of more-than-human attempts to stay alive" (Gan et al. 2017, G6). In this respect, *Locust Girl*, through the narrative trope of metamorphosis, exhibits a radical critique that seeds the deconstructive spirit in the immanent experiences of more-than-human weeds, movements, and insurgences, thereby presenting planetary imaginations in storytelling as a force for ethical thought and social change.

## Becoming Planetary: A Nomadic Praxis of Earthly Multitude

*Locust Girl* can also be read as a political fable because fable is a literary genre that features allegorical stories conveyed mainly through nonhuman creatures, such as animals, plants, and inanimate objects. The novel's specters and haunted lives are ghosts of the modern colonial matrix of power and evoke multispecies landscapes and layered temporalities that outlive anthropocentric control. Through stories of metamorphosis and becoming-animal, the novel speculates on a processual ethics and a planetary cosmopolitics that take seriously the subject's opened-ended, affective, and embodied relations to multiple others in the living environment.

The hybrid figure of the locust girl embodies a "transversalist" and non-essentialist subjectivity that cuts across opposite ends and accommodates diverse forces of alterity beyond the individual (Guattari 1995). Instead of pitting nonhuman resistance against human dominance, the novel naturalizes both as historical manifestations of the subject in the dense meshwork of life. This transversal framing enacts an implosion of fixed subjectivity, unraveling human exceptionalism and opening onto metamorphic modes of becoming. The nonhuman parts of human subjectivity are given voice by Amedea's locust, which plays an important role in reorienting her subjectivity nomadically toward earthly multitude.

The novel can be read as interrogating an anthropocentric model of subjectivity based on rational control and individual heroism. It does so by identifying the domination of what Val Plumwood calls hegemonic rationalism, which assigns political mastery to elite men over the "others" of reason: women, the body, materiality, the enslaved, and the more-than-human world (2002, 19). That masculinist and rationalist values occupy the position of power is readily apparent in the Five Kingdoms, where three out of the four ministers are male. These ministers are patriarchal authorities of the nation. They present the crystallization of historical time—"hundreds of years old" and "bound to live forever" (Bobis 2015a, 141)—and out of too much thinking for the Kingdoms, they have shrunk to the size of children. The Honourable Head, in particular, has "re-thought this earth" by restoring laws of "purity," "symmetry," and "justice" (149–50). In contrast, the novel portrays female characters in ways that suggest their subordination in "nonhistorical, naturalistic, organist, passive, [and] inert terms" (Grosz 1994, 3). This is apparent in Amedea's amnesia, after she sleeps underground for ten years due to the Kingdoms' firebomb; her female body becomes a site of trauma and non-history.

The novel uncovers the ways in which racial, sexual, and species hierarchies are invented and perpetuated through the modern colonial separation of nature and culture. Amedea is saved from her underground sleep by a girl named Beenabe. After their separation, Amedea reunites with Beenabe in the Kingdoms, where Beenabe has become a sex worker. One of the most striking aspects of Beenabe's categorization is the Kingdoms' epithet for sex workers as "green trees." This term operates as a layered metaphor: green is the most common color in the Kingdoms and the color the Strays desire the most; trees are absent in the desert but found everywhere in the "master's houses, tables, beds, chairs, even their spoons" (Bobis 2015a, 50). A "green tree" functions as a euphemism for the precarious subject status of a sex worker, who occupies an ambiguous position less human than a Kingdoms' citizen and more human than a Stray. This fluid and unstable categorization expresses the novel's broader critique of biopolitical control. Beenabe's experience further highlights the entanglement of gendered and racialized subjection. Her residence, labeled "the impure room" (166), reflects the way purity and pollution are mobilized as mechanisms of social control. Her service is framed within a liberal multicultural economy of reciprocity, where hospitality is conditioned upon subjugation and her labor required as a "return payment" for the "gifts of the Kingdoms" (140). After Amedea is charged with breaching the Kingdoms' laws, Beenabe is pressured to testify against her, a moment that reveals the tenuous benevolence of a liberal humanist discourse that can be easily withdrawn if the migrant fails to prove her loyalty. After she fails to accuse Amedea, Beenabe falls victim to nationalist violence, betrayed and lynched by hateful citizens.

At times, *Locust Girl*'s concern with colonial binaries risks a didacticism based on either/or distinctions, but the novel also depicts characters whose hybridity and liminality disturb categorical divisions (Herrero 2017, 959). Bobis highlights the promiscuous potential of liminality and impurity to breach the sealed borders of the human and the imagined nation. Because the female gender never quite made it into full humanity in patriarchal history, her allegiance to the category of the human is at best negotiable and never to be taken for granted (Braidotti 2006b, 130). A "green tree" also refers to growth and abundance, and, accordingly, its "impurity" can bridge conceptual gaps between recognizable and unrecognizable subjectivities to remap the human and the nation as creolized. Beenabe's death challenges how reciprocity is framed by a liberal humanist politics of recognition and instead invites questions: Who sets the rules of reciprocity? How can the dispossessed reciprocate? The novel does not offer a singular answer, but Beenabe's refusal to condemn Amedea, shown in the ambiguous answers in her testimony, introduces an alternative feminist ethics of care that exceeds top-down state politics of inclusion and exclusion.

The novel destabilizes the myth of liberal universalism, which unifies and forgets differences under state-sanctioned narratives. In doing so, it unearths the submerged colonial structures and their ongoing erasure of alternative ways of being that sustain multiplicity. Beenabe is killed, and her blood shocks the Kingdoms' citizens, who are astonished by their own capacity for atrocity because they have been told that they are good people and have "never known blood in their hands" (Bobis 2015a. 169). Her death further provokes a shift in perspective for Verompe, a proudly assimilated other and the bastard son of the Minister of Mouths and a sex worker. Verompe holds out Beenabe's body to challenge the Kingdoms' arbitrary definition of legitimacy: "How do *we* plead? . . . Does the other side have no right to their peace? No. Because their peace threatens our own and more legitimate peace?" (169–70). Verompe, who lives as a citizen in the Kingdoms, discards assimilationist ideologies and starts to identify as a Stray, and then a hybrid: "My blood runs from both sides. I am contaminated. . . . Blood is red on both sides of the border. I am witness and victim and culprit" (170). His transformation ruptures the purity narratives that define the Kingdoms and exposes the arbitrary nature of their boundaries.

Crucially, Bobis deploys motifs of metamorphosis and the uncanny not only to portray more-than-human emergence, but also to unveil the entangled worlds that are already there, yet obscured by hegemonic modernity. The uncanny here operates as an ecological device to unmoor stable realities by revealing the monstrosity and livability of life in the wake of anthropogenic ruins. Rather than functioning solely as an instrument of estrangement, the uncanny in Bobis's fiction is staged through the body and the senses, forging a relational strategy that recombines self and other, human and nature, mind and body, and homeliness and unhomeliness. This porous use of the uncanny is made visible through the novel's main animal creature: the locust.

Within contemporary ecological discourse, the locust is often framed as an insect pest exacerbated by climate change, with scientific studies linking extreme weather like droughts and erratic rainfall to intensified desert locust outbreaks and migratory swarms, which have devastated crops and resulted in food insecurity across parts of East Africa, Asia, and the Middle East (Meynard et al. 2020, 3753). Yet the locust resists an easy interpretation by gaining a paradoxical doubling in Bobis's novel. It designates both a climate threat and an agent of multispecies entanglement, signaling modern destruction while simultaneously gesturing toward a precarious symbiosis, as the insect is depicted to embody both plague and survival in a time of planetary catastrophe. This tension is particularly apparent in its relationship to the Strays, who not merely fear the locust as a predatory pest but consume it as a source of food: "Good for protein. . . . The locust crackled between my teeth" (Bobis 2015a, 3); "They ate grains. . . . Then we ate them. . . . Then they eat their eaters[;] . . . they clambered out after the silence and nibbled at the dead" (8). The eerie, visceral sensation of a locust crackling between one's teeth invites bodily responses from readers, despite the fact that locusts have been for millennia a food source for humans and animals in many cultures. The act of eating blurs the line between predator and prey, sustenance and devastation, situating humans and animals in an ecological web of vulnerability and interdependence that shape planetary life.

The thick mobility of climate migration brings together stories of human displacement with those of migratory nonhuman life. These climate migrants compel us to notice the beasts of anthropocentric violence that transmutes life's dynamic entanglement. Locusts are typically shy, solitary, harmless, and ecologically beneficial in grassland ecosystems, until climatic conditions drastically transform them into swarming gregarious creatures that migrate over long distances, devastating crops and pasture along the way (Egonyu et al. 2021). Climate migration thus reflects how refugees and locusts share modern narratives of projected monstrosity and externalized culpability. By shedding light on this interspecies affinity and entangled survival, *Locust Girl* engages with the dark ecologies of the Anthropocene to attune us to multispecies insurgence in strange nature. While the Strays and the locusts feed on each other, the embedding of a locust in Amedea's forehead disrupts this opposition through a radical form of multispecies coexistence:

> *We listen to the other's dreams*
> *In the other's skin—once a locust*
> *And a girl, then a locust girl*
> *Dreaming a single dream* (Bobis 2015a, 9)

The main feature of Amedea's locust is that it gathers sounds and whirrs, and therefore it is a sensory receptor and communicator. When Amedea and Beenabe despair in the desert, the locust sings their way through the wilderness: "It was this whirring that kept us moving. It whirred towards other sounds, or led us towards them. . . . It seemed to carry on a conversation with even a faraway sound and always our feet could not resist" (36–37). An antenna that listens to and intuits alterity, the locust shapes Amedea's relationship to the cosmos with an ontological openness invested in nonhuman sentience: "A stray gust of wind, a rolling pebble, dust from a rock, and my brow itched in response" (37). It unsettles the monotone of the Kingdoms' propaganda by enunciating polyphonic sounds as Amedea walks the living landscape, "'It's only one, but it sings like two' . . . three notes . . . all at the same time" (35). Through a cartographical immersion of other voices under her skin, where the landscape shapes her processual, multisensorial, and storied becomings, the locust helps Amedea embody a nomadic version of subjectivity.

The nomadic mode of being, according to Gilles Deleuze, affirms that differential relations generate qualitative variations in experiences that in turn give rise to the thinking subject. This subject emerges through a continuous process of internal differentiation (difference-in-itself) and non-identity rather than conforming to existing identities to make sense of the environment (Deleuze 2006, 56–57). It is through the immanence of differences and the passages between singularities in the world that relations of movement and becoming are produced, contributing to a subjectivity in flux. If Deleuzian differentiation reveals nomadic subjectivity as a continuous emergence and processual becoming, Karen Barad further emphasizes how differentiation is always entangled and co-constitutive. In Barad's concept of "agential separability," differentiation is not about radical exteriority or individuation but an entangled process of co-constitution, where relationalities precede individuated beings (2007, 392). Through this lens, differentiation is not a break or moving away from the other, but an ongoing intra-action of responsiveness and responsibilities to the other within lively relationalities that also constitute the self.

Actualized in a process of differentiation and (re)singularization, the nomadic subject, like Amedea, is not sovereign but embodying a "subject-in-becoming" and a "vector of subjectivation" capable of affecting and being affected by a multiplicity of others within the environment (Braidotti 2006b, 126). The multitude of alterations aligns with Félix Guattari's concept of "chaosmosis," or autopoietic self-making, which Rosi Braidotti extends to the nomadic body. For Braidotti, the nomadic mode of subjectivity operates through creative transversality, where interconnections among humans, nonhumans, and inorganic matters actualizes an ethics and praxis to recompose life in an non-anthropocentric and egalitarian manner (2006b, 126). Following this eco-philosophy of nomadism, time is not a measurable quantity as in linear modern and capitalist thought, but reconfigured as a lived force that facilitates ongoing transformations and shifting relationships of becoming-withs.

There is thus a micropolitics of planetarity in the novel's central theme of border crossing: Amedea, the Stray, becomes locust girl, the Nomad. The nomadic subject is planetary and disrupts the nature-culture divide, for while the subject is the relay point of transversal interconnections, the earth is the ecosocial ground for all encounters and provides the material support that animates and sustains the nomadic existence. Further, as Braidotti suggests, the nomadic subject is constituted by "a folding-in of external influences and a simultaneous unfolding-outwards of affects" (2006a, 135). This affectivity is characteristic of Amedea, who has to relearn emotion and language after resurfacing from her amnesia. Her relearning of the world occurs through affective, sensory, and corporeal experiences of wonder and the unexpected. For example, when Beenabe rubs earth onto Amedea's body to cover her uneven skin color, the locust whirs "with pleasure" and starts to sing in "melodic" tunes (Bobis 2015a, 34), allowing Amedea to feel love and care. In contrast, when the locust replays the traumatizing sobs of Cho-choli, Amedea senses that her skull will "split" with "invasion" (43) and thus remembers pain and suffering. Throughout the novel, the locust allows Amedea to listen, sense, process, and respond to the affective intensities of her surroundings. Her body becomes more vulnerable and her subjectivity more empathic and complex.

While nomadic thought has been critiqued for lacking accountability to a politics of location (Wuthnow 2002, 184), *Locust Girl* invites us to consider whether nomadic thought might provide an embodied framework for nurturing feminist, antiracist, and decolonial senses of place, even as it grapples with the anthropocentric powers of displacement. Amedea's corporeality challenges the Kingdoms' imposed distinction between the human and the nonhuman and their affective structuring of the Strays as bodies of shame. Her difference arouses fear in Beenabe and other Strays. Shining Lumi, a shamanic swindler who deems Amedea's singing a competition, accuses her of being monstrous and marked with "the plague" (Bobis 2015a, 87). By avoiding romantic idealism, the novel addresses how multispecies kinmaking in a human-centric environment is a practice of sustained struggle and negotiation.

Because the locust can sing, it plays a crucial role in recuperating the marginalized group's ability to self-represent, reconnect with ancestral memory, and mobilize new collectivities beyond human frames. While lining up for rations, which the Kingdoms occasionally offer to show mercy, Amedea discredits Shining Lumi, who promises that a skull she owns can sing, though it never does. Hopeful supplicants keep queuing up outside Shining Lumi's tent, paying her with their rations and pleading for her skull to sing out the stories of loved ones who have disappeared. Fearful of committing the Kingdoms' "singingcrime," Shining Lumi shamelessly practices the "crime of hope," spreading rumors that the skull will sing in due time (93). A prophetic old man, Fa-us, exhorts Amedea to disavow rumors—spread by both Shining Lumi and the Kingdoms—with singing:

"Plague them with songs, Child. . . . Rumors are not stories, are not songs. Rumors are in the air and we only catch and copy them, but songs are in the lungs and the throat. . . . And stories are lived in the bones" (54). Amedea's locust, which starts to sing in the voices of the supplicants' lost ones, provokes the Strays' collective singing and transformation. Grandfather Opi, for example, sings about the deep bond they used to have with the natural environment before the drought, remembering the vivid colors, taste of fresh water, golden grains, beautiful stones, and the meat from the animals that once grazed among the green (102). One by one, the despairing supplicants sing out their memories and stories, which fuse into the "longest song after a very long time of silence" (103).

The distinction between song and rumor in the novel parallels the difference Deleuze and Guattari discern between becoming and imitating. "Becoming is never imitating" but the "double": The painter, while painting a bird, can only become-bird to the extent that the bird becomes something else, a pure line or color (1987, 336). Singing, here, is a relational, embodied, and iterative articulation of the self in its intra-active becoming with the world. It rejects the privatization of the future in service of the nation or speculative capitalism, as the Kingdoms' songs and Shinging Lumi's rumors do. Amedea's singing, on the contrary, resurrects the repressed affectivity of the subjugated and frees their relational energy to become nomadic. It reclaims the local desires and struggles for entangled ways of becoming that hold the potential for new alternative solidarities, decolonial futures, and political life against Anthropocene subjectivity. Amedea's individual becoming leads to the Strays' collective becoming and, as the novel's ending reveals, the planetary becoming of the human species.

A planetary cosmopolitics is fully manifested in Amedea's final metamorphosis. Charged with transgressing the border and singing unauthorized songs, Amedea is brought to the Kingdoms' Supreme Court, where the novel reaches its climax. When she refuses to testify against Amedea, Beenabe is killed by outraged citizens. Angry citizens need a criminal to blame, and in order to appease them, Amedea takes on the role of the culprit. She gathers the unheard voices: Her throat swells and her eyes, cheeks, chest, and belly grow, and then her whole body expands, pushed to accommodate "all voices from all sides of the border, both desert and green haven" (Bobis 2015a, 173). The strain of embodying this multiplicity makes her implode and catch fire. She is airborne and comes out of her chrysalis, growing wings and truly becoming the locust girl. The uncanny reappears in this scene: The implosion that is associated with climate combustion and the

Kingdoms' firebombs becomes here a redemptive act of love and sacrifice. Like a phoenix rising from the ashes, Amedea is reborn.

The locust girl's self-sacrifice imagines the planetary impossible. In an interview, Bobis comments that through Amedea's self-immolation she intended to appeal to selfless and unconditional love for others (2015b). Amedea's metamorphosis imagines a nomadic being that cross-fertilizes between biotic and abiotic forces and fuses corporeal desires with earthly energies. This metamorphosis is channeled through fire to offer a queer genealogy of reproduction, at once ancestral and future-oriented, which is not grounded in the sexual logics of reproduction and family, but what releases and intensifies desire into the cosmic or inhuman realm (Clark and Yusoff 2018, 9). The fire's release of the trapped locust from Amedea's human body suggests an emancipation of our subterranean desires and affective organs from their normative indexing, as a way of dismantling the old metaphysics of anthropocentric time and subjectivity in favor of cosmic and multispecies existence. This also leads to the novel's preeminent message—that every one of us harbors a locust within, only waiting to be released. Toward the end of the novel, Bobis addresses readers as deep listeners to the locust's song:

> Can you hear that little flutter?
> It's an insect heart.
> Too close for you?
> Ah, in you.
> Now you know what we've always shared.
> No border can deny it.
> It's small and snug, and not quite hidden.
> Don't despair, it will settle. In you
> It will settle. Like the wind.
> The wind is kind. It leads me home. (Bobis 2015a, 178)

Amedea's self-immolation explores the more-than-human subjectification that implodes the skin of humanism. Her implosion allegorizes a planetary regeneration of the political anatomy of our society through an individual's metamorphosis. Becoming planetary in this aspect is an ethical choice of multiplicity. Yet, while *Locust Girl* calls forth planetary love and idealism into our imagination, this idealism deconstructs itself, deconstructs love, and deconstructs how we care for each other and for the planet. What Bobis reminds the reader, by juxtaposing the Kingdoms' exclusive love for its own citizens and the locust girl's unbiased love for an earthly multitude, is that love is not always ethical. Love asserted in the name of sameness and homogeneity is different from a love that is genuinely open to differences, mutuality, and transformations in the living world. Michael Hardt examines the concept of love as a diving force for social change, by questioning the forms of narcissistic love that exclude difference, conceived in "reactionary political projects" of fascism and nationalism and around conventional identity categories based on class, race, gender, and sexuality (2011, 677). A genuinely political concept of love, Hardt argues, "must transform us, that is, it must designate a becoming such that in love, in our encounter with others we constantly become different" (2011, 678).

In other words, love would involve risk and operate in a relational ontology of multiplicity, vulnerability, and differentiation to engender social transformation. It is with this transformative politics of love that the planetary impossible in *Locust Girl* must be imagined and read. It is also alongside this transformative love that planetarity is a promise devoid of completeness or any finite destination. The border crossing by the nomadic locust girl embodies this notion, demonstrating that hope lies not in a finite endpoint but in the collective and ongoing work of cultivating ethical and compassionate encounters with alterity. In these ethical encounters, difference and otherness cease being a reason for fear, exclusions, or exploitation; they become, rather, the gifts of time in the dynamism of life's possibility.

I have explored *Locust Girl* alongside a nomadic praxis of planetarity, which insists on ecologizing an ethics of alterity toward multispecies futures. With its environmental and pluralist focus, planetarity may appear to be a universal ideal that erases human and species asymmetries, but Bobis's novel demonstrates that a planetary ecology of solidarity does not need to lose political edge. Written from diasporic, feminist, and decolonial concerns for alterity, the speculative poetics of *Locust Girl* develops planetarity as an episteme of differentiation that recovers refugee and Indigenous rights to climate mobility against settler colonial enclosure. The novel's depiction of a post-apocalyptic world of climate ruins implodes colonial racism, exclusive borders, and extractive capitalism—practices that intersect through externalized discourses about climate migration at a time of Western humanist existential crisis. In the uncanny future-as-pasts-to-come, climate change and capitalist competition for resources may resurrect and intensify haunted lives, matters, and landscapes that arise from racial, gender, and species violence, further fragmenting the planet and rendering it spectral.

By insisting on the imperative to nomadize futures, Bobis's novel provokes readerly and social metamorphosis that must be constantly speculated into being. The locust girl embodies a cosmological orientation of our political community through an ontology of movement and borderland consciousness. Her thick mobility recuperates a planetary ethics of alterity and multiplicity that braves anthropocentric fires and militarized borders. In this light, the autopoiesis of the nomadic body is also sympoiesis, a process of becoming-with and making-with a multitude of earthly others in acts of collaborative survival and movement toward building a habitable earth in troubled times (Haraway 2016, 137). In Bobis's novel, we see a double meaning of planetarity: as a political ecology of differentiation that historicizes vulnerability, inequality, and (neo)colonial forms of exploitation; and as a relational ethics of multitude that bridges competing localities and ontological worlds toward shared care for the environment. With this dual vision, Bobis's novel must be shifted away from a multiculturalist interpretation of diasporic fiction and repositioned within a situated practice of planetarity. The situated practice holds open space for literary imaginations, reading methods, and relational existence that may promise more transformative pathways for reworlding a damaged planet. It also attunes us to witnessing and participating in the nomadic movements and metamorphoses that renew diasporic subjectivities and collectivities at "the end of the world."

5

# Global Excess, Planetary Deviance

## *Migrant Workers, Waste, and the Geo-Cyborg*

> For their detractors and haters, immigrants embody—visibly, tangibly, in the flesh—the inarticulate yet hurtful and painful presentiment of their own disposability.
>
> —Zygmunt Bauman, *Wasted Lives*

> The scar on my nail has become a piece of iron taken root inside me. It has a strong permeating power, having entered my body and spread in my blood. It howls, and in the endless long years, imposes inner gravity upon my being. It forces me to bear the weight and walk on.
>
> —Zheng Xiaoqiong, "Iron"

"I'd expected that I would be releasing some of the burdens from my parents, but the truth is, I ended up as their burden," says Shang Jiaojiao, a Chinese migrant worker poisoned by n-hexane. N-hexane, a petroleum-based solvent for cleaning electronics like smartphone touch screens, can cause nerve damage and paralysis with prolonged exposure. Despite its known neurotoxicity, n-hexane is still widely used in electronic factories for faster evaporation and lower cost. Shang is one of many migrant workers featured in *Complicit* (2017), a documentary film directed by Heather White and Lynn Zhang on the chemical exposure by Chinese migrant workers in the global supply chain of technological devices. The film also gives voice to other workers with occupational illnesses, including Yi Yeting, a labor activist who has leukemia from exposure to benzene at Foxconn, a key supplier for Apple and other major brands. Although recognized as a carcinogen, benzene is widely used across manufacturing industries to synthesize various chemicals and consumer products such as plastics, lubricants, detergents, drugs, and pesticides. Chronic exposure poses health risks of leukemia, reproductive harm, and other blood disorders. Despite its general ban as a solvent in worker activities in Western countries, it continues to be used in Chinese factories due to low cost. Workers are at risk of inhaling benzene in the air or absorbing it through their skin.

Shang and Yi represent just the tip of the iceberg of the numerous rural-to-urban Chinese migrant workers, also known as *nongmingong or floating populations*, who arrive in cities young and hopeful, only to have their dreams and health corroded by toxic chemicals, backbreaking labor, unjust compensation, and a discriminatory household registration system. Early in the film, a young worker shares her urban dreams while on a train to Guangzhou, saying, "My dream? My dream was to leave, to leave the countryside and the mountains behind. . . . I imagined it [the city] must be a place like paradise." Yet midway into the film, we see a father and his son suffering from leukemia. They are weary from their struggle to get compensation in the city, and, in the end, the father simply suggests to his ailing son, "Let's go back home." With this juxtaposition the filmmakers invite the viewer to witness the shattered urban dreams of migrant workers. Exploited by corporate avarice and relentless urbanization, Chinese migrant workers tell stories of disposable human populations in the shadows of technological and neoliberal progress. They are laborers at the assembly lines of globalization and the scaffolders of urban infrastructure, yet they remain the unseen masses. Their labor is erased from shiny end products and glimmering skyscrapers, and their rights to urban welfare and belonging are denied. Expropriated yet expendable, they become *excess* humans in the machinery of urban modernity.

The documentary title, *Complicit*, points to a second meaning of excess. As modern culture becomes increasingly fixated on newer and flashier technology, all consumers of smartphones and gadgets are complicit in the biochemical regimes of transnational capitalism that ensure richer countries outsource toxicity, labor exploitation, and waste to poorer countries with less stringent environmental and worker safety regulations. The documentary is particularly poignant when contrasted with an Apple slogan, "Until every thing we touch enhances each life it touches" (Worldwide Developers Conference 2013). But we see a spectral doubling of touch in the film when an n-hexane-poisoned worker recounts, "Wiping is the only thing

I did beside eating and sleeping," and "Sometimes I can wipe over seven hundred [touch]screens a day." This doubling reflects how the embodied act of touch in the digital age mediates chemical intimacies between humans and matters, bodies and systems, and sustenance and excess. Global technological excess operates on two opposing yet interconnected fronts. On one side, in-built obsolescence and infinite upgrades drive consumption. On the other, reckless dumping and throwaway culture pollute our planet's ecosystems and disproportionately harm migrant laborers and communities of color who manufacture and recycle electronics or live near toxic waste. From the extraction of raw materials to production, consumption, and the eventual deluge of electronic waste, the notion of excess make visible a planetary racial and class order in the life cycle of technology. The daily comforts afforded by modern technology are continually expressed in the diseased bodies and toxic environments of migrant and factory workers.

Thinking with e-waste raises ethical concerns about the chemical sociality that emerge between humans, technology, and discard under neoliberal globalization. These complex entanglements of migrant labor, chemical agents, environmental health, industrial capitalism, and government systems animate the "toxic intimacies of empire" at the intersection of molecular and transnational scales (Hsu and Vázquez 2022; Chen 2023). E-waste geographies reveal geosocial formations of techno-capitalism that network on multiple temporal, spatial, and material scales in the Anthropocene. In 2019, for instance, the world produced a staggering 53.6 million metric tonnes of e-waste, a distressing 21 percent increase since 2014, with only 17.4 percent recycled in an environmentally sound manner (Forti et al. 2020, 23). E-waste ranges from large household items like refrigerators, air conditioners, microwaves, and televisions to smaller electronics like laptops, LED lamps, cameras, VR headsets, and mobile phones. These discarded products contain harmful substances like plastics, flame retardants, and toxic chemicals like lead, mercury, cadmium, and PCBs, alongside metals like copper, gold, platinum, and rare earth elements that can be repurposed for commercial use. However, improper or informal recycling of e-waste can lead to toxic pollution of air, water, and soil and pose health hazards to humans and animals.

A prevalent narrative of e-waste and environmental justice has focused on the illegal dumping of toxic waste from the Global North into the Global South. This practice is frequently cited as an example of waste colonialism. Each year, a significant volume of undocumented e-waste is either disposed to landfill or illegally exported from Europe, North America, and

Oceania to vulnerable communities in Asia and Africa. Due to high labor costs and strict environmental laws, wealthier nations tend to ship waste to developing nations, where the waste is disassembled, scavenged, and recycled by informal industries using crude techniques such as open burning and dissolving circuit boards in acid to trace metals (B. Robinson 2009, 184). In an effort to curtail the transboundary movements of hazardous waste, the United Nations established the Basel Convention in 1992. But nations have exploited loopholes to continue the illegal trade. Notorious global e-waste dumping sites include Guiyu in southeast China and Agbogbloshie in Ghana. Embedded informal recycling economies, migrant labor abuse, local corruption, and toxic landscapes make these places hotspots for international journalists and NGOs such as the Basel Action Network (BAN) and Greenpeace to promote environmental activism.

Despite banning e-waste imports in 2000 and facing rising domestic waste, China remained one of the largest recipients of global e-waste by 2013, receiving ongoing shipments from the United States, Europe, South Korea, and Japan for metal recycling (F. Wang et al. 2013, 13). Informal e-waste trade, or "backyard" recycling, remains widespread in China. Many e-waste trade networks and workshops have thrived around electronics manufacturing hubs, notably in Guiyu and Longtang on the Pearl River Delta and Taizhou on the Yangtze River Delta (F. Wang et al. 2013, 22). Despite having caused appalling environmental and health damage, informal recycling remains a vital source of income for the poor in these regions. Before the official ban, Guiyu, a small town in Guangdong province, was dubbed the world's e-waste junkyard. Home to an estimated 150,000 people, including 100,000 migrants, Guiyu harbors over three hundred companies and three thousand household workshops dedicated to e-waste recycling (F. Wang et al. 2013, 22). Migrant workers from outlying agrarian areas in Hunan and Anhui provinces, including women and children, manually process e-waste for as little as USD 1.5 a day (F. Wang et al. 2013, 22). Lacking proper protection, these workers face toxic exposure through inhalation, skin contact, and ingestion of contaminated food and water. The health risks are dire, including lead poisoning, cancer, birth defects, and organ damage. By proximity to waste, they bear its indelible mark. Guiyu's ecosystems suffer too, as numerous studies report high concentrations of heavy metals in air, water, soil, fish, riverbank sediment, waterbirds, crops, and vegetables. Meanwhile, many local businessmen have moved out of Guiyu, avoiding hazardous environment and overseeing the work from a distance (Mujezinovic 2019).

Migrant workers in China cast plural understandings of environmental justice onto the relational chemicality of waste, defamiliarizing the North-to-South dumping narrative with complex e-waste geographies. A reductive storyline of global dumping obscures how state-led development and class hierarchies in Asia and Africa displace rural populations and landscapes. The socioeconomic infrastructures within Guiyu, for instance, intersect with global environmental injustice, revealing the local-global networks behind China's rise to world power. With China overtaking the United States as the largest e-waste generator in 2016, much of the e-waste in Guiyu now comes from domestic discards and internal flows (K. Wang et al. 2020, 5). As a hub of transnational capital and export-led factories of electronics, textiles, and toys, Guangdong province relies on migrant labor and e-waste recycling to facilitate its participation in transnational capital. Having transformed Guiyu from agricultural impoverishment to industrial prosperity, e-waste has proven to be an economic mainstay for developmentalist local authorities and communities. In this context, e-waste is not just a repository of toxins but also a source of resources, secondary manufacturing materials, and sustenance. Waste sociality thus emerges from situated and dynamic knowledge-making practices that define what is waste, value, and justice in specific contexts.

Against the slow violence of e-waste toxicity, it is important to make visible the stories of dispossessed communities for the sake of environmental justice. The politics of visibility, however, may not be as straightforward as it seems. In his analysis of photographs of e-waste salvagers in Agbogbloshie such as those in *Permanent Error* by photographer Pieter Hugo, Cajetan Iheka describes the slipperiness between witnessing and repression in the function of the camera, explaining that while images can give visibility to marginalized individuals, they can also fix them in static narratives that overlook their complexity (2017, 79). He emphasizes that naming subjects is a helpful practice to counter homogeneity and foreground singularity. This contradiction described by Iheka is present in the media representation of Guiyu. Photographs of workers or innocent Chinese children sitting among mountains of e-waste cables and circuit boards frequently appear in the campaigns of environmental organizations such as BAN and Greenpeace. Despite their humanitarian intentions, these campaigns often produce images that obscure individual names and subjectivities. In doing so, they inadvertently contribute to a pathologizing tendency in global environmental justice narratives, one that risks framing people of color and migrant workers as passive victims without agency.

Environmental NGOs and international media often portray e-waste as toxic pollutants resulting from North-to-South dumping. But local communities participating in the e-waste economy frequently view it as a valuable resource for economic survival. This friction invites us to register competing worldings of environmental justice, where normative environmentalist narratives of able-bodiedness, victimhood, and fast hope need to be reconfigured through the situated human-waste sociality in local lived ecologies. For instance, in a study on Guiyu, locals for whom green NGOs advocate have sometimes resisted outside attention and representation. One waste worker remarked, "There is pollution everywhere. . . . Why must they keep jostling with Guiyu?" (K. Wang et al. 2020, 2177). Of relevance here is Karen Thornber's concept of "ecoambiguity," which examines people's complex and contradictory attitudes toward environmental harm globally, with particular attention to modernizing nations in East Asia (2012). A straight opposition between environmental pollution and economic development is nuanced by the ambiguity of pragmatic acquiescence here, where Guiyu locals are not indifferent to the harm but see it as a "normal" part of life, aware of the toxicity while relying on it for survival. Other scholars have discussed the "art of unnoticing" among many Chinese people, where apparent apathy toward, deliberate ignorance of, or complicity with petrochemical pollution may be interpreted not as docile acceptance but as small steps at reclaiming agency in precarious lifeworlds (Lou 2022).

When considering the vexed figure of the e-waste worker, we need to consider Christof Mauch's concept of "slow hope" to expand our understanding of environmental justice beyond a fixation on doom (2019). If we listen carefully to the untold stories of slow hope, we should realize that intoxicated communities may negotiate agency in delayed and contextual ways, much as the slow violence and toxic exposure they experience has been multiscalar and accumulative. Slow hope suggests a situated approach to justice and hope to account for distributed agency and ecological afterlives in toxic landscapes. Slowness itself can be a biopolitical instrument of violence and a necessary rhythm of survival. In moving beyond damage-based research, Michelle Murphy uses "alterlife" to index not only forms of life systematically harmed by chemical exposures, but also "being in the mess of consumption, subsistence, and side effect" and "being in the contradictions of existing in worlds that demand chemical exposures as the conditions for eating, drinking, breathing" (2017, 497). An altered life is also a life open to alteration, and these molecular entanglements of capitalism shape both vulnerabilities and potentials of future life (Murphy 2017,

497). The challenge of slow hope thus calls forth a slow activism, one that simultaneously aims to dismantle the infrastructures of capitalist techno-modernity that trash and transmute racial and working-class bodies while also noticing micro, modest, and grassroots attempts at continued survival in more-than-human networks.

An important decolonial inquiry is to shine light not merely on e-waste's toxic damage but also on the infrastructures that consistently institute its toxicology. As Zygmunt Bauman points out, wasted humans and human waste are inevitable by-products of modern *order-building*—wherein "each order casts some parts of the extant population as 'out of place,' 'unfit' or 'undesirable'"—and of *economic progress*, which cannot advance without devaluing formerly effective ways of life and stripping their practitioners of means of subsistence (2004, 5). Bauman's words echo Mary Douglas's famous argument in *Purity and Danger*: "Dirt is the by-product of a systematic ordering and classification of matter, in so far as ordering involves rejecting inappropriate elements" (1966, 36). Dirt exists in the eyes of the beholder. Waste is thus not an isolated phenomenon; it always points to a system behind it.

Migrant workers and e-waste, as two expressions of excess in modernity, illustrate how attention to discard and contamination posits questions about the dominant economic and political order. Waste, whether human or nonhuman, is not a given category with intrinsic qualities; rather, it manifests systems of power and control in society. E-waste and toxic exposure materialize the contradictions of industrial capitalism's relentless pursuit of technological advancement, characterized by planned obsolescence, profit-driven depravity, and resource extraction. Migrant workers, alongside refugees and other marginalized communities, are displaced by capitalist global modernity that renders certain populations destitute and uprooted, imposes classifications of subjecthood and citizenship, and establishes boundaries between the desirable and the abject. Migrant bodies and waste shine light on the political processes of becoming superfluous, as they play an instrumental role in how the dominant discourse defines order and progress.

But waste also embodies ambivalence and transmutation. Bauman describes waste as "the midwife of all creation" and "a unique blend of attraction and repulsion" that evokes both awe and fear (2004, 22). The insatiable appetite for new designs in modern society promotes the transmutation and alienation of waste, which paradoxically signals both the thrilling sign of progress and a threatening return of what is left behind. As a result, waste must be disposed and made invisible to maintain the illusion of progress. In progressive narratives, human waste or wasted humans must be separated from the embodied self and kept at a distance to preserve the hygiene and desirability of modern lifestyles, precisely because waste carries a surplus to identity that can transgress orders. Bauman aptly explains that immigrants embody the anxieties of modernity because, to their detractors and haters, they "embody—visibly, tangibly, in the flesh—the inarticulate yet hurtful and painful presentiment of their own disposability" (2004, 56). This is reflected in the forced demolition of migrant slum villages and ghettos in major Chinese cities like Beijing, Shanghai, and Shenzhen that owe much of their growth to migrant labor. The growing mass of waste is a disturbing reminder to the modern psyche, epitomizing both modernity's compulsive drive for progress and the precariousness and disposability of progress itself.

Deviance is a potent and layered concept to make ecological and political interventions. I have turned to the notion of deviance in order to move beyond a dichotomy of domination and damage toward alternative ways of conceiving excess as capitalist modernity's inherent contradictions—contradictions that give rise to uneven ecologies, feral effects, and chemical alterlives. Deviant phenomena of toxicity, chemical exposure, and environmental illness are permeable, leaky, and unwanted reminders of order's untidiness. Toxicity itself can be viewed as a form of excess, by dismantling consumer capitalist myths of separating product from waste. Deviance alerts us to paradoxes: On one hand, it betrays modernity's risky designs that brew precarious and toxic modes of life; on the other, it expresses unruly material agencies and molecular animacies that elude biopolitical and technological control. Deviance figures the migrant worker in distributed agencies that require situated ethical obligations to make visible the toxic intimacies in local, national, and global networks. Traversing bodies and chemicals, organisms and machines, and products and waste, migrant worker ecologies help us unearth the circulatory flows of toxic substances and the racial and class grammars of inhuman subjection. Attuning to these entanglements presents ethico-political possibilities for imagining unexpected forms of survival.

### The Geo-Cyborg: Transversal Thinking in the Technocene

Migrant worker ecologies shed multiscalar, heterotemporal, and transversal perspectives into the accelerated crossover between the globe and the planet in an epoch of self-devouring growth. They bring into focus the simultaneous processes of excess and deviance that characterize naturecultures of the Technocene. As technology continues to shape modern existence, the global technosphere wreaks profound geologic damage by consuming energy on an unprecedented scale, far exceeding its capacity to recycle waste and carbon. The geologic processes of technology are noted by Peter Haff, who adopts the term "technosphere" to describe humanity's enmeshment in an "interlinked set of communication, transportation, bureaucratic and other systems" that metabolize fossil fuels and extract the earth's energy resources at an enormous magnitude, but which has thus far failed to effectively recycle its own waste (2004, 395). Modern technologies' reliance on natural resource extraction, and their failure to adequately address waste and pollution, make them a geomorphic force of the earth's history. The future time of technology folds into geologic time.

The simultaneity of excess and deviance in the Technocene gives rise to a new planetary figure—what I call the *geo-cyborg*—a posthuman cultural imaginary that acknowledges the generative kinship between increasingly integrated categories: the globe and the planet, the technosphere and the geobiosphere, mechanism and organism, product and waste. If the Anthropocene announces humanity's geologic agency mobilized by capital and technology, then the geo-cyborg captures at once the promise and the debris of human hubris. Capitalist extraction and technological development profoundly alter the earth's ecosystems, enfolding plastics, carbon, and petrochemicals into geologic strata. The geo-cyborg embodies the inhuman intimacies and becomings of technological subjects, where extraction converges with sedimentation and deep time seeps into the human accumulation of product and capital. As Yusoff reminds us, becoming geologic helps us conceptualize a more ecologically excessive notion of subjectivity, one that abandons discrete, identity-making subjects to open life to nonhuman and inhuman forces (2013, 384). Inspired by Yusoff's use of "geosocial strata" to explore "the structures of exchange between geologic strata and social worlds" (2017, 105). I invoke the geo-cyborg as a geosocial figure that articulates how ecological subjectivities emerge from the geomorphic acts of techno-capitalism. The geo-cyborg charts transversal, ghostly, and porous crossings between human and inhuman worlds. It disrupts the linear tempo of modern technoculture and excavates the stratified surplus of colonial racial histories and capitalist world ecology.

Thinking with the geo-cyborg allows me to collapse the boundaries between *geos*, *bios*, and machine, while acknowledging that planetary backfires are unevenly felt. Thus, the *migrant worker geo-cyborg* sits at the ethical and political contact zone between transnational labor and incalculable risks, expanding a politics of location by attending to molecular movements across colonial racial powers, surplus value production, biological bodies, petrochemical toxins, and technology. Queering normative notions of commodity and waste, the migrant worker geo-cyborg assembles a temporal, spatial, and material realm of transmutation and a political ecology that embodies the inhuman socialities of techno-capitalism. It speaks of human, mineralogical, and ecological ghosts in the machine, foreshadowing the future return of our inhuman beginnings. Centering the geo-cyborg affirms how the world altered by techno-capitalism is not closed but remains open. Embodying modernity's elation and fear, the geo-cyborg is planetary deviance rewriting the stories of global success and excess.

The geo-cyborg intervenes in scholarly discourses on labor, matter, and posthuman ethics. Donna Haraway's "The Cyborg Manifesto," Karen Barad's "agential realism," and Stacy Alaimo's "transcorporeality" offer insights into a posthuman ethics. Haraway's cyborg illuminates both the global grid of technological control over the planet, including the domination, appropriation, and abstraction of bodies such as female factory workers, and the subversive potential of impure identities to resist biopolitical hierarchies (1991, 154). The cyborg can reinforce or transform racial, class, and gender structures, contingent upon the ethical values embedded in its creation and evolution. In a similarly dynamic account of power structures, Barad sees apparatuses as iteratively reproduced and contested through the intra-activity of matter and meaning. Despite pessimistic views of Fordist assembly lines, Barad suggests that factory materiality is neither immutable nor fixed but is continually reshaped by "human, nonhuman, and cyborgian forms of agency" (2007, 238). Referencing Leela Fernandes's *Producing Workers*, Barad points out that capitalist spaces like jute mills are constrained yet not fully determined, as workers, machines, managers, materials, and environs relationally constitute each other. This perspective invites a posthuman ethics that reworks boundaries, including unjust and toxic labor conditions, by revealing the more-than-human agencies embedded within industrial sites. Expanding on the intra-activity of bodies and places, Alaimo develops a transcorporeal ethics that configures humans as made by "an ever-emergent world of risky knowledge, mangle practices, and disturbing, potentially deviant material agencies" (2010, 116). Transcorporeality calls for an ethics of exposure and emergence accountable to a material world that is not external but is always the very substance of more-than-human existence.

Taken together, these theories are helpful for understanding migrant workers and their environments as sites of emergent material intra-activity and assemblages of labor, technology, and nature. A posthumanist ethics of the geo-cyborg insists on accounting for the entangled, contingent, and inhuman kinds of agency for reworking hegemonic colonial, racial, class, and gender structures. When viewed iteratively, the geo-cyborg reveals how planetarity emerges not from an external place but from reorienting the human to the plural temporalities, technological mediations, and material agencies that make up the liveliness of worlds. As a corporeal amalgamation of planetary forces and global infrastructures, the geo-cyborg invites an ethical stance responsive to the uneven biochemical intimacies of technological planetarization and the lived creation of cyborgian and mineralogical agencies at the grassroots level. An eco-ethics of alterity and interdependence proves useful here, as responsibility entails rethinking what is excluded from mattering, including migrant workers' worldmaking practices and the toxic transcorporeality of techno-capitalism. Toxicity dissolves individual boundaries to reveal techno-planetary formations, while it also demands an onto-epistemic humility toward dispersed flows that may exceed technoscientific measure. For migrant workers, latent, slow, and accumulated toxicities shape the lived precarities of industrial capitalism and racialized labor.

What literary and cultural forms can the geo-cyborg assume? How are migrant workers enmeshed within deep time? This chapter explores the recalcitrant materiality of migrant worker geo-cyborgs in Chinese writers Zheng Xiaoqiong's poetry and prose and Chen Qiufan's science fiction novel *Waste Tide*. These literary works provide platforms for examining how neoliberal capitalism seeks to discipline migrant laborers into passive cyborgs, denying their self-realization through modern progressive narratives of racial and class excess. The migrant geo-cyborg characters portrayed by Zheng and Chen, however, subvert the linearity of techno-capitalism that alienates bodies and ecosystems for surplus value extraction. Instead, they embody an unruly geosocial corporeality that transmutes across *geos*, *bios*, and machine. Rather than embodying solely utopian or dystopian qualities, the migrant geo-cyborg carries an ambiguity and frames deviance as simultaneous manifestations of toxic exposure and the potential for alterlife. These selected works invite multiple interpretive frames—molecular intimacies of empire, toxic waste and slow violence, becoming geologic, plural Anthropocene temporalities, technological doubleness, and posthuman ethics—suggesting the geo-cyborg as a pertinent cultural imaginary for articulating the multifaceted nature of planetary challenges in the Technocene. By tracing the accelerating exchanges between global excess and planetary deviance in the neoliberal age, this chapter develops the geo-cyborg to examine the geosocial processes where human progress is continually extracted at the expense of promised futures.

## Zheng Xiaoqiong's Assembling and Disassembling the Migrant Worker Geo-Cyborg

"If there is a traffic jam on the highway from Dongguan to Shenzhen, 70% of the world's computers will suffer a shortage of electronic parts," remarked Li Zupan, IBM's deputy general manager for the Asia Pacific in 2000 (Yu 2021). Li's comment quickly gained popularity, adding to the many epithets of Dongguan, a leading export and manufacturing city known as "the world factory." Nestled in the Pearl River Delta, near metropolises like Guangzhou, Shenzhen, and Hong Kong, Dongguan has transformed dramatically since the reform and opening-up policy of 1978. It has changed from "the land of fish and rice" to a booming hub for manufacturing and foreign investment. As of 2018, Dongguan boasted over one million registered factories across various industries, from labor-intensive industries like electronics, textiles, and toys to advanced sectors including smartphones and robotics (Keegan 2018). Once known for the Imperial Qing dynasty's destruction of British opium, Dongguan is now ranked as one of China's top investment cities for multinational companies ("Dongguan" 2022). It becomes a hub for major corporations such as Nokia, Samsung, Philips, Foxconn, and Nestle, alongside Chinese tech firms Huawei, Oppo, and Vivo. In state and online media, Dongguan's success is often quantified in impressive numbers: "One in five computers in the world is made in Dongguan," "One in five sweaters in the world is made in Dongguan," "One in four smartphones in the world is made in Dongguan" ("World's Factory" 2007), and "Dongguan's GDP surpassed one trillion yuan in 2021" ("GDP" 2022).

The quantification of Dongguan's industrial success circulates a celebratory narrative of China's rise that shadows the human and environmental tolls of rapid urbanization. The city's impressive production statistics mask the experiences of migrant workers who reveal histories of displacement and precarity behind capitalist expansion. Since the 1980s, China's embrace of global capitalism and pursuit of consumer materialism have driven the mass mobilization of hundreds of millions of rural migrants. Despite supporting urban economies and lifestyles, these migrants remain excluded from the middle-class prosperity they help create. In 2023 alone, an estimated 297.53 million migrant workers participated in China's internal migration (National Bureau of Statistics 2024). Manufacturing centers like Shen Zhen and Dongguan host a migrant population that far outweighs the size of their local urban populations. In 2017, Dongguan had 6.26 million migrant workers, comprising 75.78% of the total population and nearly triple the size of the local population (Du et al. 2020, 4).

The structural inequalities in China, particularly the *hukou* (household registration) system, pose barriers for rural migrants seeking to settle in cities. The *hukou* system segregates the population by their rural or urban origins and limits access to public services and social welfare for those without an urban *hukou*. This institution keeps rural migrants in a state of mobility, relegating them to a floating, transient, and expendable underclass confined to the margins of urban spaces in slum villages and industrial sweatshops. In Zhou Xiaojing's study, slum villages, factory cities, and hollow home villages are parts of emergent "migrant landscapes" in China that expose the incremental destruction of agricultural communities and nonhuman habitats, a geography of slow violence that remains invisible in official narratives of modern miracles (2017, 276). Within these landscapes lie untold stories of migrant workers' dreams, family separation, and experiences of "loss, alienation, and exile," which are structurally produced by local, regional, and transnational networks of capital, labor, materials, and products (Zhou 2017, 279).

Given structural constraints like the *hukou* system, what factors continuously draw rural migrants to cities? Besides economic incentives, a significant impetus is the cultural representation of migration within Chinese official discourse, which propagates an urban-rural binary to legitimize developmentalism. The association of the countryside with backwardness is potent in the Chinese urban imagination, wherein rural migrants are often scapegoated for "rising crime rates, moral depravity, public health and hygiene concerns, and many other contemporary social ills" (Dooling 2017, 137). This urban bias serves to defend against the perceived threat of migrant liminality to urban senses of place. It also reflects how postsocialist China defines ideal citizenship by perpetuating urban-rural differences and essentializing peasantry as morally and culturally inferior. Scholars have examined how the concept of *suzhi*, or modern civility, has been neoliberalized in Chinese state discourse as a biopolitical technology to stigmatize and commodify rural migrant bodies within the market economy. As Yan Hairong suggests, Chinese governing elites, state media, and poverty-relief campaigns derogate rural migrants as lacking *suzhi* and in need of employment and discipline for the sake of civilization (2003, 494). This rhetoric subsumes heterogeneous individualities under a universal discourse of human development, which then normalizes the capitalist extraction of surplus value from migrant labor. It also privatizes structural inequality as a matter of individual responsibility and moral pressure.

Moreover, a developmentalist discourse might influence migrant workers' self-perception of rural identity and mobility. In *Made in China* (2005), Pun Ngai traces the production of social desire through ethnographic interviews with young, unmarried women migrant workers, known as *dagongmei*. Her study reveals how these women migrant workers view the modern city as a space for economic necessity, self-growth, and opportunities to challenge patriarchy, despite their awareness of the deplorable conditions of factory life (2005, 66–67). Ngai focuses on migrant workers' own knowledge practices and their active making of gender, class, and community, including practices that sometimes reinforce dominant ideologies. Considering the workers' own worldmaking practices broadens avenues for negotiating and remaking the politics ecology of global factories, where overlapping state, capital, and patriarchal structures seek to mechanize the ecologies, bodies, affects, and subjectivities of Chinese migrant workers for capitalist reproduction.

If Dongguan's label as a "migrant workers' paradise" is a neoliberal facade that conceals structural inequalities under the veneer of economic promise, then Zheng Xiaoqiong's poetry and prose offers a counternarrative grounded in grassroots modernity. Born in rural Sichun province, Zheng moved to Dongguan in 2001, where she spent seven years working as a migrant laborer on assembly lines in various factories before transitioning to a literary career. Her work resists a seamless narrative of neoliberal triumph by illuminating the corporeal and ecological excesses inherent in migrant bodies and ecologies that surpass industrial mechanization. Drawing on her lived experiences in furniture, hardware, and plastic factories, Zheng transforms these insights into flesh-cutting and powerful verses that cast globalization and urbanization against a backdrop of migrant exploitation, industrial illness, and environmental loss. She portrays production as inextricably linked with destruction and waste. Industrial terraforming displaces peasants and rural landscapes, while the making of the docile and disciplined worker's body necessitates the unmaking of the lived and ecological body. I argue that this dual process of manufacturing and discarding positions the migrant workers in her ecopoetics as geo-cyborg figures—geosocial beings who embody the transversal contradictions of industrial capitalism and challenge the linear myths of forward time and relentless growth.

In the poem "A Female Migrant Worker, Youth Confined in a Seat on the Assembly Line," Zheng traces the impacts of global capitalism by depicting the journey of a young woman from an inland village to the assembly line of a costal factory. There the woman worker is "fixing her dreams and youth on a product" that eventually ends up on a store shelf in the United States (2016, 98). The disembodied product of globalization is manufactured through this female migrant worker's body in the forms of her lost youth, exhaustion, diseased lungs, irregular menstruation, convulsive coughs, and red, swollen eyes. Parallel to the worker's diseased body, "green lychee trees" are felled by machines to create development zones and new factories. In this short poem, attention is drawn to the mobile entanglements within the factory that enmesh the woman migrant worker in a web of social and environmental injustices, local and global movements, and technical and material agencies. Zheng makes visible these thick mobilities and networks of globalization that are often obscured and depoliticized from the perspective of consumers.

Consider the poem "Disassemble," which intertwines the processes of assembly (putting together) and disassembly (taking apart):

> I disassemble my bones, soul, flesh, blood, and heartbeat
> Into screws, film, plastic articles, splinters, and hooks
> Which are assembled, recombined, labeled. I disassemble my
>     childhood
> Into illusory memories, times past, and emotions. I disassemble
>     my
>     dreams
> Into tears and disappointment, my body into illness and love
> I disassemble blueprints into products, wages, overtime, IOU
>     chits, and
>     insomnia.
> So, too, do I disassemble the three-dimensional society into flat
>     disasters, villages, and homesickness.
> . . . . . .
> How did the diseases of industry penetrate our bodies?

This tribulation belongs to our times, or to the masses.
But I still love deeply this age of industry, the industrial hardware
factory,
Love its wheels, wings, the bearings of motor vehicles,
Love the clarity of pain it brings me, the happiness and
misfortune.
In this era I will disassemble myself into springs,
Switch valves, wires, steel needles, and a street lamp.
I'll return again to the furnace to forge myself
Into shape, to hack myself into one sharp nail
To be nailed to the wall of our era. (2007, 107)

This poem assembles and disassembles the migrant worker's body across movements of making and unmaking, building and rusting, industry and individuality, and production and waste. It portrays how the production process in a hardware factory simultaneously erodes the health, aspirations, and individuality of the worker. The finished products are sedimented with the sweat and tears of laboring bodies. The poet denounces how industrial capitalism flattens the "three-dimensional society" and reduces the cultural memories of vernacular landscapes to mere functional blueprints. By juxtaposing incommensurate temporalities, inhabited time and capitalist time, the poem mourns the alienation of migrant workers from the landscape and its once meaningful web of physical and spiritual life. Zheng invokes an aesthetics of the industrial sublime in a way reminiscent of Edward Burtynsky's epic photographs about toxic landscapes. While both Zheng and Burtynsky can be said to use infrastructural criticism to orient the audience to a paradoxical sense of awe and horror at the monumental scale of industrial processes and ruins, Zheng's poem brings an embodied intimacy to bear on these vast scales of industrial spectacle, disassembling the body from within.

Zheng's use of poetic forms above, including enjambment, collage, and parallelism, builds a cumulative yet fragmented tempo that conveys the relentless process of physical and metaphorical disassembly in the context of industrial labor. The use of enjambment, or incomplete syntax at the end of a line, functions to depict the disjointed and repetitive labor of the migrant worker who assembles mundane mechanical objects like "screws, film, plastic articles, splinters, and hooks," each fragment disconnected from a coherent whole. Moving from industrial hardware to embodied experiences of dreams, insomnia, and homesickness, however, the poem also rehumanizes the affective and embodied experiences of migrant workers against industrial dehumanization. The poem's collage of industrial materials invites an ecocritical reading: It lampoons the commodity fetishism of consumer culture, reflects how the value and appeal of products are detached from the migrant labor and landscapes involved in their creation, and calls for distributed accountability for the toxic materialities that remain inconspicuous until they accumulate and gain size.

Yet we can hear slow hope in this poem. The concluding lines shift from a sense of defeat to reclamation of agency, as the speaker shifts from victimhood to dissent. Instead of succumbing to the industrial machinery's violent infiltration, causing disease and homesickness, her body becomes a site of resistance. The intra-action between human and nonhuman bodies suggests that the worker is not simply a passive victim but an active participant reshaping her relationships with the material world. This subversion is expressed in how the worker retains capacity for love, pain, and willingness to be reforged, which are qualities that industrial processes cannot fully eradicate. The speaker expresses a contradictory love for the industrial age that acknowledges both suffering and a kind of purpose. The final line crystallizes this defiance: the worker's body transmutes into a "sharp nail" that punctures the industrial wall designed to flatten, segregate, and obliterate individuals, communities, and ecosystems. The wayward nail offers a powerful metaphor for the worker's lingering agency to leave a mark on the system even as it seeks to erase those who sustain it.

The concept of the migrant geo-cyborg raises questions about how capitalist technologies separate geologic (*geos*) and biophysical (*bios*) entities by reducing them to inanimate matters for value extraction. This separation is evident in the disciplining of cyborg-like laborers in China's pursuit of transnational capital. Migrant workers on assembly lines are subjected to a system of "automatism" that treats them like machines, distorting and producing their relationship with natural and social environments (Gong 2018, 261). In reading Zheng's poetry below, we can notice the ways she reinterprets capitalist production as an ongoing environmental phenomenon, where the artificial division between *geos*, *bios*, and machines enforced by capitalist biopolitics is contested through the intra-activities and eco-mobilities of bodies, places, matters, and toxins. The separation between life and nonlife, or what Povinelli calls geontopower (2016, 5), reflects a capitalist governance of existence that intensifies under China's neoliberal market economy, where laboring bodies and mineral deposits are rendered extractable as industrial components. As the worker and the machine become interchangeable units of capitalist production, distinctions between life and nonlife, production and stratification, and extraction and erosion no longer hold in the Anthropocene, but industrial capital seeks to police these boundaries for profit.

At the same time, Zheng's poetry reveals how the material collapse between *geos*, *bios*, and machines is unevenly distributed along colonial and racial lines. The artificial distinction between animate and inanimate matter does not just structure industrial labor but also informs the biopolitical governance of bodies deemed disposable under racial capitalism. The concept of animacy remains pertinent here. As discussed earlier, Mel Chen has explored how animacy hierarchies expose perceptions of life and agency within biopolitical institutions of race, sexuality, and health. Chen explains that the racialization of toxins functions to debilitate people of color as "self-perpetuating," "de-sentient," "poorly judging subjects," and "subjects whose subjectivity is alienable or insufficient" (2023, 43). This racialized pathology has deep colonial roots, manifesting throughout history, from the Yellow Peril fears of the nineteenth century to the Covid-19 pandemic of 2019, during which Chinese and Asian peoples were accused as a sort of contamination, morally threatening, and less than human. Racialization thus obscures global environmental injustice and systemic inequalities, denying the networked transnational mobility and accountability of toxins that render colored bodies and Global South communities expendable.

Zheng's poetics decolonizes the discourse of racial pathology by depicting how Chinese migrant worker ecologies reanimate toxic substances as part of a broader ecological entanglement, comprising of the molecular and geomorphic intimacies, scales, and accountabilities of transnational capital. In this light, her work poetically enriches our understanding of how capital accumulation, power relations, and the web of life are co-produced in historical processes, or what Moore terms capitalist world-ecology (3). In the following, I explore three relational narrative strategies within Zheng's ecopoetics that foster alternatives of geosocial thinking and planetary deviance within capitalist world-ecology: first, recuperating the material agency of geologic elements from industrial coding and restoring the mineralogical subjectivities of migrant workers as a means for claiming distributed agency; second, rendering visible disavowed illnesses, injuries, and toxic exposures to question the biochemical regimes of globalization; and, finally, forging alliances between female migrant worker bodies and earth bodies to call for an ecofeminist collective against intersecting forms of injustice.

Iron, a geologic mineral and chemical element, appears repeatedly in Zheng's work as a metal emblematic of the industrial age. In her contemplation, iron is geontological because it embodies the material-discursive agency of industrial processes—cold, hard, and unyielding—violently distinguishing between the lively and inert while reshaping lives and landscapes in the name of growth. In her prose piece "Iron," Zheng depicts it as the knife of industrialization: "Iron often cuts through country with its hardness and coldness, and country suffers pain" (2018). The extraction and manipulation of iron reflects the modern capitalist drive to tame molecules into pliable matter. In a metalwork factory scene, Zheng describes ironwork: "There I saw pieces of hard iron twist and turn, being cut, bifurcated, drilled, curled, ground, into products of required shapes, sizes, and thickness" (2018). The transformation of iron is directly tied to capitalist production in the web of life, as the "becoming iron" of migrant workers and natural ecosystems embodies the inhuman forces of industrial order building. In another poem, "Life," a worker's "shadow of fatigue on the machine . . . moves slowly / Turns around, bends, as dumb as a piece of cast iron" (2007, 102). Here migrant workers become extensions of the industrial apparatus. In "A Female Migrant Worker," the poet observes that "the moon rusting on the machine / is haggard, hazy, opaque" (2016, 98). These poetic images of iron shadows and a rusty moon conjure a mechanized mode of existence, where industrial geontopowers reproduce by siphoning the vitality of life and matter that are exposed to the relentless cycle of production.

Meanwhile, Zheng reimagines iron as a geopolitical and geosocial matter of the Capitalocene, which bridges the living and the dead, industrial future and geologic past, and beginning and becoming. Iron is imbued with geomorphic agency that can shift humans from global agents to planetary subjects. Vital to human and animal health, iron embodies our earthly ancestry and mineral kinship. In "Iron," the chilling sound of iron being cut resonates as the mineral's protest against industrial manipulation, a sentiment Zheng perceives as an earthly outcry: "I had firmly believed the cacophonous and chaotic sound was iron's struggle and scream in breaking" (2018). Hence iron, alongside other industrial matters, assembles the mineralogical, geologic, and inhuman becoming of the migrant worker, as Zheng expresses a visceral connection: "I felt that the sound was coming from my bones, and the unwieldy machines was slicing my body, my soul" (2018). The narrative stages an intersection between the inhuman forces of industrial capitalism and the inhuman origins of human existence to suggest a queer coupling: the becoming geo-cyborg of the migrant worker. This geologic solidarity aligns iron and the worker in collective pain and scream against capitalist capture, invoking a geopoetics of migrant worker activism by forming a mineralogical alliance with the very substance of the earth.

Illnesses, injuries, and toxicity are mobile and deviant by-products of industrial capitalism. Machine-swallowed body parts of migrant workers emerge as ghostly residues that haunt the assumed singular future of modern progress. Zheng depicts the uneven allocation of harm and risk to vulnerable bodies. She recounts an incident where her fingernail was sliced by a lathe cutter, leading to an encounter in the hospital with other workers who had maimed fingers, hands, legs, or heads. The workers' pain is acute and unending, as she observes: "Such pain was violent, cacophonous, penetrating their bones, their souls, and they were to live with this pain forever hanging over them" (2018). This bodily damage darkens their future, while their moaning is iron-clamped by a work-injury compensation system in China described by some as currently more ornamental than adequate (Sun 2014, 56).

Zheng calls attention to the permeable and often unpredictable movement of interchanges across biological bodies, places, and matters. In the poem "Lungs," the migrant worker's body emerges as a filter for industrial pollutants: "Moving in his body are welding dust, lead dust, cement dust. . . . His diseased lungs are wheezing violently in this industrial age" (2016, 101). The fated, rotting, clogged lungs of the working class are as much an environmental illness as they are a social and institutional malaise. Alaimo's notion of "the proletarian lung" calls for situated, transcorporeal analyses of lasting structures of class, race, and gender that are irreducible to a medical discourse (2010, 28). Similarly, Zheng situates Chinese migrant workers' occupational illness and environmental health within intersectional structures of capitalism, race, and class, while showing how their wounded health and unmappable pain exceed the grasp of institutions that seek to measure, contain, or even compensate them.

The phenomenon of female migrant workers in China sheds light on the environmental and labor inequalities at the intersection of globalization, urbanization, and patriarchy. Local and transnational capital colludes with patriarchal norms and the *hukou* system to maximize labor extraction from the *dagongmei*, who often subsume their prime years, typically between eighteen and twenty-five, to urban factories before facing family and societal expectations of marriage and reproduction (Ngai 2005, 6). The growth of unskilled, labor-intensive, and low-paid industries such as electronics, garments, and toy production in the Pearl River Delta shows a preference for hiring young female laborers. These women are "less likely to get pregnant, more willing to work long hours, have nimble fingers," and are "less experienced in asking for their statutory rights" (*China Labor Bulletin* 2004). Beyond global factories, *dagongmei* find employment in fields like the service industry, massage, and the underground sex industry. Motivated by factors like money, independence, and flexibility, many *dagongmei* transition, either voluntarily or under duress, from factory work to sex work. This transition makes them vulnerable to negative social perceptions, physical violence, sexual harassment, and venereal diseases (Tsang 2018, 897). The sexual exploitation of *dagongmei* is also a transnational operation. In cities like Dongguan, the ascent of global capital has been accompanied by a booming sexscape where businessmen from Taiwan and Hong Kong visit for sex services or keep mistresses. These intersecting class and sexual relations turn the bodies of female migrant workers into sites of contestation, which are shaped by local and global forces, tradition and change, as well as individual and collective aspirations in a rapidly globalizing China.

Zheng frequently invokes imagery that entangles female and earth bodies to interrogate the gendered violence of patriarchal capitalism. This strategy recurs throughout her work as an inquiry into how the hegemony of industrial time overrides other temporalities like ecological seasonal cycles and female workers' bodily rhythms. Mechanical clock time obstructs "the ferocious river of the female body" wherein "confused tides no longer fluctuate according to season" (Zheng 2016, 98). In "Screaming Earthworms," she calls attention to capitalist cyborgism by using natural images to reimagine women migrant workers: "a dormant earthworm" with arteries blocked by urban concrete (2016, 99), "a gold mine" drained, excavated, and eroticized by the glittering "masculine metropolis" (99), and "a plum tree with syphilis and venereal diseases" sown by an emerging market economy (100). These images demonstrate that while women and the earth support the city's foundation, they are pushed downward as the city rises. The poet's figurative transmutation of the woman's body into a screaming earthworm also counters normative narratives of resistance that disregard or trivialize modest, persistent, and micro-acts of transgression. These mirco-acts of defiance may manifest in female workers' "dream, scream, and bodily pain" (Ngai 2005, 166). The scream, existing in the liminality between the conscious and the unconscious, between self and world, is an authentic act of resistance, a means of self-extension, and a testament to the female migrant worker's struggle to "realize a worn-out body" (Ngai

2005, 187). A screaming body is not a defeated body, but rather a defiant one that demands deep, attentive listening. By mobilizing corporeal assemblages and building alliances between female workers bodies and earth bodies—river, land, and earthworm in writhing screams—the poet suggests that despite capitalist capture, the body's ongoing metabolism and the ecosystem's life cycles will continue to extend themselves, even in blocked and toxified ways.

Geosocial processes of assembling and disassembling, extraction and ruination, and production and toxicity coexist in Zheng's oeuvre, sedimenting an uncanny ecology of *geos*, *bios*, and machines that is immanently produced by the self-consuming practices of modernization. Zheng's geo-cyborg imagination cannot be reduced to dichotomous readings of nostalgic nature versus malevolent modernity, nor do her migrant workers regain agency through radical class abolition. In her work, the affective texture of a global, technological, and industrial modernity is nuanced, mixing felt experiences of loss, excitement, awe, guilt, screams, anger, and deviance that characterize grassroots migrant ecologies in situated and thick manners. Affective ambiguity is palpable in "Disassemble," where Zheng asserts, "But I still love deeply this age of industry . . . Love the clarity of pain it brings me, the happiness and misfortune" (2007, 107). Paradox is also evident in the growth of Chinese migrant literature and subcultures, which have benefited from technologies such as the internet that provide self-expressive platforms for migrant writers like Zheng, despite state surveillance. If development is an unyielding wheel, Zheng's work truthfully articulates that, just as there is no return to a pristine countryside, there is no easy escape for the working-class poor in China, whose existence is inevitably enmeshed in the cyborgian geontologies of techno-capitalism. Her work calls for ongoing situated ethical commitments to structural inequality and injustice, while recognizing the geomorphic and mineralogical forms of agency and resistance among the laboring masses.

Through an analysis of the migrant geo-cyborg imaginary in Zheng's work, I intend to show how her entanglement of production and waste undoes a colonial capitalist logic of separability, unearthing the geosocial excess in global factories and ethically recalibrating what matters. Her writing experiments with a more-than-human poetics of worldmaking in industrial sweatshops, where migrant and earthly bodies are not passive resources but what iteratively emerge through a politics of slow hope rather than overt subversion. As she reflects in "Iron," the scar on her wounded nail has become "a piece of iron taken root" within her, spreading through her blood, howling the initial pain, imparting gravity to her being, and compelling her to "bear the weight and walk on" (2018). This rooted iron speaks of the *becoming geo-cyborg* of the migrant worker in the Technocene, a reassembled body that combine the *geos*, the *bios*, and the machine in an ecological subjectivity. Zheng's injured and scabbed finger and the searing edge of her poetics constitute decolonial markers of planetary defiance. They insist that grassroots laborers be acknowledged and remembered, akin to a stubborn iron nail embedded in the flat wall of industrial capitalism. Her work suggests that even within enclosed spaces like industrial sweatshops, there exist ethical and political possibilities to imagine planetary subjects to come.

## Deviant Toxicity and Prosthetic Decoloniality: Geo-Cyborg Futures in *Waste Tide*

While the geo-cyborg imagination in Zheng Xiaoqiong's ecopoetics is expressed through literary realism, it takes on a speculative form in Chen Qiufan's science fiction novel *Waste Tide* (2013; translated into English in 2019). Set in the futuristic town of Silicon Isle, a fictionalized version of the global e-waste hub of Guiyu, China, Chen's novel grapples with the complex interplay between technology and toxicity, human and posthuman, and global neoliberalism and local insurgency within the transnational e-waste trade. Chen brings into imaginative focus the geosocial ambivalence of migrant workers, who soak up the toxic waste of techno-modernity while simultaneously embodying a potent political counterforce for decolonial uprisings against colonial capitalist infrastructures and stratification.

In a world inundated with prosthetics and augmented reality technology, Silicon Isle presents a dystopian picture where informal e-waste recycling has enshrouded the town in choking fumes and contaminated water, soil, and air to the brink of uninhabitability. The economic and social landscape is starkly divided between the powerful clans and nouveau rich natives at the top and a migrant labor force, known as the "waste people," at the bottom. Scott Brandle, an American envoy from a multinational corporation, arrives on Silicon Isle with his Chinese American translator, Chen Kaizong, under the guise of promoting green recycling. Yet his real intent is to monopolize the recycling of rare earth metals, which is a powerful component for use in electronics and lethal weaponry. The narrative takes a turn with Mimi, a female waste worker, who accidentally touches a discarded prosthetic device harboring a residual neurological virus from a World War II scientific experiment. The virus catalyzes an unforeseen metamorphosis. It interacts with the heavy-metal toxicants accumulated in Mimi's body from years of e-waste exposure, triggering her transformation into a super cyborg with capabilities of merging human and cybernetic consciousness. After surviving sexual assault and a live burial, a revived Mimi stands as a leader in the waste people's movement for justice and resistance against oppressive local and global powers.

*Waste Tide* speculates a future world where humans are altered by the geosocial materialities of the technosphere, echoing our own social reality. In this speculative future, humans are geo-cyborgs to various degrees because technology has recomposed atmospheric lifeworlds through a surplus of techno-capitalism and a deluge of toxic waste that humanity is unwilling and unable to remedy. Despite this coevolution of life and technology, the progress-minded local authorities and natives of Silicon Isle cling to a modern myth of separability, wielding technology and e-waste as geontopowers and biopolitical tactics to maintain the divide between life and nonlife. This deliberate separation of technological and ecological temporalities is encapsulated in a scene where Scott Brandle visits the Museum of Silicon Isle History. He reflects on the museum's aura of "false, shallow technological optimism" and "a rewritten history" that the natives present to outsiders (Chen 2019, 17). The museum exemplifies the geopolitical landscape of technocracy depicted in the novel. Rather than presenting technological time as a linear progression, Chen's portrayal invites us to consider how it is fractured by overlooked temporalities such as deep time. These disparate temporalities converge in the atmosphere of Silicon Isle, where the "leaden miasma" of e-waste mingles with "the sea breeze," "seeping into the pores of every living being" (29).

The emphasis on intersecting global and planetary processes makes *Waste Tide* a novel with relevance beyond the immediate Chinese context. It tackles the temporal ecologies of the Anthropocene, where phenomena such as climate change and toxic pollution reveal the distributed conditions in which life is altered by the synergies of multiple, often discordant, temporalities of geology, biology, and capitalism. As Chakrabarty reminds us, one way to view the current climate crisis is as a problem of mismatched temporalities: the small scales of human historical time and political practices entangled with the vast scales of earth systems and geologic time (2021, 49). To these scales of small and large we must add tempos and rhythms, including the regenerative cycles of ecosystems and natural resources, the metabolic tempos of biological organisms, and the fast clockwork of economistic and anthropocentric productivity. Together, these interwoven temporalities compose a multiscalar ecosocial reality. But it is not enough to merely recognize this temporal meshwork. An environmental politics attuned to attritional and unequal phenomena like toxic exposure entails an ongoing ethical translation between the timescales of the globe and those of the planet. This calls for reimagining humanity through a framework that can navigate and integrate diverse scales: a *trans-scalar sensibility*. Such a perspective challenges us to consider what aesthetic and cultural forms might embody this sensibility without slipping back to linear narratives of human mastery or decline, whether framed as pessimistic doom, heroic individualism, or techno-triumph.

In this context, science fiction has re-emerged as an appealing genre for storying alternative futures. Common narrative tropes in science fiction, including nonhuman agency, epic time-space spans, and species futures, enable a scaling-up of the human imagination in the Anthropocene (Heise 2019, 281). Chen Qiufan (Stanley Chen) is a prominent writer in "the new wave of Chinese SF" of the post-1980s generation, alongside other writers such as Liu Cixin, Han Song, Hao Jingfang, Xia Jia, and Chi Hui. As Mingwei Song suggests, many writers of the new wave have responded to China's active participation in the market economy and globalization in the postsocialist era and presented critiques of official discourses on harmonious development or technological optimism (2015, 8). Chen's sci-fi works are among the few in this wave that address environmental concerns. In *Waste Tide* and related works, he explores posthuman ethics and the breakdown of boundaries between organic and inorganic matter in the envisioning of technological planetarization. By zooming in on migrant workers and the trans-scalar mobility of e-waste, *Waste Tide* can be read as an attempt to denaturalize a progressive futurescape of technoculture in and beyond China by unearthing the discontinuous histories and residual materialities of techno-capitalism.

Focusing on ecological imperialism and outsourced toxicity, Chen's speculative experiment in *Waste Tide* unmasks the neocolonial nature of developmental agendas promoted by transnational corporations and the wealthy. The novel's opening chapter quotes a Wikipedia entry on the Basel Convention, an international treaty aimed at reducing hazardous movements of waste between nations, but concludes with a stark revelation: "The United States, the leading producer of electronic waste, has never ratified the Convention" (Chen 2019, 11). Scott Brandle's employer, TerraGreen Recycling, has pioneered technology to recycle rare earth metals from consumer e-waste. However, high labor costs and strict environmental regulations in the United States have driven the company to outsource waste and pollution to developing nations under the masquerade of a green economy. As nonrenewable resources, rare earth metals are essential for creating innovative technologies such as smartphones and military weapons, yet their extraction and processing generate considerable toxicity. With China controlling the majority of global production and facing rising demand, it has tightened export restrictions, making rare earth a vital element in global geopolitics.

In an effort to persuade the clans of Silicon Isle, Scott frames TerraGreen's proposal as a civilizing mission, designed to help locals upgrade to modern technology, restore a greener environment, and become competitive with other Global South regions such as Southeast Asia and West Africa. Meanwhile, he attempts to bribe local authorities. The hidden rationale behind these global ventures, as Scott later admits, involves "economic hit men" from multinational conglomerates who toss out "sweet lures" in the name of "progress" and "joint development," tempting local governments to sacrifice "oil fields, minerals, and the genes of endangered animals" and local laborers to "slave away like robots" (210). Over the years, Scott has facilitated various predatory projects, "from the rainforest of the Amazon to the prairie of Mozambique, from the hellish slums of southern India to the resource-abundant waters of Southeast Asia" (210). Although the novel focuses on e-waste, the inclusion of these backstories suggests that e-waste is only one exemplar of transnational capital's ecocidal and neocolonial operations, all performed under the guise of a "free market" setup.

*Waste Tide* complicates narratives of victimhood by exploring divergent and layered worlding practices within local e-waste ecologies. The novel describes Silicon Isle as a contested place where global neoliberal capital intersects with the competing powers of local government, native family clans, migrant labor, and environmental organizations. E-waste is depicted through the lens of local-global processes: transnational flows of illicit waste, state-led development, profit-seeking local elites, urban consumerism, possessive individualism, technocratic digital control, and the systemic denial of migrant workers' subjectivity and personhood. Mimi and her fellow waste people are at the nexus of intersecting class and racial infrastructures of toxic violence. Waste materially and symbolically relegates certain human beings to wasted lives. Silicon Isle's natives regard the waste people as "slaves, bugs, and disposable trash," as if they were "a completely different species," despite their own lavish lifestyles being sustained by the health and labor of the waste people (261). This polarized geography exposes the neoliberal infiltration of social belonging, foregrounding how the free market ironically reinforces barriers between human and nonhuman, clean and dirty, and center and periphery—barriers that the novel subsequently subverts.

Mimi's cyborg subjectivity may well be a quintessential example of what I term the geo-cyborg. She embodies a posthuman figure that merges technology, biology, and geology in a world of increasing transversal connectivity between the technosphere and the geobiosphere. This transversality leads to geosocial exchanges between global excess and planetary deviance: As humans accumulate capital and technology beyond ecological limits, they generate increasingly unpredictable risks from climate change to waste exposure. In other words, the geologic agency of techno-capitalist extraction and accumulation carries with it transversal processes of erosion and exposure. Mimi's becoming the geo-cyborg challenges conventional meanings of waste because she reveals how excess—migrant subjectivity, surplus value production, the laboring mass, and toxic waste—retains the potential to transgress humanist hierarchies by embodying the ambivalence of not only disposability but also deviance. The nonhuman and inhuman excesses within Mimi and the waste people already prefigure a posthuman recomposition of subjectivity and community. In this sense, the geo-cyborg is a trans-scalar imaginary, with the potential to catalyze posthuman thinking attuned to nonlinear time-space-matter and unruly ecological consequences that deflate techno-capitalist dreams of mastery. Consequently, we are compelled to think with the geo-cyborg about a renewed politics of justice, alterlife, and decoloniality that breaches a closed order of racial and class stratigraphy.

*Waste Tide* explores the ways migrant ecologies contest the myths of containment and upward mobility within colonial capitalist systems. For Silicon Isle natives, the waste people rub salt into the wound of an ancestral homeland turned into electronic junkyard due to the unfettered pursuit of possessive dreams. Although the natives reside in clean suburbs and opulent mansions, they are haunted by "a pervasive stench" from the burning of e-waste (27). This odor is a reminder that toxic pollution affects everyone regardless of social status. A local fisherman informs Mimi that the electronic power plant's wastewater contaminates the ocean and ultimately ends up in the toxic seafood sold in markets. Water, food, soil, air, and other ecological flows implicate all communities in shared, albeit uneven, risks. The natives distance themselves from the waste people as a way of denying their own disposability in a toxic world. A deep-seated self-loathing is palpable in clan director Lin's confession: "The greatest hope cherished by the people of Silicon Isle is to see their children leave this place . . . sometimes you can no longer even tell what's trash and what's not in our lives" (23–24). Mimi's suffering helps the waste people realize that trash is not an innately inferior entity, but a construct of social and class hierarchy. The awakened waste people assert, "Waste is dirty, inferior, lowly, useless, but omnipresent. They [the natives] produce waste every day, they can't live without the waste people. . . . Do they really think they can avoid us?" (197). The Silicon Isle natives' anxiety highlights a broader, unsettling truth: Global consumerism is turning the earth into a gigantic trash bin, endangering not only those closest to the garbage but also those who believe they are safe from its reach.

Temporally, Chen's depiction of the geo-cyborg employs anachronism, or what appears untimely and asynchronous, to respond to the trans-scalar challenges of the Anthropocene. Anachronism, as I have argued elsewhere, can serve as a narrative and ecological device to reclaim temporalities, subject positions, and nonhuman materialities excluded by modern progressive time (Zong 2021, 306). By cautioning against a culture of modern forgetfulness, anachronism can offer an ethical response to anthropocentrism by reinscribing history and the human subject with epistemic multiplicity, allowing us to notice nonlinear time-space and modes of inhabitation (Zong 2021, 320). *Waste Tide* uses anachronism to historicize forgotten detritus and question the violent values of imperialism, militarism, and technoscience. An anachronistic and deviant object, a virus-inflected prosthesis accidentally put on Mimi's head, catalyzes her transformation into a cyborg. Originally engineered by the high-tech company SBT for a risky brain-machine interface on chimpanzees, the prosthesis was mislabeled as medical waste by a computer system and shipped to Silicon Isle. Scott Brandle's task is to retrieve it to prevent a scandal for SBT.

A further patching of the novel's plot reveals a link between the artificial virus and Project Waste Tide, a fictionalized biochemical weapon program from World War II initiated by the Japanese American Dr. Suzuki to aid the American military in nontraditional warfare. The biochemical weapon, QNB, can infiltrate the receiver's skin and respiratory system, causing a spectrum of unpredictable symptoms, including nerve damage, coma, ataxia, loss of spatial and temporal perception, memory loss, hallucinations, and irrational fear (Chen 2019, 229). Following its defeat in Vietnam, the American military used QNB in several regional wars, including in "Afghanistan, the Persian Gulf, Sarajevo, Ethiopia," but downplayed it as "a nonlethal chemical weapon with no long term negative effects" (231). Through the leaky trajectory of an obsolete prosthesis, the novel orients readerly attention to the environmental footprints of warfare and techno-military engineering. It responds to the calamitous repercussions and enduring harm of US militarization across multiple scales. The American military's classification of QNB plays into the public's habitual perception of wartime violence as explosive and dramatic, while concealing its latent and protracted effects. The fictional scenario in *Waste Tide* resonates with real historical events like the aerial spraying of the herbicidal toxicant Agent Orange over Vietnamese land during the Vietnam War. Despite scientific studies measuring dioxin levels in human blood, soil, and animal specimens, the multigenerational health and environmental harm, along with American accountability for Agent Orange, can never be fully captured in scientific and biomedical lexicons.

These expansive networks of toxic waste show us how the biochemical materialities of bodies are entangled with toxic, debilitating, and intersecting power relations, which manifest in uneven vulnerabilities shaped by histories of technoscience, militarism, and imperialism and structures of race and capital. *Waste Tide* brings these toxic entanglements to speculative imagination by advocating for a trans-scalar aesthetic that repositions humanity in a more-than-human world of chemical alterlives. The novel centers the deviance of toxicity, not as an isolated quality, but as a leaky and pervasive condition that destabilizes time, producing plural temporalities through contextual, irreversible, and cumulative effects on ecosystems, biological metabolism, and geological strata. The character Mimi becomes a focal point for trans-scalar toxicity. Her brain has become a reactive "mine field" where heavy-metal toxins, an artificial virus, and a weakened immune system synergize incalculably under external stimuli to "trigger a chain reaction" (225). Mimi's metamorphosis underscores how a contaminated social-ecological landscape transmutes waste and migrant workers, producing messy and networked embodiments that rupture the myths of inert resources and individuated bodies.

The question remains, where does acknowledging the extensive networks of toxic chemicality leave us? In what ways can toxicity enable an altered politics of resistance for marginalized groups like Chinese migrant workers, given that it institutes the systemic erosion of their health and homes? While toxic exposure may blur boundaries and destabilize subjectivities, *Waste Tide* remains clear-eyed about the reality that toxic entanglements are reproduced by intoxicating systems of ecological imperialism, technocracy, and racial and class disparities. Rather than reducing toxic kinship to apolitical molecular fluidity, Chen's novel insists on the need to decolonize the extractive infrastructures and epistemologies that sustain toxic exposure, thus inviting us to consider these conditions as sites of not merely environmental injustice, but also networked agency from below. This dynamic plays out through the ambivalent toxicity embodied by migrant geo-cyborgs—impure life-forms transformed by geosocial and cyborgian forces, entangling excess with deviance.

The liminality of excess is critical to understanding the paradoxical role of the geo-cyborg in reimagining politics and ethics. Toxicity disrupts linear order by revealing obscured and invisible temporalities, connectivity, and alterlives; yet these same toxic processes also sustain systems that perpetuate inequality and sacrifice (Liboiron et al. Calvillo 2018, 333). Mimi embodies this ambivalence, portrayed simultaneously as a victim of the uneven distribution of toxic harm and a deviant agent within the network of toxic entanglement. Her cyborg subjectivity converges the ambivalence of toxicity and the ambiguity of e-waste, both being material reminders of the complex and indeterminate intra-actions of *geos*, *bios*, and technology in situated worlding practices. This ambivalence illustrates the geo-cyborg's dual dystopian and utopian dimensions, along with its potential for decolonial worldmaking. The geo-cyborg raises pressing questions: If migrant workers become geoagents through their intimacies with industrial toxins, can a hopeful and life-affirming politics emerge from their entanglement with substances that threaten to consume them?

The works of Zheng Xiaoqiong and Chen Qiufan in this chapter respond with a politics of slow activism that calls for sustained ethical attention to more-than-human vulnerability. In the previous section, I have discussed how Zheng Xiaoqiong's ecopoetics offers a perspective wherein the geosocial intimacies of migrant workers shift from a narrative of victimhood to liveliness and collaborative survival between migrant laborers and mineralogical matters like iron. *Waste Tide* continues to explore this theme. Toxic e-waste redefines both humans and nonhumans as vibrant, porous, and coemergent agents, but what forms of situated activism might transpire in posthuman milieus of unequal toxicity? The geo-cyborg invites us to consider posthuman environmental ethics in a world of cyborgian agencies, where subjectivity emerges through AI, biotechnology, genetic modification, and toxic pollution. More precisely, *Waste Tide* speculates on future visions and asks whether technology can support an affirmative politics of difference for marginalized communities like migrant workers, whether technological subjectivity can be reimagined as materially embedded in geontologies, and whether there can be a post-exceptionalist technological cosmopolitics that goes beyond the homogenization of efficiency and the desire for mastery.

After being tortured by local thugs, a furious Mimi awakens to the collective struggle of waste workers. That her resistance is an act against geosocial stratification is given narrative form in the novel when the thugs attempt to bury her alive in the muddy ground, leaving her to die beneath the earth: "The Mimi of yesterday had worked hard to sniff burning pieces of plastic for twenty-five yuan a day, for the hope of one day being able to care for her parents, but now, her violated body was lying underground and her soul was adrift in the night rain" (Chen 2019, 171). This near-death moment triggers her cyborg transformation. Her resourceful machine consciousness, however, needs to collaborate with her "long-suffering, fragile body" (169), resulting in two distinct yet fused identities: Mimi 0, the harmed human waste girl, and Mimi 1, the host of cybernetic intelligence. Mimi's cyborg body requires "astonishing levels of energy consumption" (309) and her hyper-metabolism demands high-energy fructose.

Mimi 0 and Mimi 1 hold divergent views during the waste people's class uprising, illustrating the tension between goal-driven pragmatism and empathetic or moral deliberation. Mimi 1's decision to incite the waste people's hatred and violence against the natives contrast with Mimi 0's empathetic stance, illustrating how cybernetic rationality prioritizes survival, efficiency, and optimization while lacking the emotional and ethical complexities typical of human consciousness. But it is Mimi 1's algorithmic processing that recognizes the evolutionary advantages of human virtues such as "pity, sympathy, shame, fairness . . . morality" (407), leading her to decide to rescue the natives during a typhoon-induced flood. This choice is based on Mimi 1's data analysis of social dynamics and her goal to help the waste people gain recognition. This demonstrates that machinic intelligence can integrate or replicate, but not necessarily feel some human moral behavior. The novel's conclusion, however, takes a dramatic turn. Scott abducts a fragile Mimi, hoping to exploit her as lucrative laboratory specimen. Though Kaizong rescues her, Mimi ultimately chooses self-destruction over the risk of losing her humanity to machines and commodification. This shift from radical resistance to political compromise is also reflected on Silicon Isle, where TerraGreen Recycling strikes a deal with the Silicon Isle government to build a recycling industrial park, pledging to allocate some profits to improve migrant workers' working conditions and address occupational illnesses.

The schism within Mimi's cyborg subjectivity encapsulates what Rosi Braidotti aptly frames as "the posthuman predicament"—the internal contradictions and paradoxes prompted by questions such as: "Where does the posthuman leave humanity?" "How does the posthuman engender its own form of inhumanity?" "How might we resist the inhuman(e) aspects of our era?" (2013, 3). Mimi's story offers a political allegory for the double-edged potential of technology to both empower and exploit, underscoring the enduring need for humanity in an increasingly mechanized world. It is tempting to interpret the schism within her cyborg subjectivity as a reflection of the technosphere's dominance over the geobiosphere, as the gendered, raced, and classed bodies of the waste people remain among the most vulnerable to modern techno-capitalism. Nevertheless, this reading risks overstating the universalizing power of technology and flattening the novel's design, which foregrounds the embodied finitude of Mimi's posthuman existence. Her cyborg body consumes vast amounts of energy: "Mimi realized that she wasn't a completely free soul, but was still tethered to that buried, dying body. As soon as her body truly died, her consciousness was going to dissipate" (Chen 2019, 177). Mimi thus embodies the author's ambivalent perspective on technological agency as potentially both liberating and enslaving and both enabled and constrained by cosmic energy. Like all cybernetic systems. her existence is bound to the planetary realities of energy, labor, and material consumption. The energy-intensive nature of Mimi's virtual subjectivity (un)earths the geologic and ecological kinship between organism and technology. This geologic gravity disrupts disembodied fantasies of technological subjectivities through AI or cybernetic transcendence and challenges any presumption of detachment from the material world, where rare earth elements and other mineral deposits are being mined for new energy technologies.

Additionally, the novel's ambiguous portrayal of technology resonates with contemporary debates over its impacts on labor markers, especially regarding the broader social tensions surrounding automation and employment. Media coverage on China's robot and AI revolution has highlighted the potential mass unemployment due to automation and the need for migrant workers to upskill and master robotics to survive the global push for high-tech productivity (C. Zhou 2019). As industrial hubs like Dongguan transition from manufacturing to Silicon Valley–style development, many migrant workers have been forced to return to their hometowns.

The need for upskilling faces barriers in existing social structures that limit migrant workers' access to education and resources. *Waste Tide* explores this through a violent encounter where clan director Lin and his thugs, equipped with "artificially enhanced shells," tear into the recycled prostheses of the waste people (Chen 2019, 381). The novel dramatizes the uncertainty over whether technology exacerbates inequalities or offers an empowering opportunity to liberate the migrant workforce from repetitive and hazardous tasks in the new wave of technology-induced displacement and vulnerability. Upon hacking into the Compound Eye, an AI surveillance system in Shantou city, Mimi witnesses a world of transhumanist apathy, where people indulge in technological stimuli and information loads but show no happiness (263). Although modern technology presents the guise of convenience and freedom, it is depicted as eroding genuine empathy and democratic values. Chen's portrayal of Mimi's self-sacrifice reminds us that empathy and justice must remain at the forefront of discussions about the role of technology in future employment and social life.

Nevertheless, the fate of the waste people in *Waste Tide* exposes how a return to humanism fails to address the political needs of the posthuman subaltern. The decision by the waste people to rescue the natives during the flood appeals to an ideal of universal humanism: "We have to show them [the natives] that we're not polluting waste or parasitic animals. We're human, the same as them. We laugh, we cry, we pity, we sympathize. We can even risk our lives to rescue them" (393). This noble act creates a temporary reconciliation in civil society, as the natives shift from fear to gratitude, and waste items such as silicone rubber, plastic fiber, LED bulbs turn into rescue rafts and emergency lights. However, the novel remains doubtful whether projects of empathy and coexistence can reorient alternative posthuman politics without simultaneously pluralizing technological subjectivity beyond its dominant modern enframing tethered to the hegemony of state and capital. Being recognized as "equal humans" does not disrupt, but rather reinforces, a universal norm of the human, a modern colonial ideal made possible by technological exploitation of life and resources on earth. We see how the waste people become once again relegated to a planetary order of racial and class disposability as TerraGreen and Silicon Isle government join hands in the neoliberal technological market. Their tokenish gesture to address environmental illness is a mere drop in the ocean compared to the renewed game of techno-capitalist globalization, as the Silicon Isle Mayor declares, "Win-win-win! A brand new future for Silicon Isle" (430).

The realist ending in *Waste Tide* begs more questions about incorporating technology in reimagining a prosthetic decoloniality in the Anthropocene. As the transversality across human, ecology, and technology intensifies, we may borrow insights from Yuk Hui's discussion of a "culture of prosthesis" for a planetary thinking of technodiversity,

> Future planetary thinking has to start with an organological motif. For this purpose, we have to cultivate and ameliorate a *culture of prosthesis* and not a *culture of replacement*. A culture of replacement sees machines as competition for the human being and that the human will be gradually replaced by machines in all domains; a culture of prosthesis recognizes the organological value of machines and goes beyond the instrumentality of machines; that is to say, to go beyond both productivity and creativity in its calculative form. As Bergson proposed, the new vocation of machines will have to deviate from the materialization of the spirit and search for the spiritualization of matter. (2024, 232)

Hui may not have mentioned Chinese migrant workers who have limited access to prosthetic technologies, but I argue that a culture of prosthesis holds potential for reorientating migrant futures beyond reductive narratives of human enhancement or displacement within a seemingly closed system of modern techno-capitalism. Instead, it opens space for imagining alternative cosmotechnics. For Hui, "Cosmotechnics as unification between the cosmic order and the moral order through technical activities" suggests that technology should be pluralized beyond a universalizing culture of capital and resituated in a broader reality in the language of coexistence between humans and nonhumans (2020, 2). The geo-cyborg imaginations of migrant workers in Chinese literature and sci-fi, as explored in this chapter, present a planetary thinking that attends to transversal kinship and prosthetic resurgence in local milieus and specific practices. In *Waste Tide*, Mimi's choice for self-destruction rejects a capitalist ethos that instrumentalizes modern technology for human domination, exemplified by outcome-driven male characters like Scott Brandle and Director Lin. In Chen's other sci-fi stories, such as "Dreaming of Plenitude" (2021) and "Do you Hear the Fungi Sing" (2022), he more directly explores how Indigenous, ethnic, and non-Western epistemologies might shape technological futures attuned to cosmic reciprocity between humans and the environment. In this sense, an alternative cosmotechnics of nonexploitative futures calls for posthuman alliances informed by local practices that do not simply integrate marginalized communities into existing techno-capitalist systems but seek to continually transform and exceed them.

If, as Francesca Ferrando reminds us, technology should neither be feared nor merely reduced to a classist project for human evolution, it can instead serve as "a mode of revealing," a praxis through which futures are dynamically enacted, where the "what" (outcome) is inseparable from the "how" (process) (2013, 29). The task for a decolonial cosmotechnics might proceed with posthuman modes of environmental activism that simultaneously aim at worldbuilding, coexistence, and prosthetic pleasure. Mimi's geo-cyborg metamorphosis represents a posthuman transformation that unsettles hegemonic technological regimes by connecting situated ethics with geosocial agency. The autonomous individual is decentered by a prosthetic self constituted through entanglements across technology, geology, and biology in thick and impure relations. Her toxic embodiment materialize an ethics and politics of exposure, where vulnerability means inhabiting "a fraught sense of political agency that emerges from the perceived loss of boundaries and sovereignty" (Alaimo 2016, 5). The precarious ecologies of migrant labor call for ongoing practices of ethics, care, and activism that can transform exploitative relations and repair life by cultivating a trans-scalar sensibility—one that accounts for delayed, nonlinear, and networked forms of violence and takes responsibility for the earthly ecosystems that sustain planetary coexistence and transformative potential.

How can migrant workers envision alternative worlds within emerging naturecultures and posthuman unevenness? The environmental narratives of Zheng Xiaoqiong and Chen Qiufan move beyond measuring migrant workers against a universal model of humanism, a model that continues to categorize them as modernity's disposable lives or robotic laborers. As I have explored in this chapter, figures of the geo-cyborg shine light on a posthuman ethos of excess and deviance that thickens the networked agencies emerging contingently and uncannily from the potent fusions of *geos*, *bios*, and technology. By recasting global excess against planetary deviance, migrant worker ecologies disrupt artificial boundaries between commodity and waste, assembling and disassembling, extraction and stratification, and nature and technology. Migrant workers are grassroots figures that prompt us to reconsider the becoming geologic of human subjectivity in the Anthropocene, drawing attention to the toxic and molecular reproduction of capitalism in a world of extraction, consumerism, and technoculture. Considering geo-cyborg migrant workers emphasizes the sustained ethical importance of responding to posthuman conditions, while expanding our imagination in the direction of slow activism and slow hope enmeshed in the mineralogical kinships and prosthetic mobilities in marginalized locales like industrial sweatshops and waste recycling sites in the Global South. Embedded in these grassroots ecologies are decolonial possibilities for planetarities from below, the worlding of subaltern survival and plural futures that elude global capitalist capture and technological mastery.

# Epilogue

# "Sowing Seeds Within the Cracks"

## *Diaspora as a Decolonial Praxis*

While writing this book, I have moved from Australia to Mui Wo, a rural town on Lantau Island, the largest outlaying island on the periphery of metropolitan Hong Kong. Once a farming area, Mui Wo is now a town with a diverse population that combines Indigenous villagers and a transnational class, including upper-and middle-class professionals, foreign expatriates, and international artists and educators drawn by the currents of financial globalization (Tang 2017, 3). Differing from the hectic or futuristic images of Hong Kong, Mui Wo offers its residents an alternative landscape of lush green hills, bicycling as a daily mode of transportation, organic farms, wetlands, and the wondrous sight of free-roaming cows and water buffaloes. These bovine species were once important to Hong Kong's agriculture as draft animals to plow rice paddies. As rice fields gave way to property development and imported food industries in the 1970s, the cows and buffaloes became "unemployed," "abandoned," and "feral." These nomadic creatures and human inhabitants of Mui Wo share space and negotiate their movements in collectively redefining communities of belonging and co-becoming. From the beach to the tourist promenade, from narrow country trails to village backyards, and around rubbish bins, multispecies response-abilities are woven through everyday contingencies, collaborations, and separations where humans and bovids are folded into the thick rhythms of each other.

My research into migrant and refugee ecologies had stirred within me conflicting feelings of hope and apprehension. I felt encouraged by the more-than-human webs of interdependencies that expand the stories of diasporic mobilities, responsibilities, and collectivities beyond humancentric and capitalist narratives. Yet I am ever aware of the danger of romanticizing these ties and downplaying the stark realities of dehumanizing politics. The migratory circuits that afforded my own borderland consciousness—diligent study leading from a rural town in China to higher education in Australia and then to an academic position in Hong Kong—are entangled with liberal humanist promises of freedom and rejection and their corollary myths of upward mobility. In the ecological milieu of Mui Wo, I encountered John, an Iranian asylum seeker, writer, and comedian living in the village. One evening, during a BBQ on the rooftop of their tiny flats, I listened to asylum seekers from Iran, Georgia, and Ukraine share their struggles with immigration hurdles, hopes of securing legal work rights, and the uncertainties ahead. I asked John what he thought of the local buffaloes that often frequent a wetland next to the flats. "The buffaloes?" he began. "I think they're awesome. They don't ask for my passport."

These words have often revisited me as I put this book together. On one hand, buffaloes and asylum seekers are subjected to a modern biopolitics of extinction that regulates life and mobility through state and capitalist territorial logics. Free-roaming bovids are nonhuman witnesses to and internal diasporas in a colonial system of artificial and often arbitrary borders of citizenship and animality that intersect ecological perceptions of feral and pest species with a cultural politics of belonging and place. On the other hand, buffaloes and asylum seekers show us the continued survival and multispecies livability within feral lifeworlds that emerge from yet also elude the monocultural designs of the Anthropocene. Grazing buffaloes with egrets perched on their backs on the urban fringes of a global financial hub are a scene of radical hope. It calls us to notice, act, and participate in the many situated and partial histories of symbiosis and collectives of mutuality beyond anthropocentric mastery.

Moreover, a feral politics of survival gains significance in the larger Hong Kong society in the wake of the 2019 protests, changes to the political environment, and outward migration waves. That Hong Kong is a lost front in the Western liberal imagination is palpable in the pity and concern from my Australian friends and relatives: "poor Hong Kong." The narrative of "the death of Hong Kong" is also pitted against celebratory claims of national integration and techno-capitalist AI futures that threaten to neutralize wetland and oceanic ecosystems with new infrastructure blueprints and island reclamations projects. In finding refuge from within and against these linear models of death and freedom, humans and animals are forced to become feral together.

Turning to these movements and passages between ferality and refuge in my current locale helps me situate this project beyond the purview of the migratory sites explored in the book's chapters. These feral forms of more-than-human survival and their interrogation of exclusive structures that reproduce static political boundaries are not just local concerns because they illuminate migrant futures and ontological impurity inherent within and between colonial, capital, and nation-state systems of control. The feralization and pathologization of migrant bodies expose a colonial logic of purity that presumes an integral bond between nation, nature, and native. Across this book, I have returned to the discourse of freedom and placed migrant, refugee, and Asian diasporic emancipatory politics in generative tensions with decolonial thought. This has led to questioning how liberal humanist institutions of freedom and mobility—property ownership, settler inclusion, sovereign bordering, and individual ethics—continue modern colonial assumptions of purity and Man, which in turn justify environmental racism against migrants and hybrid nature as security threats and contaminating pollutants. A decolonial analytic exposes the colonial racial scripts that cheapen migrant lives and labor to fuel capitalist extraction, accumulation, and reproduction in the web of life and in the name of (un)freedom. Decolonizing these structural inequalities reveals the dishonesty of borders, fences, and walls as global linear solutions to the migration "crisis" under climate change. It also unsettles the normative ecological subject by articulating and imagining expansive modes of existence and freedom that are grounded in impurity, movement, and interdependent naturecultures during migration and diaspora.

"Interdependency between women is the way to a freedom which allows the *I* to *be*, not in order to be used, but in order to be creative. This is a difference between the passive *be* and the active *being*," Audre Lorde says (1984, 111). She is talking about women as knowledge makers whose need and desire to nurture community while sustaining differences can bring about real change. By stating, "The master's tools will never dismantle the master's house," Lorde understands that difference must not only be tolerated but seen as a creative force for actualizing alternative visions of future, community, and coexistence, "to make common cause with those others identified as outside the structures in order to define and seek a world in which we can all flourish" (1984, 112). A key contribution of migrant and diasporic ecopoetics to the environmental humanities is the exploration of dwelling in borderlands and impure places as part of the sustained effort for replenishing refuges, nomadizing futures, and commoning across differences toward earthly survival. The writers and filmmakers in this book have told emplaced stories about the ambivalences of migrant and refugee ecologies, engaging with antiracist, decolonial, multispecies, and the often conflicting agendas of justice.

Diasporic movements broaden the ways in which we think about borders themselves as mobile and mutable. Alongside a posthumanist biopolitics that manipulates more-than-human agency to displace and control, we have seen incalcitrant alliances between migrants and earthly forces (animals, plants, water, fire, and minerals) in nested and extensive networks beyond the individual. Borderlands, in this study, are creative sites and material interfaces for negotiating the unsettling affects, complex responsibilities, and uneven harms of colonial capitalism in the morphology of ongoing life within planetary ruins and resurgence.

Systemic changes can be slow. Catherine E. Walsh identifies "crack making" as a decolonial praxis, conceiving decoloniality as an ongoing movement of making fissures in the modern colonial order (2018, 250). The invention of decolonial pluriversals may emerge by opening, making, and widening the cracks, alongside the practice of "sowing seeds within the cracks" (Walsh 2018, 250). It is not, therefore, enough to tell stories of migrant and refugee lives as oppressed and damaged bodies from a critique of environmental and social injustice. Nor is it enough to assert an abstract kinship with nature that harmonizes differences. We need stories, methods, and ethics that embed migrants and refugees in specific lands and places, and at the same time grapple with their capabilities as desiring, feeling, and creative beings who create with more-than-human nature in dynamic and wondrous sympoiesis.

In multiplying decolonial cracks and seedlings, *Planetarity from Below* has been a study of migrant and diasporic ecopoetics as material and discursive acts of not only environmental justice, but also ecological worldmaking. A thick notion of mobility and a processual stance of ethical doings have been my two interpretive frames for formulating a diasporic ecopraxis that holds the generative frictions between sowing seeds in cracks while staying with the trouble of colonial capitalist systems. This book has located several spheres in which diasporic cultural texts ecologize the unreconciled tensions of our Anthropocene present: wonder and possession, planetary circulation and situated politics, migration and borders, excess and deviance, and dehumanization and posthumanness. Dwelling with these tensions, the literature and films assembled in this book explore a residual ethos of unknowability by articulating ecosocial forms of migration and diaspora—wonder, aqueous, affective, ghostly, metamorphic, and deviant—that fuse elemental flows and social formations to express the rhythms, mobilities, and ultimate incalculability of migrant and nonhuman agencies in their relational coemergence. They have thus drawn us into a diasporic praxis of worlding that turns to modest, unfinished, and grassroots stories of sympoiesis on a damaged planet to rupture modern purity and the capitalist property form and make possible a migrant insurgence of post-anthropocentric ethics.

As readers who have reached the end of the book will have observed, planetary subjectivity is rather immanent to the webbed interdependencies of human and nonhuman existences that are in excess of modern progressive narratives of state, capital, and technology. A decolonial ecopoetics helps to perceive the many worldings of planetarity from below, in which people from borderlands and local histories negotiate life and responsibilities by caring with nonhuman agencies. An insurgent poetics of excess offer cues for reimagining migrant and refugee emancipatory agendas of justice, mobility, and freedom beyond a politics of control by state and capital toward alternative cosmovisions of a multispecies democracy.

Following ancestral pulses of life yet returning from the future, planetarity from below stories a political ontology of the irrepressible commons in the here and now. The irrepressible commons unfolds in the thickness of everyday sustenance, labor, and affectivity among those who sustain care for earth life from within unjust systems. The irrepressible commons are sites of endurance and solidarity, where the displaced and disposable humans and nonhumans persist, even in weedy, altered, and ghostly forms. To listen carefully to the irrepressible commons is to enter the plural worlds of planetarity from below.

# Bibliography


Abdullah, Mena, and Ray Mathew. [1965] 2019. *The Time of the Peacock*. ETT Imprint.

Adam, Barbara, and Chris Groves. 2007. *Future Matters: Action, Knowledge, Ethics*. Brill.

Adamson, Joni, and Scott Slovic. 2009. "The Shoulders We Stand On: An Introduction to Ethnicity and Ecocriticism." *MELUS* 34 (2): 5–24.

Ahuja, Neel. 2021. *Planetary Specters: Race, Migration, and Climate Change in the Twenty-First Century*. University of North Carolina Press.

Ahuja, Neel. 2012. "Species in a Planetary Frame: Eco-Cosmopolitanism, Nationalism, and *The Cove*." *Tamkang Review* 42 (2): 13–32.

Alaimo, Stacy. 2010. *Bodily Natures: Science, Environment, and the Material Self*. Indiana University Press.

Alaimo, Stacy. 2012. "States of Suspension: Trans-Corporeality at Sea." *ISLE: Interdisciplinary Studies in Literature and Environment* 19 (3): 476–93.

Alaimo, Stacy. 2016. *Exposed: Environmental Politics and Pleasures in Posthuman Times*. University of Minnesota Press.

Albrecht, Glenn, et al. 2007. "Solastalgia: The Distress Caused by Environmental Change." *Australian Psychiatry* 15 (Suppl.): S95–S98.

Ali, Kazim. 2021. *Northern Light: Power, Land, and the Memory of Water*. Milkweed Editions.

Anderson, Ben. 2009. "Affective Atmospheres." *Emotion, Space and Society* 2 (2): 77–81.

Bahng, Aimee. 2018. *Migrant Futures: Decolonizing Speculation in Financial Times*. Duke University Press.

Baldwin, Andrew. 2022. *The Other of Climate Change: Racial Futurism, Migration, Humanism*. Rowman and Littlefield.

Balkan, Stacey, and Swaralipi Nandi, eds. 2021. *Oil Fictions: World Literature and Our Contemporary Petrosphere*. Pennsylvania State University Press.

Barad, Karen. 2007. *Meeting the Universe Halfway: Quantum Physics and the Entanglement of Matter and Meaning*. Duke University Press.

Bauman, Zygmunt. 2000. *Liquid Modernity*. Polity Press.

Bauman, Zygmunt. 2004. *Wasted Lives: Modernity and Its Outcasts*. Polity Press.

Becker, George F. 1915. "On the Earth Considered as a Heat Engine." *Proceedings of the National Academy of Sciences of the United States of America* 1 (2): 81–86.

Bélanger, Danièle, and Rachel Silvey. 2019. "An Im/Mobility Turn: Power Geometries of Care and Migration." *Journal of Ethnic and Migration Studies* 46 (16): 3423–40.

Bennett, Jane. 2001. *The Enchantment of Modern Life: Attachments, Crossings, and Ethics*. Princeton University Press.

Bennett, Jane. 2010. *Vibrant Matter: A Political Ecology of Things*. Duke University Press.

Bettini, Giovanni. 2019. "And Yet It Moves! (Climate) Migration as a Symptom in the Anthropocene." *Mobilities* 14 (3): 336–50.

Bhabha, Homi. 1994. *The Location of Culture*. Routledge.

Bittel, Jason. 2015. "The Christmas Crab Massacre." *NRDC*, December 24. https://www.nrdc.org/stories/christmas-crab-massacre#:~:text=Ants%20are%20killing%20Christmas%20Island's,tiny%20wasps%20save%20the%20day%3F&text=Named%20for%20the%20day%20it,around%2045%20million%20red%20crabs

Blackstock, Michael. 2001. "Water: A First Nations' Spiritual and Ecological Perspective." *B.C. Journal of Ecosystems and Management* 1 (1): 1–14.

Bladow, Kyle, and Jennifer Ladino. 2018. "Toward an Affective Ecocriticism: Placing Feeling in the Anthropocene." In *Affective Ecocriticism: Emotion, Embodiment, Environment*, edited by Kyle Bladow and Jennifer Ladino, 1–22. University of Nebraska Press.

Blanchot, Maurice. 1989. *The Space of Literature*. Translated by Ann Smock. University of Nebraska Press.

Bleiker, Roland, et al. 2013. "The Visual Dehumanisation of Refugees." *Australian Journal of Political Science* 48 (4): 398–416.

Blum, Hester. 2013. "Introduction: Oceanic Studies." *Atlantic Studies* 10 (2): 151–55.

Bobis, Merlinda. 2015a. *Locust Girl*. Spinifex Press.

Bobis, Merlinda. 2015b. "Emily Yu Zong Interviews Merlinda Bobis." *Mascara Literary Review*, October 1. http://mascarareview.com/?s=emily+yu+zong

Boochani, Behrouz. 2018. *No Friend but the Mountains: Writing from Manus Prison*. Picador.

Boochani, Behrouz, and Arnold Zable. 2020. "Dialogue with Behrouz Boochani." *National Gallery of Victoria*. https://www.ngv.vic.gov.au/exhibition_post/arnold-zable-dialogue-with-behrouz-boochani/

Bow, Leslie. 2012. "Asian American Women's Literature and the Promise of Committed Art." In *The Cambridge History of American Women's Literature*, edited by Dale M. Bauer, 557–75. Cambridge University Press.

Bradley, Nicholas. 2021. "The Scent of the Latent Commons." In *Current, Climate: The Poetry of Rita Wong*, xiii–xxiv. Wilfrid Laurier University Press.

Braidotti, Rosi. 2003. "Feminist Philosophies." In *A Concise Companion to Feminist Theory*, edited by Mary Eagleton, 195–214. Blackwell.

Braidotti, Rosi. 2006a. "The Ethics of Becoming Imperceptible." In *Deleuze and Philosophy*, edited by Constantin Boundas, 133–59. Edinburgh University Press.

Braidotti, Rosi. 2006b. *Transpositions: On Nomadic Ethics*. Polity Press.

Braidotti, Rosi. 2013. *The Posthuman*. Polity Press.

Brathwaite, Kamau. 1999. *ConVERSations with Nathaniel Mackey*. We Press.

Brubaker, Rogers. 2005. "The 'Diaspora' Diaspora." *Ethnic and Racial Studies* 28 (1): 1–19.

Buell, Frederick. 2003. *From Apocalypse to Way of Life: Environmental Crisis in the American Century*. Routledge.

Buell, Lawrence. 2005. *The Future of Environmental Criticism: Environmental Crisis and Literary Imagination*. Blackwell.

Butler, Judith. 2009. *Frames of War: When Is Life Grievable?* Verso.

Cameron, Emilie. 2008. "Indigenous Spectrality and the Politics of Postcolonial Ghost Stories." *Cultural Geographies* 15 (3): 383–93.

Campling, Liam, and Alejandro Colás. 2021. *Capitalism and the Sea: The Maritime Factor in the Making of the Modern World*. Verso.

Carson, Rachel. [1965] 2017. *The Sense of Wonder*. HarperCollins.

Carter, David J. 2017. "Bush Legends and Pastoral Landscapes." In *Teaching Australian and New Zealand Literature*, edited by Nicholas Birns, Nicole Moore, and Sarah Shieff, 42–54. Modern Language Association of America.

Chakrabarty, Dipesh. 2021. *The Climate of History in a Planetary Age*. University of Chicago Press.

Chandler, Mielle, and Astrida Neimanis. 2013. "Water and Gestationality: What Flows Beneath Ethics." In *Thinking with Water*, edited by Cecilia Chen, Janine Macleod, and Astrida Neimanis, 61–83. McGill-Queen's University Press.

Cheah, Pheng. 2006. *Inhuman Conditions: On Cosmopolitanism and Human Rights*. Harvard University Press.

Cheah, Pheng. 2016. *What Is a World? On Postcolonial Literature as World Literature*. Duke University Press.

Chen, Cecilia, Janine Macleod, and Astrida Neimanis. 2013. "Introduction: Toward a Hydrological Turn?" In *Thinking with Water*, edited by Cecilia Chen, Janine Macleod, and Astrida Neimanis, 3–22. McGill-Queen's University Press.

Chen, Mel. 2012. *Animacies: Biopolitics, Racial Mattering, and Queer Affect*. Duke University Press.

Chen, Mel. 2023. *Race, Disability, and Chemical Intimacy Across Empire*. Duke University Press.

Chen, Qiufan. 2019. *Waste Tide*. Translated by Ken Liu. Head of Zeus.

*China Labor Bulletin*. 2004. "Dagongmei: Female Migrant Labourers." March 6.

Chow, Rey. 2002. *The Protestant Ethnic and the Spirit of Capitalism*. Columbia University Press.

Christian, Dorothy, and Rita Wong. 2013. "Untapping Watershed Mind." In *Thinking with Water*, edited by Cecilia Chen, Janine Macleod, and Astrida Neimanis, 232–53. McGill-Queen's University Press.

Christian, Dorothy, and Rita Wong. 2016. *Downstream: Reimagining Water*. Wilfrid Laurier University Press.

Chu, Kiu-Wai. 2021. "Screening Vulnerability in the Anthropocene: Island of the Hungry Ghosts and the Eco-Ethics of Refugee Cinema." *Screen* 62 (4): 577–85.

Clark, Nigel, and Kathryn Yusoff. 2018. "Queer Fire: Ecology, Combustion, and Pyrosexual Desire." *Feminist Review*, no. 118: 7–24.

Clark, Timothy. 2015. *Ecocriticism on the Edge: The Anthropocene as a Threshold Concept*. Bloomsbury.

Clifford, James. 1988. *The Predicament of Culture*. Harvard University Press.

Clifford, James. 1994. "Diasporas." *Cultural Anthropology* 9 (3): 302–38.

Cohen, Jeffrey Jerome, and Lowell Duckert. 2015. *Elemental Ecocriticism: Thinking with Earth, Air, Water, and Fire*. University of Minnesota Press.

Coleman, Daniel. 2016. "Indigenous Place and Diaspora Space." *Settler Colonial Studies* 6 (1): 61–76.

Collins, Francis L. 2022. "Geographies of Migration II: Decolonising Migration Studies." *Progress in Human Geography* 46 (5): 1241–51.

*Complicit*. 2017. Directed by Heather White and Lynn Zhang. East Village Entertainment.

Cottier, Fabien, and Idean Salehyan. 2021. "Climate Variability and Irregular Migration to the European Union." *Global Environmental Change* 69: 1–11.

Curthoys, Ann. 2000. "An Uneasy Conversation: The Multicultural and the Indigenous." In *Race, Colour and Identity in Australia and New Zealand*, edited by John Docker and Gerhard Fischer, 21–36. University of New South Wales Press.

Davis, Heather. 2022. *Plastic Matter*. Duke University Press.

Day, Iyko. 2016. *Alien Capital: Asian Racialization and the Logic of Settler Colonial Capitalism*. Duke University Press.

Deleuze, Gilles. 2003. *Francis Bacon: The Logic of Sensation*. Translated by Daniel W. Smith. Continuum.

Deleuze, Gilles. 2006. *Difference and Repetition*. Translated by Paul Patton. Bloomsbury Publishing.

Deleuze, Gilles, and Félix Guattari. 1987. *A Thousand Plateaus*. Translated by Brian Massumi. Continuum.

DeLoughrey, Elizabeth. 2011. "Introduction: Towards an Aesthetics of the Earth." In *Postcolonial Ecologies: Literatures of the Environment*, edited by Elizabeth DeLoughrey and George B. Handley, 3–39. Oxford University Press.

DeLoughrey, Elizabeth. 2014. "Satellite Planetarity and the Ends of the Earth." *Public Culture* 26 (2–73): 257–80.

DeLoughrey, Elizabeth. 2017. "Submarine Futures of the Anthropocene." *Comparative Literature* 69 (1): 32–44.

DeLoughrey, Elizabeth. 2019. *Allegories of the Anthropocene*. Duke University Press.

DeLoughrey, Elizabeth. 2022. "Mining the Seas: Speculative Fictions and Futures." In *Laws of the Sea*, edited by Irus Braverman, 145–63. Routledge.

DeLoughrey, Elizabeth, and George B. Handley, eds. 2011. *Postcolonial Ecologies: Literatures of the Environment*. Oxford University Press.

Dennis, Simone. 2008. *Christmas Island: An Anthropological Study*. Cambria Press.

Dennis, Simone. 2009. "Of Crustacean Blood and Ant Infection: Life in the Migration Exclusion Zone, Christmas Island, Australia." *Australian Journal of Anthropology* 20: 213–28.

Derrida, Jacques. 1994. *Specters of Marx*. Translated by Peggy Kamuf. Routledge.

Dimock, Wai Chee. 2008. *Through Other Continents: American Literature Across Deep Time*. Princeton University Press.

Dirlik, Arif. 1994. *What Is in a Rim? Critical Perspectives on the Pacific Region Idea*. Routledge.

"Dongguan Is Building a New Pinnacle for Attracting Foreign Investment" (东莞打造外资招引新高地). 2022. *Nanfang Daily*, January 14. https://epaper.southcn.com/nfdaily/html/202201/14/content_10001929.html

Dooling, Amy. 2017. "Representing Dagongmei (Female Migrant Workers) in Contemporary China." *Frontiers of Literary Studies in China* 11 (1): 133–56.

Douglas, Mary. 1966. *Purity and Danger: An Analysis of Concepts of Pollution and Taboo*. Routledge.

Dow, Katharine, and Janelle Lamoreaux. 2020. "Situated Kinmaking and the Population 'Problem.'" *Environmental Humanities* 12 (2): 475–91.

D'Souza, Radha. 2016. "Listening to the Elders at the Keepers of the Water Gathering." In *Downstream: Reimagining Water*, edited by Dorothy Christian and Rita Wong, 197–206. Wilfrid Laurier University Press.

Du Zhiwei , Gengzhi Huang, and Lixia Jin. 2020. "Beyond the Intention: Individual-Level Determinants and Intergenerational Differences of Floating Populations' Actual Settlement Choices in Dongguan, China." *International Journal of Environmental Research and Public Health* 17 (24): 1–15.

Economides, Louise. 2016. *The Ecology of Wonder in Romantic and Postmodern Literature*. New York: Palgrave Macmillan.

Egonyu, James P., et al. 2021. "Global Overview of Locusts as Food, Feed and Other Uses." *Global Food Security* 31: 100574.

Elias, Amy J., and Christian Moraru. 2015a. "Introduction: The Planetary Condition." In *The Planetary Turn: Relationality and Geoaesthetics in the Twenty-First Century*, edited by Amy J. Elias and Christian Moraru, xi–xxxvii. Northwestern University Press.

Elias, Amy J., and Christian Moraru, eds. 2015b. *The Planetary Turn: Relationality and Geoaesthetics in the Twenty-First Century*. Northwestern University Press.

Espiritu, Yen Le. 2014. *Body Counts: The Vietnam War and Militarized Refugees*. University of California Press.

Faber, Daniel, and Christina Schlegel. 2017. "Give Me Shelter from the Storm: Framing the Climate Refugee Crisis in the Context of Neoliberal Capitalism." *Capitalism Nature Socialism* 28 (3): 1–17.

Favell, Adrian. 2022. *The Integration Nation: Immigration and Colonial Power in Liberal Democracies*. Wiley.

Ferdinand, Malcolm. 2022. *Decolonial Ecology: Thinking from the Caribbean World*. Polity Press.

Ferrando, Francesca. 2013. "Posthumanism, Transhumanism, Antihumanism, Metahumanism, and New Materialisms: Differences and Relations." *Existenz* 8 (2): 26–32.

FirstVoices. N.d. https://www.firstvoices.com/

Fitzsimmons, Lorna, Youngsuk Chae, and Bella Adams, eds. 2014. *Asian American Literature and the Environment*. Routledge.

Forti, Vanessa, et al. 2020. *The Global E-Waste Monitor 2020: Quantities, Flows and the Circular Economy Potential*. UNU/UNITAR and ITU.

Foucault, Michel. 2010. *The Birth of Biopolitics: Lectures at the Collège de France, 1978–79*. Translated by Graham Burchell. Picador.

Fujikane, Candace. 2021. *Mapping Abundance for a Planetary Future: Kanaka Maoli and Critical Settler Cartographies in Hawai'i*. Duke University Press.

Fujikane, Candace, and Jonathan Y. Okamura, eds. 2008. *Asian Settler Colonialism: From Local Governance to the Habits of Everyday Life in Hawai'i*. University of Hawai'i Press.

Gamber, John. 2014. "Introduction: Ecocriticism and Asian American Literature." In *Asian American Literature and the Environment*, edited by Lorna Fitzsimmons, Youngsuk Chae, and Bella Adams, 1–12. Routledge.

Gan, Elaine, et al. 2017. "Introduction: Haunted Landscapes of the Anthropocene." In *Arts of Living on a Damaged Planet*, G1–14. University of Minnesota Press.

Gandhi, Evyn Lê Espiritu. 2022. *Archipelago of Resettlement: Vietnamese Refugee Settlers and Decolonization Across Guam and Israel-Palestine*. University of California Press.

"GDP of 24 Cities Exceeds One Trillion Yuan! City with Four Trillion Yuan GDP Is Born!" 2022. *China Daily*, January 12. https://cn.chinadaily.com.cn/a/2022 01/12/WS61de1875a3107be497a01c0e.html

Ghosh, Amitav. 2016. *The Great Derangement: Climate Change and the Unthinkable*. Penguin Books.

Gifford, Terry. 1999. *Pastoral*. Routledge.

Giles, Paul. 2015. "Writing for the Planet Contemporary Australian Fiction." In *The Planetary Turn: Relationality and Geoaesthetics in the Twenty-First Century*, edited by Amy J. Elias and Christian Moraru, 143–59. Northwestern University Press.

Gilroy, Paul. 1993. *The Black Atlantic: Modernity and Double Consciousness*. Harvard University Press.

Gilroy, Paul. 1994. "Diaspora." *Paragraph* 17 (3): 207–12.

Glăveanu, Vlad Petre, and Gail Womersley. 2021. "Affective Mobilities: Migration, Emotion and (Im)possibility." *Mobilities* 16 (4): 628–42.

Glissant, Édouard. 1997. *Poetics of Relation*. Translated by Betsy Wing. University of Michigan Press.

Gong, Haomin. 2018. "Ecopoetics in the Dagong Poetry in Postsocialist China: Nature, Politics, and Gender in Zheng Xiaoqiong's Poems." *ISLE: Interdisciplinary Studies in Literature and Environment* 25 (2): 257–79.

Gordon, Avery. 2008. *Ghostly Matters: Haunting and the Sociological Imagination*. 2nd ed. University of Minnesota Press.

Grosz, Elizabeth. 1994. *Volatile Bodies: Toward a Corporeal Feminism*. Allen and Unwin.

Guattari, Félix. 1995. *Chaosmosis: An Ethico-Aesthetic Paradigm*. Indiana University Press.

Gunew, Sneja. 1994. *Framing Marginality: Multicultural Literary Studies*. Melbourne University Press.

Haff, Peter K. 2004. "Technology as a Geological Phenomenon: Implications for Human Wellbeing." *Geological Society* 395: 301–9.

Hage, Ghassan. 1998. *Fantasies of White Supremacy in a Multicultural Society*. Pluto Press.

Hage, Ghassan. 2017. *Is Racism an Environmental Threat?* Wiley.

Haiven, Max. 2013. "The Dammed of the Earth: Reading the Mega-Dam for the Political Unconscious of Globalization." In *Thinking with Water*, edited by Cecilia Chen, Janine MacLeod, and Astrida Neimanis, 213–31. McGill-Queen's University Press.

Hall, Stuart. 1980. "Race, Articulation and Societies Structured in Dominance." In *Sociological Theories: Race and Colonialism*, 305–45. UNESCO.

Hall, Stuart. 1990. "Cultural Identity and Diaspora." In *Identity: Community, Culture, Difference*, edited by Jonathan Rutherford, 222–37. Lawrence & Wishart.

Haraway, Donna. 1991. *Simians, Cyborgs, and Women: The Reinvention of Nature*. Routledge.

Haraway, Donna. 2015. "Anthropocene, Capitalocene, Plantationocene, Chthulucene: Making Kin." *Environmental Humanities* 6 (1): 159–65.

Haraway, Donna. 2016. *Staying with the Trouble: Making Kin in the Chthulucene*. Duke University Press.

Hardt, Michael. 2011. "For Love or Money." *Cultural Anthropology* 26 (4): 676–82.

Hayashi, Robert T. 2011. *Haunted by Waters: A Journey Through Race and Place in the American West*. University of Iowa Press.

Heise, Ursula K. 2008. *Sense of Place and Sense of Planet: The Environmental Imagination of the Global*. Oxford University Press.

Heise, Ursula K. 2019. "Science Fiction and the Time Scales of the Anthropocene." *ELH* 86 (2): 275–304.

Hepburn, Ronald W. 1984. *Wonder and the Other Essays: Eight Studies in Aesthetics and Neighbouring Fields*. Edinburgh University Press.

Herrero, Dolores. 2017. "Post-Apocalypse Literature in the Age of Unrelenting Borders and Refugee Crises: Merlinda Bobis and Australian Fiction." *Interventions* 19: 948–61.

Høeg, Elida, and C. D. Tulloch. 2019. "Sinking Strangers: Media Representations of Climate Refugees on the BBC and Al Jazeera." *Journal of Communication Inquiry* 43 (3): 225–48.

Hsu, Hsuan L., and David J. Vázquez. 2023. "Introduction: The Molecular Intimacies of Empire." *Journal of Transnational American Studies* 13 (1): 5–14.

Hu-DeHart, Evelyn. 2000. *Across the Pacific: Asian Americans and Globalization*. Temple University Press.

Huggan, Graham. 2001. *The Postcolonial Exotic: Marketing the Margins*. Routledge.

Huggan, Graham, and Helen Tiffin. 2010. *Postcolonial Ecocriticism: Literature, Animals, Environment*. Routledge.

Hui, Yuk. 2020. "Cosmotechnics." *Angelaki* 25 (4): 1–2.

Hui, Yuk. 2024. *Machine and Sovereignty: For a Planetary Thinking*. University of Minnesota Press.

Iheka, Cajetan. 2017. *Naturalizing Africa: Ecological Violence, Agency, and Postcolonial Resistance in African Literature*. Cambridge University Press.

Iheka, Cajetan. 2021. *African Ecomedia: Network Forms, Planetary Politics*. Duke University Press.

Iovino, Serenella. 2013. "Introduction: Mediterranean Ecocriticism, or, A Blueprint for Cultural Amphibians." *Ecozon@* 4 (2): 1–14.

Iovino, Serenella. 2017. "Mediterranean Ecocriticism." *ISLE: Interdisciplinary Studies in Literature and Environment* 24 (2): 325–40.

Iovino, Serenella, and Serpil Oppermann. 2014. "Introduction: Stories Come to

Matter." In *Material Ecocriticism*, edited by Serenella Iovino and Serpil Oppermann, 1–18. Indiana University Press.

*Island of the Hungry Ghosts*. 2018. Directed by Gabrielle Brady. Chromosom Film.

Jameson, Fredric. 1994. *The Seeds of Time*. Columbia University Press.

Jameson, Fredric. 1995. "Marx's Purloined Letter." *New Left Review* 209: 75–109.

Johns-Putra, Adeline, and Kelly Sultzbach. 2022. "Introduction." In *The Cambridge Companion to Literature and Climate*, edited by Adeline Johns-Putra and Kelly Sultzbach, 1–24. Cambridge University Press.

Jones, Philip G. 2007. "Reflecting on Australia's Muslim Cameleer Heritage." In *Australia's Muslim Cameleers: Pioneers of the Inland 1860s–1930s*, edited by Philip G. Jones and Anna Kenny, 9–16. Wakefield Press.

Juncker, Jean-Claude. 2015. "State of the Union 2015: Time for Honesty, Unity and Solidarity." *European Commission*, September 9. https://ec.europa.eu/commission/presscorner/detail/en/SPEECH_15_5614

Keegan, Matthew. 2018. "Dongguan in the Spotlight: Hi-Tech Comeback for 'Factory of the World'?" *The Guardian*, February 16. https://www.theguardian.com/cities/2018/feb/16/dongguan-spotlight-china-factory-world-hi-tech

Keller, Catherine. 1996. *Apocalypse Now and Then: A Feminist Approach to the End of the World*. Beacon Press.

Kirksey, Eben, and Sophie Chao. 2022. "Introduction: Who Benefits from Multispecies Justice?" In *The Promise of Multispecies Justice*, edited by Sophie Chao, Karin Bolender, and Eben Kirksey, 1–21. Duke University Press.

Koshy, Susan, et al. 2022. "Introduction." In *Colonial Racial Capitalism*, edited by Susan Koshy et al., 1–30. Duke University Press.

Krøijer, Stine, and Cecilie Rubow. 2022. "Introduction: Enchanted Ecologies and Ethics of Care." *Environmental Humanities* 14 (2): 375–84.

Lai, Larissa. 2013. "Epistemologies of Respect: A Poetics of Asian/Indigenous Relation." In *Critical Collaborations: Indigeneity, Diaspora, and Ecology in Canadian Literary Studies*, edited by Smaro Kamboureli and Christl Verduyn, 99–126. Wilfrid Laurier University Press.

Latour, Bruno. 1993. *We Have Never Been Modern*. Harvard University Press.

Latour, Bruno. 1998. "To Modernize or to Ecologize? That's the Question." In *Remaking Reality: Nature at the Millennium*, edited by N. Castree and B. Willems-Braun, 221–42. Routledge.

Latour, Bruno. 2004. "Whose Cosmos, Which Cosmopolitics? Comments on the Peace Terms of Ulrich Beck." *Common Knowledge* 10 (3): 450–62.

Le, Quynh Nhu. 2019. *Unsettled Solidarities: Asian and Indigenous Cross-Representations in the Américas*. Temple University Press.

Lee, Poh Lin. 2013. "Making Now Precious: Working with Survivors of Torture and Asylum Seekers." *International Journal of Narrative Therapy and Community Work* 1: 1–10.

Lee, Poh Lin. 2018. "Narrative Practice and Sandplay: Practice-Based Stories of Collaboration with People Seeking Asylum Held in Mandatory Detention." *Journal of Systemic Therapy* 7 (2): 1–16.

Lefebvre, Henri. 1991. *The Production of Space*. Translated by Donald Nicholson-Smith. Blackwell.

Li, David Leiwei. 1998. *Imagining the Nation: Asian American Literature and Cultural Consent*. Stanford University Press.

Liboiron, Max, Manuel Tironi, and Nerea Calvillo. 2018. "Toxic Politics: Acting in a Permanently Polluted World." *Social Studies of Science* 48 (3): 331–49.

Linton, Jamie. 2010. *What Is Water? The History of a Modern Abstraction*. University of British Columbia Press.

Lorde, Audre. 1984. *Sister Outsider: Essays and Speeches*. PDF adapted for IB English use, 2020–2021.

Lou, Loretta Ieng Tak. 2022. "The Art of Unnoticing: Risk Perception and Contrived Ignorance in China." *American Ethnologist* 49 (4): 580–94.

Lowe, Ian. 2022. "Migration Boost Is Bad News for Australia's Environment—We Mustn't Ignore That." *The Conversation*, September 5.

Lowe, Lisa. 2015. *The Intimacies of Four Continents*. Duke University Press.

Lye, Colleen. 2005. *America's Asia: Racial Form and American Literature, 1893–1945*. Princeton University Press.

Malak, Amin. 1994. "'The World is Your People': The Time of the Peacock and the Evolution of an Australian Identity." *Kunapipi* 16 (2): 43–47.

Mansfield, Nick. 2008. "'There is a Specter Haunting . . .': Ghosts, Their Bodies, Some Philosophers, a Novel and the Cultural Politics of Climate Change." *Borderlands* 7 (1). www.borderlands.net.au/vol7no1_2008/mansfield_climate.htm. Accessed July 15, 2018.

Maracle, Lee. 2016. "Water." In *Downstream: Reimagining Water*, edited by Dorothy Christian and Rita Wong, 33–38. Wilfrid Laurier University Press.

Massey, Doreen. 1994. *Space, Place, and Gender*. University of Minnesota Press.

Mayblin, Lucy, and Joe Turner. 2021. *Migration Studies and Colonialism*. Polity Press.

Mauch, Christof. 2019. "Slow Hope: Rethinking Ecologies of Crisis and Fear." *RCC Perspectives: Transformations in Environment and Society* 1: 1–43.

Mbembe, Achille. 2019. *Necropolitics*. Duke University Press.

Means, Alexander J. 2022. "Foucault, Biopolitics, and the Critique of State Reason." *Educational Philosophy and Theory* 54 (12): 1968–69.

Melamed, Jodi. 2011. *Represent and Destroy: Rationalizing Violence in the New Racial Capitalism*. University of Minnesota Press.

Meynard, Christine N., et al. 2020. "On the Relative Role of Climate Change and Management in the Current Desert Locust Outbreak in East Africa." *Global Change Biology* 26 (7): 3753–55.

Mezzadra, Sandro. 2011. "The Gaze of Autonomy: Capitalism, Migration, and

Social Struggles." In *The Contested Politics of Mobility: Borderzones and Irregularity*, edited by Vicki Squire, translated by Rodrigo Nunes, 121–42. Routledge.

Mezzadra, Sandro, and Brett Neilson. 2018. "Lampedusa." In *Posthuman Glossary*, edited by Rosi Braidotti and Maria Hlavajova, 228–30. Bloomsbury.

Milstein, Tema, and José Castro-Sotomayor. 2020. "Ecocultural Identity: An Introduction." In *Routledge Handbook of Ecocultural Identity*, edited by Tema Milstein and José Castro-Sotomayor, xvii–xxiii. Routledge.

Moore, Donald S., Jake Kosek, and Anand Pandian. 2003. "Introduction: The Cultural Politics of Race and Nature." In *Race, Nature, and the Politics of Difference*, edited by Donald S. Moore, Jake Kosek, and Anand Pandian, 1–70. Duke University Press.

Moore, Jason W. 2015. *Capitalism in the Web of Life: Ecology and the Accumulation of Capital*. Verso.

Morrison, Toni. 1995. "The Site of Memory." In *Inventing the Truth: The Art and Craft of Memoir*, 2nd ed., edited by William Zinsser, 83–102. Houghton Mifflin.

Morton, Timothy. 2009. *Ecology Without Nature*. Harvard University Press.

Morton, Timothy. 2010. "Thinking Ecology: The Mesh, the Strange Stranger, and the Beautiful Soul." *Collapse* 6: 265–93.

Morton-Robinson, Aileen. 2015. *The White Possessive: Property, Power, and Indigenous Sovereignty*. University of Minnesota Press.

Mujezinovic, Davor. 2019. "Electronic Waste in Guiyu: A City Under Change?" *Environment & Society Portal, Arcadia*, no. 29 (Summer). Rachel Carson Center for Environment and Society. https://doi.org/10.5282/rcc/8805

Murphy, Michelle. 2017. "Alterlife and Decolonial Chemical Relations." *Cultural Anthropology* 32 (4): 494–503.

Nail, Thomas. 2015. *The Figure of the Migrant*. Stanford University Press.

Nail, Thomas. 2019. "Migrant Climate in the Kinocene." *Mobilities* 14 (3): 375–80.

National Bureau of Statistics, China. 2024. "2023 Monitor Report on Rural Migrant Workers." May 1. https://www.gov.cn/lianbo/bumen/202405/content_6948813.htm

Neimanis, Astrida. 2009. "Bodies of Water, Human Rights and the Hydrocommons." *TOPIA: Canadian Journal of Cultural Studies* 21: 161–82.

Neimanis, Astrida. 2012. "Hydrofeminism: Or on Becoming a Body of Water." In *Undutiful Daughters: Mobilizing Future Concepts, Bodies and Subjectivities*, edited by Henriette Gunkel, Chrysanthi Nigianni, and Fanny Söderbäck, 96–115. Palgrave Macmillan.

Neimanis, Astrida. 2016. "Water and Knowledge." In *Downstream: Reimagining Water*, edited by Dorothy Christian and Rita Wong, 51–68. Wilfrid Laurier University Press.

Neimanis, Astrida. 2017. *Bodies of Water: Posthuman Feminist Phenomenology*. Bloomsbury.

Ngai, Pun. 2005. *Made in China: Women Factory Workers in a Global Workplace*. Duke University Press.

Nicolas, Robert. 2020. *Theft Is Property! Dispossession and Critical Theory*. Duke University Press.

Nixon, Rob. 2011. *Slow Violence and the Environmentalism of the Poor*. Harvard University Press.

Nugent, Ciara. 2022. "How Arizona's Border Wall Could Stop Animals Escaping from Climate Change." *Time Magazine*, December 15. https://time.com/6241549/arizona-border-wall-mexico-animals-climate-change/. Accessed December 1, 2023.

Nüsser, Marcus, and Ravi Baghel. 2017. "The Emergence of Technological Hydroscapes in the Anthropocene: Socio-Hydrology and Development Paradigms of Large Dams." In *Handbook on Geographies of Technology*, edited by Barney Warf, 287–301. Edward Elgar.

Oppermann, Serpil. 2023. *Ecologies of a Storied Planet in the Anthropocene*. West Virginia University Press.

Oppermann, Serpil. 2017. "Introducing Migrant Ecologies in an (Un)Bordered World." *ISLE: Interdisciplinary Studies in Literature and Environment* 24 (2): 243–56.

Oppermann, Serpil, and Zhou Xiaojing, eds. 2017. Migrant Ecologies in an (Un) bordered World. *ISLE: Interdisciplinary Studies in Literature and Environment 24 (2)*.

Orwell, George. 1949. *1984*. Secker and Warburg.

Palumbo-Liu, David, ed. 1995. *The Ethnic Canon: Histories, Institutions, and Interventions*. University of Minnesota Press.

Parker, Noel, and Nick Vaughan-Williams. 2012. "Critical Border Studies: Broadening and Deepening the 'Lines in the Sand' Agenda." *Geopolitics* 17 (4): 727–33.

Parsons, Howard L. 1969. "A Philosophy of Wonder." *Philosophy and Phenomenological Research* 30 (1): 84–101.

Perera, Suvendrini. 2002. "A Line in the Sea." *Race & Class* 44 (2): 23–39.

Perera, Suvendrini. 2013. "Oceanic Corpo-Graphies, Refugee Bodies and the Making and Unmaking of Waters." *Feminist Review* 103 (1): 58–79.

Plumwood, Val. 2002. *Environmental Culture: The Ecological Crisis of Reason*. Routledge.

Povinelli, Elizabeth A. 2016. *Geontologies: A Requiem to Late Liberalism*. Duke University Press.

Pratt, Mary Louise. 1992. *Imperial Eyes: Travel Writing and Transculturation*. Routledge.

Preston, Jen. 2013. "Neoliberal Settler Colonialism, Canada and the Tar Sands." *Race & Class* 55 (2): 42–59.

Pugh, Jonathan. 2018. "Relationality and Island Studies in the Anthropocene." *Island Studies Journal* 13 (2): 93–110.

Pugliese, Joseph. 2020. *Biopolitics of the More-Than-Human*. Duke University Press.

Puig de la Bellacasa, Maria. 2017. *Matters of Care: Speculative Ethics in More Than Human Worlds*. University of Minnesota Press.

Ray, Sarah Jaquette. 2013. *The Ecological Other: Environmental Exclusion in American Culture*. University of Arizona Press.

Rhook, Nadia. 2015. "'Turban-Clad' British Subjects: Tracking the Circuits of Mobility, Visibility, and Sexuality in Settler Nation-Making." *Transfers* 5 (3): 104–22.

Rigby, Kate. 2006. "Writing After Nature." *Australian Humanities Review* 39–40 (September). https://australianhumanitiesreview.org/2006/09/01/writing-after-nature/. Accessed February 1, 2025.

Robinson, Brett H. 2009. "E-Waste: An Assessment of Global Production and Environmental Impacts." *Science of the Total Environment* 408 (2): 183–91.

Robinson, Cedric. 1983. *Black Marxism: The Making of the Black Radical Tradition*. Zed Books.

Rose, Deborah Bird. 2011. *Wild Dog Dreaming: Love and Extinction*. University of Virginia Press.

Rose, Deborah Bird. 2022. *Shimmer: Flying Fox Exuberance in Worlds of Peril*. Edinburgh University Press.

Rubenstein, Mary-Jane. 2008. *Strange Wonder: The Closure of Metaphysics and the Opening of Awe*. Columbia University Press.

Safran, William. 1991. "Diasporas in Modern Societies: Myths of Homeland and Return." *Diaspora: A Journal of Transnational Studies* 1 (1): 83–99.

Santa Ana, Jeffrey. 2015. *Racial Feelings: Asian America in a Capitalist Culture*. Temple University Press.

Santa Ana, Jeffrey, et al. 2022. *Empire and Environment: Ecological Ruin in the Transpacific*. University of Michigan Press.

Saranillio, Dean Itsuji. 2013. "Why Asian Settler Colonialism Matters: A Thought Piece on Critiques, Debates, and Indigenous Difference." *Settler Colonial Studies* 3 (3–4): 280–94.

Saskatchewan Environmental Society. 2015. *The Legacy of Uranium Mining in Saskatchewan: The Unacceptable Environmental Impacts of Uranium Mining*. March.

Seigworth, Gregory J., and Melissa Gregg. 2010. "An Inventory of Shimmers." In *The Affect Theory Reader*, edited by Melissa Gregg and Gregory J. Seigworth, 1–25. Duke University Press.

Selby, Jan, et al. 2017. "Climate Change and the Syrian Civil War Revisited." *Political Geography* 60: 232–44.

Shapcott, Thomas. 2019. "Introduction." In *The Time of the Peacock*, by Mena Abdullah and Rey Mathew, 3–7. ETT Imprint.

Shaw, Allison K., and Kathryn A. Kelly. 2013. "Linking El Niño, Local Rainfall, and Migration Timing in a Tropical Migratory Species." *Global Change Biology* 19: 3283–90.

Simal-Gonzalez, Begona. 2020. *Ecocriticism and Asian American Literature*. Palgrave Macmillan.

Smith, Nicolas. 1999. "The Howl and the Pussy: Feral Cats and Wild Dogs in the Australian Imagination." *Australian Journal of Anthropology* 10 (3): 288–305.

Smith, Sara, and Pavithra Vasudevan. 2020. "Earth Beyond Repair: Race and Apocalypse in Collective Imagination." *Environment and Planning D: Society and Space* 38 (1): 91–110.

Song, Mingwei. 2015. "After 1989: The New Wave of Chinese Science Fiction." *China Perspectives*, 1: 7–13.

Spennemann, Dirk H. R. 2018. "Patterns of Late Nineteenth and Early Twentieth Century Land Use by Punjabi Hawkers in Southern New South Wales, Australia." *Journal of Sikh and Punjab Studies* 25 (2): 225–73.

Spennemann, Dirk H. R. 2021. "Slamming the Door Shut: Patterns of Punjabi Immigration to Victoria (Australia) During the Late Nineteenth and Early Twentieth Century." *South Asian Diaspora* 13 (2): 129–42.

Spivak, Gayatri Chakravorty. 2003. *Death of a Discipline*. Columbia University Press.

Steffen, Will, et al. 2020. "The Emergence and Evolution of Earth System Science." *Nature Reviews Earth & Environment* 1: 54–63.

Steinberg, Philip, and Kimberley Peters. 2015. "Wet Ontologies, Fluid Spaces: Giving Depth to Volume Through Oceanic Thinking." *Environment and Planning D: Society and Space* 33 (2): 247–64.

Stiegler, Bernard, with Paolo Vignola and Mitra Azar. 2021. "Introduction—Decarbonization and Deproletarianization: *Gagner sa vie* in the Twenty-First Century." In *Bifurcate: "There Is No Alternative"*, edited by Bernard Stiegler with the Internation Collective, translated by Daniel Ross, 18–44. Verso.

Sun, Wanning. 2014. *Subaltern China: Rural Migrants, Media, and Cultural Practices*. Rowman & Littlefield.

Sundberg, Juanita. 2023. "'Trash-Talk' and the Production of Quotidian Geopolitical Boundaries in the United States–Mexico Borderlands." *Social and Cultural Geography* 13 (1): 871–90.

Surma, Anna. 2018. "In a Different Voice: 'A Letter from Manus Island' as Poetic Manifesto." *Continuum* 32 (4): 518–26.

Suzuki, Erin. 2021. *Ocean Passages: Navigating Pacific Islander and Asian American Literatures*. Temple University Press.

Suzuki, Erin, and Aimee Bahng. 2020. "The Transpacific Subject in Asian American Culture." *Oxford Research Encyclopedia of Literature*. January. https://oxfordre.com/literature/view/10.1093/acrefore/9780190201098.001.0001/acrefore-9780190201098-e-877. Accessed December 24, 2023.

Tang, Kin-Ling. 2017. *Encountering Development in the Age of Global Capitalism: A Case Study*. Springer.

Todd, Zoe. 2015. "Indigenizing the Anthropocene." In *Art in the Anthropocene: Encounters Among Aesthetics, Politics, Environment, and Epistemology*, edited by Heather Davis and Etienne Turpin, 241–54. Open Humanities Press.

Tofighian, Omid. 2018. "Translator's Tale: A Window to the Mountains." In *No Friend but the Mountains: Writing from Manus Prison*, by Behrouz Boochani, xiii–xxxvi. Sydney: Picador.

Tofighian, Omid, and Behrouz Boochani. 2021. "The Weaponisation of Time: Indefinite Detention as Torture." In *Stealing Time: Migration, Temporalities and State Violence*, edited by Monish Bhatia and Victoria Canning, 65–82. Palgrave.

Trigger, David, et al. 2008. "Ecological Restoration, Cultural Preferences and the Negotiation of 'Nativeness' in Australia." *Geoforum* 39 (3): 1273–83.

Tsang, Eileen Yuk-ha. 2018. "Finding Hope as a 'Tempting Girl' in China: Sex Work, Indentured Mobility, and Cosmopolitan Individuals." *Deviant Behavior* 39 (7): 896–909.

Tsing, Anna. 2015. *The Mushroom at the End of the World: On the Possibility of Life in Capitalist Ruins*. Princeton University Press.

Tsing, Anna, et al., eds. 2017. *Arts of Living on a Damaged Planet*. University of Minnesota Press.

Tuan, Yi-Fu. [1977] 2001. *Space and Place: The Perspective of Experience*. 8th ed. University of Minnesota Press.

Tuck, Eve, and K. Wayne Yang. 2012. "Decolonization Is Not a Metaphor." *Decolonization: Indigeneity, Education & Society* 1 (1): 1–4.

Turner, Bethaney. 2021. "3 Ways Community Gardens Often Exclude Migrants and Refugees—and How to Turn This Around." *The Conversation*, August 13. https://theconversation.com/3-ways-community-gardens-often-exclude-migrants-and-refugees-and-how-to-turn-this-around-164547. Accessed September 15, 2022.

Turner, Joe, and Dan Bailey. 2021. "'Ecobordering': Casting Immigration Control as Environmental Protection." *Environmental Politics* 31 (1): 110–31.

UNHCR. 2019. "Concerns over States Contracting Private Security Companies in Migration Situations." December 20. https://www.ohchr.org/en/stories/2019/12/concerns-over-states-contracting-private-security-companies-migration-situations

Van Dooren, Thom, and Matthew Chrulew, eds. 2022. *Kin: Thinking With Deborah Bird Rose*. Duke University Press.

Walker, David. 1999. *Anxious Nation: Australia and the Rise and Fall of Asia, 1850–1939*. University of Queensland Press.

Walsh, Catherine E., and Walter D. Mignolo. 2018. *On Decoloniality: Concepts, Analytics, Praxis*. Duke University Press.

Wang, Feng, et al. 2013. "E-Waste in China: A Country Report." UNU-ISP. April 5.

Wang, Kun, Qian Junxi, and Liu Lixiong. 2020. "Understanding Environmental Pollutions of Informal E-Waste Clustering in Global South via Multi-Scalar Regulatory Frameworks: A Case Study of Guiyu Town, China." *International Journal of Environmental Research and Public Health* 17 (2802): 1–18.

Ward, Russel. 1992. "The Australian Legend." In *Images of Australia*, edited by Gillian Whitlock and David Carter, 92–110. University of Queensland Press.

Waterhouse, Richard. 2000. "Australian Legends: Representations of the Bush, 1813–1913." *Australian Historical Studies* 31 (115): 201–21.

Watson, Lilla. 2004. "A Contribution to Change: Cooperation out of Conflict." Keynote address, "Celebrating Difference, Embracing Equality" conference, Hobart, September 21–24.

Weik von Mossner, Alexa. 2012. "The Human Face of Global Warming: Varieties of Eco-Cosmopolitanism in Climate Change Documentaries." *Revista Canaria de Estudios Ingleses* 64: 145–59.

Whitlock, Gillian. 2020. "No Friend but the Mountains: How Should I Read This?" *Biography* 43 (4): 705–23.

Whyte, Kyle Powys, and Chris Cuomo. 2018. "Ethics of Caring in Environmental Ethics: Indigenous and Feminist Philosophies." In *The Oxford Handbook of Environmental Ethics*, edited by Stephen M. Gardiner and Allen Thompson, 1–17. Oxford University Press.

Willmott, Glenn. 2018. *Reading for Wonder: Ecology, Ethics, Enchantment*. Palgrave Macmillan.

Wilson, Sheena, Imre Szeman, and Adam Carlson. 2017. "On Petrocultures: Or, Why We Need to Understand Oil to Understand Everything Else." In *Petrocultures: Oil, Politics, Culture*, edited by Sheena Wilson, Imre Szeman, and Adam Carlson, 3–19. McGill-Queen's University Press.

Woinarski, John. 2018. *A Bat's End: The Christmas Island Pipistrelle and Extinction in Australia*. CSIRO Publishing.

Wong, Rita. 2008. "Decolonizasian: Reading Asian and First Nations Relations in Literature." *Asian Canadian Studies* 199: 158–80.

Wong, Rita. 2015. *Undercurrent*. Gibsons, Nightwood Editions.

Wong, Rita, and Christian Dorothy. 2016. "Introduction: Re-Storying Waters, Re-Storying Relations." In *Downstream: Reimagining Water*, edited by Dorothy Christian and Rita Wong, 1–25. Wilfrid Laurier University Press.

"'World's Factory' Dongguan, Guangdong Is Transforming 'Attracting Investment' into 'Attracting Talents.'" ("世界工廠"廣東東莞將"招商引資"變為"選

商引智"). 2007. December 7. http://big5.www.gov.cn/gate/big5/www.gov.cn/ztzl/2007-12/07/content_827611.htm

Wuthnow, Julie. 2002. "Deleuze in the Postcolonial: On Nomads and Indigenous Politics." *Feminist Theory* 3 (2): 183–200.

Yan, Hairong. 2003. "Neoliberal Governmentality and Neohumanism: Organizing Suzhi/Value Flow Through Labor Recruitment Networks." *Cultural Anthropology* 18 (4): 493–523.

Ybarra, Priscilla Solis. 2016. *Writing the Goodlife: Mexican American Literature and the Environment*. University of Arizona Press.

Yu, Changheng. 2021. "The Strength and Spirit of Dongguan, the 'World's Factory.'" ("世界工厂"东莞的硬核与温度). *21Jingji*, November 17. http://www.21jingji.com/article/20211117/herald/6fae919237fd8827e7b5181a4669199d.html

Yusoff, Kathryn. 2013. "Geologic Life: Prehistory, Climate, Futures in the Anthropocene." *Environment and Planning D: Society and Space* 31 (5): 779–95.

Yusoff, Kathryn. 2017. "Geosocial Strata." *Theory, Culture & Society* 34 (2–3): 105–27.

Yusoff, Kathryn. 2018. *A Billion Black Anthropocenes or None*. University of Minnesota Press.

Yusoff, Kathryn, and Jennifer Gabrys. 2011. "Climate Change: Geoengineering and Geologic Politics." *WIREs Climate Change* 2 (4): 516–34.

Zheng, Xiaoqiong. 2007. "Eight Poems." Translated by Zhou Xiaojing. *Chinese Literature Today* 6 (1): 98–109.

Zheng, Xiaoqiong. 2016. "Selected Poems of Zheng Xiaoqiong." Translated by Zhou Xiaojing. *Verge: Studies in Global Asias* 2 (1): 97–104.

Zheng, Xiaoqiong. 2018. "Iron." Translated by Isabelle Li. *Sydney Review of Books*, November 22.

Zhou, Cissy. 2019. "Could Robotic Automation Replace China's 100 Million Workers in Its Manufacturing Industry?" *South China Morning Post*, February 14. https://www.scmp.com/economy/china-economy/article/2185993/man-vs-machine-chinas-workforce-starting-feel-strain-threat

Zhou, Xiaojing. 2017. "Slow Violence in Migrant Landscapes: 'Hollow Villages' and Tourist River Towns in China." *ISLE: Interdisciplinary Studies in Literature and Environment* 24 (2): 274–91.

Zhou, Xiaojing. 2021. *Migrant Ecologies: Zheng Xiaoqiong's Women Migrant Workers*. Rowman & Littlefield.

Zong, Emily Yu. 2016. "'I Protest, Therefore I Am': Cosmo-Multiculturalism, Suburban Dreams, and Difference as Abjection in Hsu-Ming Teo's *Behind the Moon*." *Journal of Intercultural Studies* 37 (3): 234–49.

Zong, Emily Yu. 2020. "Post-Apocalyptic Specters and Critical Planetarity in Merlinda Bobis's *Locust Girl*." *Ariel: A Review of International English Literature* 51 (4): 57–76.

Zong, Emily Yu. 2021. "Anachronism in the Anthropocene: Plural Temporalities and the Art of Noticing in Ruth Ozeki's *A Tale for the Time Being*." *LIT: Literature Interpretation Theory* 32 (4): 305–21.
Zong, Emily Yu. 2023. "The Making of the Asian Australian Novel." In *The Cambridge History of the Australian Novel*, edited by David Carter, 502–19. Cambridge University Press.

# Index